PAT CHOATE

SAVING CAPITALISM

Pat Choate is the author of *Dangerous Business, Hot Property, Agents of Influence, The High-Flex Society,* and *America in Ruins,* and coauthor with Ross Perot of *Save Your Job, Save Our Country.* In 1996, he was Ross Perot's vice presidential running mate. He lives with his wife outside Washington, D.C.

ALSO BY PAT CHOATE

Dangerous Business: The Risks of Globalization for America

Hot Property: The Stealing of Ideas in an Age of Globalization

Save Your Job, Save Our Country (with Ross Perot)

Agents of Influence: How Japan's Lobbyists in the United States Manipulate America's Political and Economic System

The High-Flex Society: Shaping America's Economic Future (with J. K. Linger)

America in Ruins: The Decaying Infrastructure (with Susan Walter)

Being Number One: Rebuilding the U.S. Economy (with Gail Garfield Schwartz)

SAVING CAPITALISM

SAVING CAPITALISM

Keeping America Strong

PAT CHOATE

VINTAGE BOOKS
A Division of Random House, Inc.
New York

A VINTAGE BOOKS ORIGINAL, SEPTEMBER 2009

Library of Congress Cataloging-in-Publication Data
Choate, Pat.
Saving capitalism : keeping America strong / Pat Choate.
p. cm.
Includes bibliographical references.
ISBN 978-0-307-47483-4 (pbk.)
1. United States—Economic policy—2001–2.
2. Capitalism—United States. I. Title.
HC108.83.C46 2009
330.973—dc22 2009026836

Book design by R. Bull

www.vintagebooks.com

Printed in the United States of America
10 9 8 7 6 5 4 3 2 1

For Kay

CHAIRMAN WAXMAN: You found a flaw?

MR. GREENSPAN: I found a flaw in the model that I perceived is the critical functioning structure that defines how the world works, so to speak.

CHAIRMAN WAXMAN: In other words, you found that your view of the world, your ideology, was not right, it was not working.

MR. GREENSPAN: Precisely. That's precisely the reason I was shocked, because I had been going for forty years or more with very considerable evidence that it was working exceptionally well.

—*The Financial Crisis and the Role of Federal Regulators*, Congressman Henry Waxman (D-CA) and Dr. Alan Greenspan, former chairman of the Federal Reserve, House Committee on Oversight and Government Reform hearing, October 23, 2008

We remain the most prosperous, powerful nation on earth. Our workers are no less productive than when this crisis began. Our minds are no less inventive, our goods and services no less needed than they were last week or last month or last year. Our capacity remains undiminished. But our time of standing pat, of protecting narrow interests and putting off unpleasant decisions—that time has surely passed. Starting today, we must pick ourselves up, dust ourselves off, and begin again the work of remaking America.

—President Barack Obama, inaugural address, January 20, 2009

CONTENTS

PROLOGUE

President Franklin D. Roosevelt not only saved the American economy, he saved market capitalism itself. Seventy-five years later, President Barack Obama now faces the same challenge, but in a far more complex and economically integrated world.

When Roosevelt took office in 1933, a quarter of all American workers were unemployed, nine thousand banks had failed, and $140 billion of depositors' money had disappeared. Confronted with a seemingly dead economy, Americans were willing to try just about anything.

In contrast, President Obama has taken charge near the beginning of this economic crisis, not at its low point. Consequently, he must forge solutions at a moment when many Americans—including a majority of the membership in Congress—still view free-market absolutism as something akin to a secular religion and any deviations from it as that old political demon "socialism."

The arithmetic of this economic collapse is staggering. In 2008 and early 2009, the crash wiped out more than 40 percent of the world's wealth, destroyed more than seven million American jobs, and shrank the U.S. gross domestic product by almost 6 percent. Moreover, the decline in global production closely parallels the decline in the early years of the Great Depression. Economists Barry Eichengreen and Kevin H. O'Rourke report that since April 2008:

- World industrial production continues to track closely the 1930s' fall, with no clear signs of turnaround.

- German, British, Canadian, and U.S. industrial output are closely matching their respective rates of fall in the 1930s;
- Italy and France are doing worse; and
- Japan's industrial output is experiencing an even worse decline than in the early 1930s.

The existing economic descriptors are inadequate for this crisis. Therefore, this book will identify the current economic crisis as a depression, with a lowercase *d*.

This depression is neither a normal cyclical downturn nor a traditional finance-driven crash, although the money industry did collapse spectacularly in 2008. Rather, it is something far more fundamental, the economic equivalent of a powerful earthquake caused by shifting tectonic plates deep within the earth. The United States is in the midst of a basic structural shift in the global economy that reaches to the very core of its economic institutions. Where American leaders once believed globalization would lead to the widespread adoption of market capitalism, this depression has brought into focus a different reality—the rise of state capitalism.

State capitalism is the system under which national governments own all the basic natural resources such as oil and natural gas and control or greatly support major industries that produce everything from baby food to spacecraft. Many of these governments also possess multitrillion-dollar sovereign wealth funds, giant pools of public capital that potentially enable them to purchase any corporation or industry in the world, regardless of size, cost, or importance.

While the great economic conflict of the twentieth century was capitalism versus Marxism, the battle in the twenty-first century will be state versus market capitalism. And market capitalism is already losing badly. No private corporation can compete for long against the state-owned and state-operated enterprises of nations such as China or the state-backed corporations of Japan, Korea, Taiwan, or Germany.

The collapse of the tech bubble of the 1990s and the credit and housing bubbles of the early 2000s largely distracted attention from these fundamental structural changes. After these economic mirages broke, the extent of state capitalism became more visible and the consequences more tangible. Foremost of the costs is the deindustrialization of the United States.

Over the past three decades, U.S. corporate leaders responded to this emerging form of competition by monopolizing entire industries and outsourcing production and jobs to places where labor, environmental, and other regulatory costs are lower and profits are higher. In the process, they stripped away much of America's industrial base, including industries vital to national security.

In response, Americans imported almost $6 trillion more in goods from abroad than they exported from 1981 to 2008. The country paid for those goods by exhausting its savings, selling assets, and assuming massive debt, including from foreign sources. Wall Street became a casino that gambled away America's wealth. Now our financial system is crippled, and millions of Americans have no savings, no jobs, no credit, and few prospects of recouping their losses.

The longer-term consequences are simple. People without assets, jobs, and credit cannot buy the goods and services made and sold by others. They become poorer and their lives more difficult.

The obvious question is why did America's leaders fail to anticipate this depression and then respond so slowly and so incompetently?

Some observers did understand the situation and even tried to forestall the depression, but rigid ideology and intense partisanship blinded the politicians who were in charge. For most of the past thirty years, these market absolutists held the zealous convictions that markets are self-regulating, the gains from industrial outsourcing exceed the costs, federal budget deficits are irrelevant, and mounting trade deficits are immaterial.

The governing ethos was "Government is the problem, not the solution"—hardly a suitable foundation for national economic policy.

This depression, moreover, is about more than the rise of state capitalism, massive financial failures, and absolutist ideology. It is also about the degradation of democracy and capitalism. The checks and balances of the American form of government failed spectacularly over the past three decades. Our nation presented to the world an economic model that seemed indifferent to the well-being of the people of the United States, let alone those of other nations. Public and private leaders have tolerated chicanery, inequality, tax evasion, financial looting, mass exploitation of poor foreigners, and ruin of the common good.

Not surprisingly, nations are rejecting market capitalism throughout the world. By April 2009, barely a majority of Americans thought capitalism was superior to socialism, although most respondents could define neither. The tragedy is that capitalism, properly regulated, is the most efficient means in the world to allocate scarce resources and stimulate economic innovation and growth. However, as we have experienced, market capitalism is also a fragile thing, constantly vulnerable to political manipulation, ideologues, rogues, and other enemies.

We are at an in-between time—a tumultuous moment when free-market absolutism is dying, but a widely acceptable form of sustainable twenty-first-century capitalism has not yet been born. In this interim, the Obama stimulus package is beginning to slow the downward economic slide, but it is too economically anemic, too politically timid, and too rigidly beholden to old economic rules to reignite the U.S. and world economies. For that, America needs stronger measures and they are needed now.

This book argues that systemic change is required if America is to emerge from this depression capable of reclaiming its economic and political sovereignty. The goal must be restoration of a responsible capitalism that can provide long-term, sustainable, noninflationary growth that improves the lives of all Americans. Actions are needed that are powerful enough to turn away economic disaster, yet fully within the power of the nation to initiate and complete. The following six game-changing proposals meet that test:

1. Impose strict federal supervision of all financial institutions of any form doing business in the United States and provide for an adequate, honestly valued, and sound currency.
2. Replace the federal income and corporate taxes with either a value-added, flat, or fair tax; balance the federal budget; and then begin paying down the national debt.
3. Balance U.S. trade accounts with the rest of the world in a way that is neither protectionist nor mercantilist and deals with state capitalism pragmatically.
4. Strengthen the American social net so that every American worker has the opportunity for education, training, health care, employment, minimal income, and a pension sufficient for a dignified retirement.
5. Develop a national capital budget of public works investments and then launch a massive infrastructure construction program that will create millions of new jobs for workers who will build the domestic facilities America needs now and in the future.
6. Create a national innovation strategy that will facilitate decades of creativity, investment, and the generation of employment opportunities in America.

As President Roosevelt's most difficult mission seven decades ago was saving capitalism, President Obama's principal challenge now is the same.

SAVING CAPITALISM

CHAPTER ONE

MONEY

An unending economic hurricane has been ripping apart the U.S. and world economies since December 2007. In the seventeen months between then and April 2009, the number of unemployed Americans increased by seven million. By April 2009, almost 5.4 million of the nation's 45 million home loans, worth more than $717 billion, were delinquent or in foreclosure.

Although the pace of decline seemed to be slowing by the early summer of 2009, far worse is yet to come in 2010. The Treasury Department's stress test of the nineteen largest banks in early 2009 revealed that they could be forced to write off as much as a fresh $600 billion by the end of 2010, increasing their losses to more than $1 trillion. Most of those mortgage defaults will be by people now at work, who once were thought financially immune to such distress, but now are likely to lose their jobs and then their family homes.

The lender of last resort, the federal government, has tried to blunt this depression with unprecedented levels of money infusions into the U.S. economy. Despite federal commitments of almost $9 trillion for direct investments, $1.7 trillion for guarantees, and $1.4 trillion for loans, plus a cut of the Federal Reserve loan rate to banks of almost zero, the prolonged freeze in credit markets cracked only slightly by the spring of 2009.

In the last quarter of 2008 and the first of 2009, auto production fell by half and global trade declined at the fastest pace since the Great Depression. The governments of Europe, Japan, and China are engaged in massive bailouts of their economies. Yet the bottom of this depression is not visible, let alone a domestic or global upturn.

America's money industry is directly to blame for much of the world's economic meltdown. It gambled with other people's money and lost, used faulty risk-assessment tools, and knowingly sold fraudulent assets, including hundreds of billions of dollars of subprime mortgages, for vast profits. The administrations of Bill Clinton and George W. Bush enabled Wall Street's recklessness by scrapping the regulatory safeguards Franklin Roosevelt had erected in the 1930s. Equally significant, the U.S. Federal Reserve System, Securities and Exchange Commission, and Treasury Department failed to exercise their oversight authority adequately.

The salvage program put into place by both the Bush and Obama administrations is designed to restore the U.S. financial system to the way it was before the crash of 2008, with the same oligarchs in control but with a bit more regulation. If that is all that is accomplished, we will have learned nothing and can be sure that we will have a repeat of the behavior that brought us to this crisis.

We must think bigger about what America wants from the money industry and act accordingly. A strong capitalist system requires an equally strong financial sector, whose integrity is safeguarded by strict federal supervision of all money institutions, bans on Wall Street speculation with other people's money, and an adequate and sound currency, thereby ensuring a steady flow of capital and credit to American businesses of all sizes.

We need a money industry that uses the great reservoirs of other people's money that it holds to serve the real economy, as it did successfully for several decades in the post–World War II era, as opposed to the recent exploitation of privileged access for compensation-based looting, speculation, and selfish schemes.

American capitalism needs a long era of dull but prudent banking, overseen by suspicious federal regulators.

The free-market absolutism of the past thirty years, most notably the last ten, created such an antigovernment, antiregulatory bias, coupled with the fantasy that the market always knows best and always regulates itself, that the very will to regulate disappeared at the top levels of American government, academia, and business. For sure, other factors affected this crisis, as subsequent chapters will reveal, but it all came together as a perfect storm in the money industry.

Here are the essentials of what happened and recommendations for rebuilding America's financial system.

THE MONEY INDUSTRY

The economic origins of the present crash are the oil shocks of the 1970s, when many major oil-producing countries created their production cartel, the Organization of the Petroleum Exporting Countries (OPEC), and radically increased the price of crude oil. The OPEC nations deposited much of their money for safekeeping in major U.S. banks such as Chase Manhattan, Citibank, Chemical Bank, and Bank of America. These banks recycled hundreds of billions of petrodollar deposits as loans for developing countries, eagerly and often imprudently offering high-interest financing to countries such as Argentina, Brazil, Mexico, Nigeria, Ivory Coast, and the Philippines—nations whose leaders repeatedly stole part of the proceeds, wasted part, and used a little for the intended development.

Forgetting how nations defaulted on loans during economic crises in the 1800s and during the Great Depression, Walter Wriston, chairman of Citibank, then considered America's leading banker, proclaimed in the late 1970s that lending to governments was safe because sovereign nations do not default.

Wriston's maxim was totally wrong. In 1982, when Argentina, Brazil, and Mexico defaulted on more than $300 billion of debt, much of it owed to Citibank, the Federal Reserve and Treasury had to scramble to prevent major U.S. financial institutions, including Citibank, from collapsing. By the end of the 1980s, developing nations had defaulted on more than $1.3 trillion of debt, most of which was owed to U.S. banks. A Washington Post Book Company study revealed that more than one thousand U.S. banks were technically bankrupt by 1992.

Despite the rhetoric of market absolutism embraced by every U.S. president from 1981 to 2008, Washington had to bail out the financial services industry eight times, even as it cancelled many of the financial regulations that governed the industry.

1. In 1982, the Federal Reserve and the Treasury bailed out U.S. banks holding Mexican, Argentine, and Brazilian debt.
2. In 1984, Continental Illinois received a $4 billion rescue package.
3. In the late 1980s, the Federal Reserve paid out large loans to save 350 banks that later failed.
4. Between 1989 and 1992, Congress provided $250 billion to support hundreds of insolvent savings and loan institutions.
5. From 1990 to 1992, federal banking authorities provided $4 billion to save the Bank of New England and arranged for Citibank to get capital from Saudi Arabia.
6. In 1994, Congress provided Mexico a $50 billion loan to bail out Goldman Sachs and other U.S. financial institutions that had bought high-yield Mexican debt.
7. In 1997, the Treasury pushed the International Monetary Fund (IMF) to rescue East Asian currencies in order to save American lenders.
8. In 1998, the Federal Reserve saved Long-Term Capital

> Management, a massive hedge fund whose investors included leaders from U.S. finance.

Misfeasance, malfeasance, and malversation (corruption of officials) distinguished the finances of this era.

Despite these repeated bailouts and Wall Street's widespread abuse of its clients, federal regulators were extraordinarily tolerant. When a financial institution failed to obey or fulfill a law, regulation, contract, or agreement, punishment was mostly limited to a warning or a fine, sometimes in the hundreds of millions of dollars, followed by a corporate announcement that the company neither admitted nor denied any guilt. Such federal wink-and-nod acceptance facilitated the rise of a gambling culture in the great financial houses where solvency and soundness once reigned.

A FAVORED INDUSTRY

As this lenience suggests, the "money" industry was, and remains, favored in Washington. Although never naming it as such, the federal government in the latter part of the twentieth century put into place, step by step, a long-term national industrial policy that privileged the financial industry over all others, particularly manufacturing. The benefits to finance were enormous, and the consequences to manufacturing were devastating.

By the 1980s, finance dominated the American economy, and what finance wanted was quick cash. Beginning with the merger mania of that decade and continuing through the buyouts, privatization, and outsourcing of subsequent years, our leaders sacrificed the real economy for the financial one. Where our best and brightest graduates had once sought their fortunes in the corporations that created wealth by producing goods and services, these talented young people were soon seeking jobs in financial firms where they sought quick fortunes manipulating paper wealth.

Consequently, the number of jobs in the financial sector (the winner) grew and those in manufacturing (the loser) declined. The math is clear. Between 1981 and 2009, manufacturing employment fell from 18.7 million jobs to barely 12 million, a 40 percent loss, while finance grew from 5.1 million jobs to 8.1 million, a 60 percent increase. America lost almost three jobs for every one it gained in that exchange.

In the process, the Wall Street–driven outsourcing of industrial and service jobs over the past three decades has devastated America's middle class. First, families tried to cope by having both adults work outside the home. When joint incomes were insufficient to maintain family lifestyles and pay bills, families went into debt to credit card companies at usurious rates. During this time, banking institutions financed hundreds of thousands of mortgages, often to unqualified borrowers. Then millions of families borrowed against the equity in their homes to pay off other debts, putting themselves on the financial edge. Millions of those mortgages were "subprime" because the money industry made them to people without the means to service the debt, which the lenders knew.

As many in the American middle class increasingly found themselves in a financial bind, elected federal leaders actually worsened the situation in 2005 by enacting changes in laws that prevented borrowers from discharging credit card and other debt they owed through bankruptcy. Consequently, starting over became impossible for millions of Americans who became legal "debt slaves" to the money industry. When some in Congress tried in 2009 to reverse these bankruptcy laws on credit cards, plus allow bankruptcy judges to alter mortgage terms, they were defeated. But when the money industry crashed because of its greed and incompetence, the same elected officials rushed to bail it out with unseemly, and ultimately costly, haste.

The money industry's demonstrated capacity to obtain trillions of dollars in bailout grants and loans from Washington reflects its extraordinary political power. Indeed, no other special interest has similar influence with the White House, Congress, and both political parties. The fountainhead of that influence is their massive political contributions and lobbying expenditures. Senator Dick Durbin, assistant Senate majority leader, described the dynamics bluntly in an April 2009 radio interview: "And the banks—hard to believe in a time when we're facing a banking crisis that many of the banks created—are still the most powerful lobby on Capitol Hill. And they frankly own the place."

In March 2009, two watchdog groups, Essential Information and the Consumer Education Foundation, released *Sold Out,* a report that documents $1.7 billion in campaign contributions made by the finance industry from 1998 to 2008, plus another $3.4 billion spent on lobbying. Year by year, company by company, politician by politician, the report identifies who gave what to whom. It also identifies former congressional staff members, ex-members of the House and Senate, and former White House and other executive branch officials whom the finance industry hired as lobbyists and what they did.

Such lobbying is Washington's growth industry, producing about $10 billion in business annually. It is changing the very concept of public service. Over the past decade, for instance, more than thirty-three thousand people registered as lobbyists with the Senate Office of Public Records, including half of all senators and representatives who left office. Washington's revolving door is simply out of control.

THE MONEY INDUSTRY'S PEOPLE

Money buys access and position in Washington. Thus, our political leaders regularly appoint money people to senior positions in both Republican and Democratic administrations.

For instance, President Clinton's principal economic advisor and later treasury secretary was Robert Rubin, former cochairman of Goldman Sachs and subsequent director and senior advisor at Citigroup. Rubin mentored Lawrence Summers, who succeeded him as treasury secretary in 1999, and Timothy F. Geithner, who worked for both Rubin and Summers.

While advising candidate Obama in the 2008 elections, Summers also worked as a part-time managing director at the $30 billion hedge fund D. E. Shaw, which paid him $5.2 million for one-day-a-week's work over a two-year period. He also received $2.7 million for forty speeches, primarily to large Wall Street companies including Citigroup, JPMorgan Chase, and Goldman Sachs, later beneficiaries of the federal bailouts that he now oversees.

Geithner became chairman of the Federal Reserve Bank of New York in November 2003, was responsible for overseeing the New York banks, and was intimately involved in the federal bailouts of Wall Street financial institutions when they failed. President Obama appointed him treasury secretary in 2009, and the U.S. Senate confirmed him for the position. His chief of staff is Mark Patterson, who left his job as a top lobbyist for Goldman Sachs in April 2009. Michael Paese, who had been the top staffer at the House Financial Services Committee, which helped structure the bailout of Wall Street in 2008, filled the resulting vacuum at Goldman's Washington office.

After leaving office in 2001, Bill Clinton advised several Wall Street investment funds, while his vice president, Al Gore, is cofounder of Generation Investment Management with David Blood, an investment banker formerly of Goldman Sachs. Lombard Odier Darier Hentsch & Cie, a Swiss bank, is the largest investor in the fund, whose assets include stock in companies such a Novo Nordisk A/S, the world's largest insulin maker, and Johnson Controls, which makes auto seats and batteries.

The giant hedge fund Paulson & Co. in 2008 hired Alan Greenspan, former chairman of the Federal Reserve (1987–2006).

This fund made a reported $15 billion profit in 2007 by shorting stocks of those holding subprime mortgages.

The Bush family has long been connected with Wall Street; Prescott Bush, father of George H. W. Bush and grandfather of George W. Bush, headed the investment firm Brown Brothers Harriman in the 1930s and 1940s. After George H. W. Bush left the presidency, he advised the Carlyle Group, a major investment fund, and Citigroup.

John W. Snow, who was George W. Bush's treasury secretary from February 2003 to June 2006, became chairman of Cerberus, a private investment firm that does billions of dollars of contract work for the federal government, owned Chrysler, and was the recipient of $4 billion in federal rescue funds in late 2008. Henry Paulson, the ex-chairman of Goldman Sachs, replaced Snow at the Treasury and led the bailout of the financial industry, including Goldman Sachs, which got a $10 billion investment by the Treasury at about the same time investor Warren Buffett bought into the firm for $5 billion. The deal Paulson negotiated with his old firm gave taxpayers less than half what Buffett got, but at twice the price.

- Buffett received 43.5 million options worth $1.8 billion for his $5 billion. Taxpayers got only 9.5 million options worth $500 million for their $10 billion investment.
- Buffett is being paid 10 percent interest on his preferred stock. Taxpayers get 5 percent for five years and then 9 percent for five years.
- Buffett has a 10 percent call premium. Taxpayers have no premium rights.
- Buffett got $5 billion of present value for this $5 billion investment. Taxpayers have $4.9 billion of present value for their $10 billion.

During Paulson's tenure in 2008, Goldman Sachs received another $13 billion of taxpayer monies from the funds paid out by insurance giant AIG, which received $180 billion in federal bailout monies.

President George W. Bush's budget and policy director in his first term and chief of staff in his second was Joshua Bolten, who headed Goldman Sachs's European government affairs division from 1994 to 1999.

In 2001, President George W. Bush appointed Robert Zoellick the United States trade representative. He served as deputy secretary of state in 2005–2006 and afterward as vice chairman, international, of the Goldman Sachs Group, managing director, and chairman of Goldman Sachs's board of international advisors. In July 2007, George W. Bush appointed Zoellick to be the eleventh president of the World Bank.

President Obama's chief of staff is Rahm Emanuel, who worked in the Clinton campaign in 1992 and later became a senior White House advisor. He left the White House in 1998 and became an investment banker at Wasserstein Perella for thirty months, where he made a reported $16 million for his services. In 2000, President Clinton appointed him to what is known as a "plum position"—on the board of directors for the Federal Home Loan Mortgage Corporation (Freddie Mac)—which paid him $31,000 in 2000 and $231,000 in 2001. He resigned that position to successfully run for Congress in 2002. Emanuel was the leading recipient in the 2008 election cycle of money from Wall Street. His leading contributors were Goldman Sachs, JPMorgan Chase, Citigroup, Morgan Stanley, and UBS. He led the Democrats' effort in the 2006 election cycle to take control of Congress. He was a major conduit of political contributions to the Democrats from the money industry.

The finance chair for the Obama campaign in 2008 was Penny Pritzker, a Chicago financier and close Obama advisor. In the 1990s, she led the Superior Bank of Chicago, a pioneer in making and then packaging subprime mortgages that Merrill Lynch then marketed. Foreshadowing the economic collapse of 2008, Superior Bank failed in 2001 with more than $1 billion of insured and uninsured deposits. As part of a settlement, the Pritzker family paid $100 million and agreed to pay another $335 million over fifteen years. In late 2008, Penny Pritzker withdrew her name from consideration as commerce secretary.

These are only the top jobs filled by Wall Street. Many lesser positions, such as assistant secretary of treasury, commerce, and state, are filled by people from the money industry, too. Almost inevitably, when these individuals leave public office, they will return to finance or lobby on behalf of that industry. A shift from a Republican to a Democratic president, or the reverse, is meaningless, as one group of insiders from the same companies replaces another, all of whom are on the same team. In sum, Wall Street controls and runs those parts of our federal government that affect it.

FAILED SELF-REGULATION

The present economic crisis is eerily reminiscent of the one faced by newly elected president Franklin D. Roosevelt more than seven decades ago, when Wall Street experienced one of its manic moments and the nation was in a financial bust. In his March 4, 1933, inaugural address, FDR captured the essence of the problem and his intended solution in a few elegant sentences:

> *[I]n our progress toward a resumption of work we require two safeguards against a return of the evils of the old order; there must be a strict supervision of all banking and credits and investments; there must be an end to speculation with other people's money, and there must be provision for an adequate but sound currency.*

Roosevelt quickly kept his promise. Two days after taking office, he declared a bank "holiday" and persuaded Congress to enact the Emergency Banking Act, which created a de facto deposit insurance program at the Federal Reserve. Only seven days after closing, one thousand banks reopened and people began putting their money back into them. Less than three months later, in June 1933, Congress enacted the Banking Act of 1933, informally known as Glass-Steagall in honor of its sponsors, Senator Carter Glass (D-VA) and Representative Henry B. Steagall (D-AL). The act separated commercial and investment banking, because Congress had found in its hearings that the actions of bankers and brokers were sometimes indistinguishable, thereby creating clear conflicts of interest and opportunity for fraud. In the crash of 1929, Congress found that banks had gambled deposits and savings on stocks that fell in value, thereby breaking the banks and ruining millions of depositors. FDR's goal was to build a wall between banks (where people and businesses deposited their money for safety) and securities organizations (where brokers and investors took investment risks).

The Glass-Steagall Act also created the Federal Deposit Insurance Corporation (FDIC), which guaranteed deposits up to a set amount. Prior to the bank holiday, more than nine thousand banks had failed, wiping out the savings of millions of Americans. More than anything, the FDIC restored confidence in America's banks. Between 1934 and 1941, the agency managed only 370 failures.

FROM BANKING TO GAMBLING

As bankers who lived through the Great Depression were replaced around the 1960s by a new generation, the banks became more aggressive, striving for more assets, deposits, and income. By the 1990s, the big banks' fondest dream was repeal of the Glass-Steagall Act provisions separating deposit and brokerage functions. They finally got their chance in 1999, when Senator Phil Gramm (R-TX), Representative Jim Leach (R-IA), and

Representative Thomas Bliley (R-VA) introduced legislation to revoke the Banking Act of 1933.

The banks' advocates made two principal arguments: They were losing market share to foreign competitors, and their securities activities would be low risk. Treasury Secretary Lawrence Summers supported passage of the bill, and President Clinton signed it into law in November 1999. With that, the federal government allowed the major banks to underwrite and trade mortgage-backed securities and collateralized debt obligations, which turned out to be a classic example of "be careful what you ask for." The Heritage Foundation reports that in 2001 "newly originated subprime, Alt-A (slightly less risky) and home equity lines (second mortgages) totaled $330 billion and amounted to 15 percent of all residential mortgages." By 2006, at the peak of the bubble, they totaled $1.1 trillion in new loans and 48 percent of the total—more than a tripling of volume. The money industry was gorging itself, taking high fees for disbursing weak paper.

After the Internet bubble burst in 2000, when many investors in technology stocks lost money, the Federal Reserve eased credit dramatically, thereby stimulating growth in the housing industry. As the bubble expanded, the money industry issued millions of mortgages to people unable to pay back their debt. To reduce risk and generate revenue, banks packaged dozens of these subprime mortgages with good ones into securities they sold around the world—a process known as collateralizing mortgages. The buyers of these collateralized mortgages relied on the reputed solvency, soundness, and integrity of American banks and the credit ratings of those instruments by companies such as Moody's and Standard & Poor's.

To reduce their potential losses, the banks bought insurance from AIG and others in the form of a special type of derivative called a credit default swap (CDS). The *New York Times* defines a derivative as "a risk shifting insurance contract whose value is derived from the value of an underlying asset such as a physical commodity, an interest rate, a corporate stock, a currency, a stock index, or virtually any other tradable instrument upon which the parties can agree."

Such private derivative sales greatly concerned some U.S. regulators. Even as repeal of Glass-Steagall was working its way through Congress, a related battle royal was under way among the Treasury, the Federal Reserve, and the Commodity Futures Trading Commission (CFTC) over whether to regulate these swaps. Futures contracts on commodities are an ancient form of insurance used by farmers, miners, and other producers and their customers to hedge their risk. Futures are standardized exchange-traded derivatives that are regulated. But these mortgage-based derivative swaps were a new type of insurance, one in which two parties entered into a private contract. If company A bought an insurance contract from company B and A had a loss, B had to pay.

Brooksley Born, chair of the CFTC and former head of the derivative practice at the Washington, D.C., law firm of Arnold & Porter, concluded in the late 1990s that because these two-party private deals had enormous potential for abuse, the federal government should regulate them and make the transactions transparent. Treasury Secretary Rubin, Federal Reserve Chairman Greenspan, and Deputy Treasury Secretary Summers stoutly opposed her proposal, arguing that transparency and regulatory costs might drive business offshore, and powerful members of Congress were soon warning Born to stop pushing for regulation. A disgusted Born resigned in the summer of 1999.

As the Clinton administration was coming to a close, Senator Gramm, working with then treasury secretary Summers, pushed into law another financial deregulation bill, the Commodity Futures Modernization Act of 2000, which explicitly prohibited the regulation of energy futures and exempted credit default swaps from both regulation and federal oversight. The Enron debacle quickly followed when that corporation's traders went wild with the buying, selling, and trading of energy futures contracts. The Houston-based company, with more than $100 billion of reported revenue in 2000, used trades in energy futures to almost bankrupt the State of California, and then it miscalculated and bankrupted itself in 2001.

Foremost of the contract sellers was AIG, the world's largest insurance company, which until this crisis had a rare and coveted AAA credit rating. If someone wanted insurance against the risk of a subprime mortgage default, a corporation failing, credit card receivables, or a host of other debt security risks, AIG analysts would calculate that risk, set a price, and make a contract guaranteeing the purchaser against loss. As part of the deal, AIG also agreed to provide the insured party collateral if the debt securities being insured declined in value or if AIG's corporate-debt rating fell below AAA.

A small group of in-house economic model makers analyzed the risk of each derivative contract. The modelers convinced AIG management that their formulas had reduced the risk of loss to almost zero. Thus, unlike normal insurance, in which a capital reserve is maintained to pay off losses or hedging contracts are bought to reduce risk, AIG's CDS contracts were written "naked"—no capital reserve for losses was established—and AIG bought no offsetting insurance. AIG's liability soon rose to more than $440 billion. Knowingly or not, AIG management was betting the world's largest insurance company, which otherwise was exceptionally well run, on the skills of its small "geek squad" of economic model makers. In the first several years, and with a booming economy, their risk models worked and AIG made large profits from its derivatives business. Then the risk models failed.

FEDERAL PERMISSION TO GAMBLE

Others, of course, noted AIG's success. In late April 2004, senior representatives of Bear Stearns, Goldman Sachs, Morgan Stanley,

Merrill Lynch, and Lehman Brothers, led by Goldman Sachs chairman Henry Paulson, met in Washington with the commissioners of the Securities and Exchange Commission (SEC). They requested that the SEC release them from its "net capital" rule, which required banks and their brokerage units to keep a dollar in reserve for every $12 of risk they took. The SEC not only granted the request, it ruled that any bank with assets of $5 billion or more could use its own model of risk to determine the debt-to-liability ratio for its own brokerage units. With that, the SEC gave the big banks government permission to gamble with their capital. Soon firms such as Bear Stearns had $33 of debt for every dollar of equity.

After the SEC issued that ruling, the banks' brokerage units began buying, selling, and trading hundreds of billions of dollars of these two-party insurance contracts. By December 2008, the FDIC reported that the aggregate face value of derivatives held by U.S. commercial banks was $201 trillion, which was more than thirteen times the gross domestic product of the United States. Eric Dinallo, the insurance superintendent for New York, estimated that in 2008 almost 80 percent of the estimated $62 trillion in credit default swaps in existence were speculative.

The Office of the Comptroller of the Currency reported that five large commercial banks held the overwhelming majority of those derivatives: JPMorgan Chase ($87 trillion), Bank of America ($38 trillion), Citibank ($35 trillion), Wachovia ($4 trillion), and HSBC ($4 trillion). The three largest banks were highly leveraged. Collectively, JPMorgan Chase, Bank of America, and Citibank had $160 trillion of liabilities and total assets of $4.3 trillion, an equity-to-liability ratio of 38 to one, making the banks extraordinarily vulnerable to even the slightest downturn in the economy. What the banks' managers and boards seemed to have forgotten is that, in a downturn, leverage works in reverse. Unfortunately, in the spring of 2007, the economy began to slow and the world of American finance began to fall apart.

In June 2007, two of Bear Stearns's hedge funds, heavily invested in the weakening subprime market, collapsed. In March 2008, the parent firm failed and JPMorgan Chase bought it all for less than the value of Bear Stearns's New York headquarters building in a sale arranged by its lender, the Federal Reserve. As difficult as it was to imagine, the financial world went from bad to worse.

On September 7, 2008, the federal government effectively nationalized mortgage lenders Fannie Mae (Federal National Mortgage Association) and Freddie Mac, which then owned or guaranteed about half of the $12 trillion U.S. mortgage market, creating a panic among investors worldwide who held $5.2 trillion of debt guaranteed by those two institutions.

On September 14, Merrill Lynch sold itself to Bank of America, and the next day Lehman Brothers filed for Chapter 11 bankruptcy, leaving its investors worldwide in a lurch. On September 17, the Federal Reserve bailed out AIG with an infusion of $85 billion, taking 79.5 percent equity in the insurance giant. Six days later, the national media reported that the FBI was investigating the possibility of fraud by twenty-six corporate executives from Lehman Brothers, AIG, Fannie Mae, and Freddie Mac.

Of the institutions that had met with the SEC barely four years earlier, only Goldman Sachs and JPMorgan Chase remained, and Goldman Sachs was in desperate need of a massive federal bailout.

BAILOUT

On September 19, 2008, Treasury Secretary Henry Paulson formally asked Congress for $700 billion in bailout monies to buy the toxic assets held by the nation's largest banks. He presented Congress a three-page draft bill that would give him complete authority to use the federal funds and total immunity for his actions. Even for members of Congress who had long benefited from the money industry's massive political contributions, such autocratic control by a Wall Street insider was unacceptable. Undeterred, Wall Street mounted a massive lobbying campaign led by the Bush White House and Treasury Department to enact its proposed bailout legislation. But events soon took over.

In the two-week interim before Congress took up this bill, the FDIC seized Washington Mutual and sold its assets to JPMorgan Chase. Four days later, the FDIC sold the banking operations of Wachovia, one of the nation's largest banks, to Citigroup. In a move to help the acquiring banks, the Treasury changed tax regulations to allow a bank acquiring another to write off all the acquired bank's losses for tax purposes—an unannounced action by Paulson that was worth more than $100 billion to the acquiring banks.

Also in that interim, a longer, more detailed piece of federal bailout legislation was written by the administration and leaders of the Democratically controlled House and Senate that left real control with Paulson. Without congressional hearings, expert testimony, or any of the other trappings of the normal legislative process, including little more than pro forma time for debate, the Bush administration and the Democratic leadership tried to stampede Congress into enacting the $700 billion bailout of the money industry. Resistance from Republicans and a handful of progressive Democrats, led by Representative Marcy Kaptur (D-OH), enabled opponents in the House of Representatives to defeat the bailout bill on its first vote, plus plant some ideas that later bore fruit.

THE ISAAC PROPOSALS

Many House members had been in Congress during the savings and loan crisis of the 1980s and remembered how the FDIC had smoothly handled three thousand bank and thrift failures, which represented $100 billion of insolvency reconciled at a total cost of $2 billion, none of which was taxpayer money. They invited William M. Isaac, who led the FDIC during that crisis, to advise them on the new financial debacle now before them.

The bailout alternative Isaac proposed was the issuance of FDIC "net worth certificates," a program designed to shore up the capital of weak banks so that they would have more time to work out their problems. No subsidy or cash would be required from the taxpayers. It was an elegant idea that worked almost flawlessly during the 1980s crisis.

Under this program, the FDIC purchased net worth certificates (subordinated debentures) in those banks the agency determined could survive if given a little time. The banks used the notes to boost their capital. The FDIC paid for the certificates by issuing its senior notes (guaranteed by the U.S. government) to the banks. No cash changed hands and the interest rate on each instrument was the same, avoiding both any cost to the FDIC and any bank-paid subsidies. This no-cost exchange was possible because the FDIC is backed by the full faith and credit of the United States government.

As part of the deal, the FDIC would strictly oversee the banks' operations, including the hiring, retention, and pay of executives and employees. None of the problems with controversial executive bonuses that plagued the bailout in 2009 were encountered under the FDIC approach. The FDIC liquidated or merged banks too weak to survive.

One of the main problems with Paulson's original $700 billion bailout plan was that it produced virtually no financial leverage—$700 billion purchased only $700 billion of assets. If the banks used the money to expand their capital, Isaac argued, the banks would be able to loan seven to ten dollars for every dollar they received. Thus, recapitalization of a bank would get far more leverage from taxpayer money than simply buying bad assets.

The Bush administration and Congress ignored the Isaac approach, added $150 billion of pork projects to the bailout package, and pushed the bill through the Senate and House just before the 2008 elections. Isaac's logic prevailed, however, in the longer term, and the Treasury began using the public monies to capitalize the banks rather than to buy toxic assets.

The Treasury's big failure was rejecting the inclusion of a "public purpose" provision in the legislation that would have required the recipient banks to lend the new monies and not use it for bonuses and dividends. These omissions, of course, were no accident, because many members of Congress had rejected the idea, and Paulson rejected it as well. The Obama stimulus program enacted in February 2009, moreover, contained a specific provision, put in at the recommendation of the Treasury, that allowed bailout recipients to honor bonus contracts made prior to that date, language that became public after AIG gave its risk analysis personnel $160 million in bonuses in March 2009. An enormous public outcry ensued.

MARK TO MARKET

More significant, a long-standing, obscure SEC accounting rule resulted in the diversion of billions of bailout dollars from their intended purpose at the very moment American finance was in meltdown. Under the SEC's "mark-to-market" accounting rule, banks are required to keep a certain amount of capital for every dollar of liability they have on their books. If the value of collateral drops, as it does when housing and stock prices fall, a bank instantly has to put up more capital and reevaluate the value of its collateral at what are often fire-sale rates. Thus, just at the moment the nation needs more lending from banks, the SEC is forcing the banks to use much of their capital to shore up the fire-sale values of the collateral they already hold on existing loans.

Isaac and his congressional allies argued the mark-to-market rule should be changed so that bankers could count their collateral at the real price they could get if eventually given time to market it prudently. The SEC refused to make the change initially. For critical months, much of the federal bailout money went to banks' capital reserves, rather than into loans, where it could do the most good.

The Financial Accounting Standards Board (FASB), a private organization dominated by the major accounting firms, establishes accounting rules for the SEC and the public sector. In April 2009, the board eased its rules slightly but still continued to force reduction of value on the banks' books for securities they intend to hold to maturity. These rules, at the critical moment in the financial crisis, had the effect of diverting capital to reserves faster than the federal government could provide bailouts.

The political problem with the Isaac plan was that it required the FDIC to oversee the bailouts. The FDIC, an independent agency skilled in bank collapses and nonpartisan in its approach, does not engage in the political or crony-capitalist games played in the Treasury Department under its ex–Wall Street insider leadership. FDIC employees are not part of the Wall Street–Washington club and almost certainly would never have allowed the extraordinary salaries and bonuses permitted by the Treasury or the 100 cents on the dollar payments made by AIG out of its $180 billion of public monies.

Most significantly, the Paulson plan failed to assure global money interests that America's financial industry was stable and trustworthy. Credit markets froze worldwide in the fall of 2008. Banks were afraid to lend even overnight funds to one another, fearing they might not get back their money. When the Federal Reserve and the Treasury allowed Lehman Brothers to fail, the act was seen as a repudiation of the "too big to fail" position the United States had long held. Previously, foreign investors and lenders had had the assurance that if they put their money into the largest U.S. financial institutions it was totally safe, because Washington monitored and regulated the soundness of those banks and thus would not allow them to fail. For a nation borrowing hundreds of billions of dollars annually, global trust was invaluable. With this one decision to allow Lehman to fail, however, Federal Reserve Chairman Ben Bernanke and Treasury Secretary Henry Paulson shattered that confidence.

The consequences of the resulting credit freeze were obvious immediately. American companies became unable to borrow the monies needed to make payrolls in the last quarter of 2008 and the first of 2009, or to finance consumers who wanted to buy autos, homes, or anything else. Suddenly, American business had to revert to cash-on-the-barrelhead operations common to developing countries, and thousands of employers began laying off workers and shutting down production. Unintentionally, the Treasury and the Federal Reserve had triggered a systemic failure of the U.S. financial system.

SAVING WALL STREET

A fail-safe mechanism exists in U.S. law if a meltdown of the U.S. financial system is imminent. The Federal Deposit Insurance Act allows the treasury secretary to declare a national emergency once in receipt of a letter from the Federal Reserve board and the FDIC board, and with approval of the president, that warns the U.S. financial system is in danger of systemic collapse.

That moment arrived in early October 2008. Though he disguised it in almost incomprehensible language to hide the severity of the moment, Secretary Paulson declared an emergency on October 14, 2008. This allowed the FDIC to guarantee, with the backing of the full faith and credit of the United States, the newly issued senior unsecured debt of insured depository institutions, most U.S. holding companies, and non-interest-bearing transaction accounts at FDIC-insured institutions. In effect, the Bush administration very quietly put everything owned by everyone in America on the line to save Wall Street. Amazingly, the declaration went unnoticed and uncommented upon during the final days of the 2008 presidential campaign.

Trying to break the credit crunch, the United States guaranteed both foreign and domestic financial institutions that their deposits in the U.S. money industry were secure. Trust in the system, however, was unshakably broken, and global markets deemed the guarantee insufficient. It was as though the world held its collective breath, waiting for the Bush administration to exit and that of Barack Obama to take charge.

Between the November 2008 election and the inauguration of the new president, Obama and Bush financial advisors worked closely. They made the transition rapidly in part because of Obama's appointment of Tim Geithner to be treasury secretary. Yet the Geithner solutions were little more than repackaged versions of the Paulson proposals.

In quick succession, the Obama administration persuaded a Democratic Congress to accept a special program to buy credit card assets, another to aid with subprime mortgages, and a third to loan hundreds of billions of dollars in nonrecourse loans to private investors to assume Wall Street's toxic assets. *Nonrecourse* means that if the deal goes bad, all the taxpayer gets back is the toxic asset.

The Public-Private Investment Program created by the Obama administration is a Rube Goldberg structure in which the public loans private investors about thirteen dollars for every dollar of their private equity. The purpose of these high-leverage loans is to get private investors to inject capital into banks by buying their bad assets. Because those assets are toxic, however, this scheme will produce little new capital. Both Joseph Stiglitz and Paul Krugman, two Nobel laureates in economics, have harshly criticized the plan, as have many other economists. Their criticism is that by taking timid actions that protect existing equity holders in the largest banks, the government has made real reform impossible, leaving the country with its largest banks crippled, thereby dragging down the economy, as happened in Japan in the 1990s, when that government failed to seize and recapitalize its failed banks.

The net effect of the Paulson-Geithner plans is to save Wall Street equity holders by shifting the cost of the bailout to U.S. taxpayers. Better and far less expensive options exist. One is the Isaac plan rejected by the Bush administration. Another is a proposal by Andrew M. Rosenfield, who teaches at the University of Chicago Law School and runs an investment firm. He suggests that the U.S. government seize the insolvent banks, as current law allows; inject cash in the form of Treasury notes (a variant of the Isaac plan); and remove the banks' bad assets, which are then held by the Treasury while it waits to see what they are really worth. Then the government would auction off the bank with a clean balance sheet. The result would be a new bank with ample capital to lend.

WHAT TO DO

The money industry is the heart and arterial system of the American economy. It collects and allocates the funds required to operate an economy that annually produces and distributes more than $14 trillion in goods and services. It does all this, moreover, through millions of daily, individual, uncoordinated decisions. A sound financial system, owned and operated by the private sector, is the anchor of any national effort to keep America strong and capitalistic.

Most of America's 8,300 national, regional, and community banks and other financial institutions did not gamble with their depositors' and investors' money. They operate prudently, serve their depositors and clients well, and are in sound financial health.

Those infected with the spirit of manic risk-taking were primarily executives in America's largest banks and investment houses, which dominate the money industry. These gamblers destroyed a quarter or more of the national wealth, wiped out the pensions of many working people, denied educations to young people, pushed families out of their homes, destroyed the dreams of millions of people, and perhaps worst of all raised serious doubts about the economic integrity of America and the viability of capitalism among billions of people worldwide. No terrorist in the world could have weakened America and capitalism more.

American capitalism requires a financial system that is once again solvent, stable, safe, and trustworthy, and provides capital and credit for productive activities. The challenge faced by President Obama, as with FDR before him, is to impose "strict supervision of all banking and credits and investments," end "speculation with other people's money," and provide "for an adequate but sound currency." The following recommendations and actions will help.

SUNSHINE

A historic economic debacle has been under way for almost two years, and Americans need to understand its dynamics. From the limited information now available, we know there has been massive incompetence, fraud, outright theft, and a systemic failure of both public and private safeguards. With the American financial system spiraling out of control and world-famous banks, insurance companies, and investment houses toppling one after another like falling dominoes, the absence of public oversight is striking. Nothing—no major congressional hearings, no presidential commission—so far has been convened. America needs to know how this crisis happened so that we can prevent a repeat.

From January 1933 to July 1934, the Senate Banking and Currency Committee held hearings that drove Depression-era regulatory change in the finance industry. Led by Ferdinand Pecora, the committee's chief counsel, the seventeen months of hearings, resulting in twelve thousand pages of documents and testimony under oath, exposed the shenanigans of Wall Street insiders whom Pecora described as "the Street's mightiest and best-informed men." The hearings revealed the double-dealing supposedly reputable firms used to swindle their customers, including selling more than $25 billion of worthless stock in the years before the crash of 1929 (about $500 billion in 2008 dollars). The hearings stripped away the mystery and sanctity of Wall Street practices and revealed many of the "demigods" of finance to be mere crooks. Substitute the names, firms, and practices in Pecora's best-selling 1939 book, *Wall Street Under Oath: The Story of Our Modern Money Changers,* with those involved in the current scandal and his description seems absolutely contemporary.

Pecora concluded that while the great financial institutions did perform a necessary function, the manner of their performance and the terrific concentration of power from many sources in their hands were more threatening. "The bankers," he wrote, "were neither a national asset nor a national danger—they were both."

The actions of Wall Street today are as corrupt as then and cannot withstand public scrutiny, which the leaders of the largest banks and investment houses know. For Wall Street, therefore, public hearings and federal regulation are of such significance that they cannot be left to chance. The *New York Times* revealed in June 2009 that nine of the largest participants in the derivatives business decided during the middle of the Wall Street collapse (November 2008) to form a new lobbying organization—the CDS Dealers Consortium. Then they hired well-connected Washington lobbyists and began work to derail federal regulation of derivatives, just as they had done in 2000 through the efforts of Senator Phil Gramm. The irony is that five of the nine firms took monies from the federal government because their bad derivatives gambles had taken them and the global economy to the brink of disaster. Now they wanted to resume trading using taxpayers' money as their stake.

In May 2009, Congress passed and the president signed Public Law 111-21, which authorized the creation of a Financial Crisis Inquiry Commission (FCIC). Modeled on the 9/11 Commission, the FCIC is to investigate the causes of the failure of the U.S. financial system. The commission will be composed of ten members—six of whom shall be appointed by the Senate and House Democratic leaders and four of whom will be appointed by their Republican counterparts. The commission will have the power to subpoena witnesses and its final report is due on December 15, 2010.

The commission begins with major structural problems, not the least of which is that three of the four congressional leaders making the appointments to the committee supported earlier legislation that deregulated the financial industry, and all four are major beneficiaries of campaign funds from the industry. An honest report would include revelations that are sure to embarrass many members of Congress. While Congress authorized the commission to focus on causes, it does not seek recommendations as to how to prevent a recurrence. Equally significant, the report will not be made public until after the 2010 midterm elections. The risk is that the commission will serve as political cover for Congress to postpone any meaningful financial reforms until 2011, which probably means no action until the next financial crisis.

If it soon becomes obvious that elected leaders are too reluctant to examine the issues and make recommendations for change, then a major nonprofit, nonpartisan foundation should step up, provide funding, and name a blue-ribbon panel to do the job. America needs to know.

CLEAN HOUSE

Fraud is the cancer of the American financial system. It has metastasized under financial deregulation, intimately involving some of the "best" people in our communities and the nation. If capitalism is to thrive, our government must cut out that cancer. Arrests, trials, and jail time will come as no surprise, as the prevalence of fraud in the money industry is well known by many insiders. An intense cleansing is required.

In October 2004, Chris Swecker, assistant director of the FBI's Criminal Investigative Division, testified before the House Financial Services Subcommittee on Housing and Community Opportunity. He described to the committee the FBI's efforts since 2002 to stop mortgage fraud for profit. He explained how the FBI had intercepted a mortgage fraud scheme by several insiders at the First Beneficial Mortgage Corporation against the Fannie Mae and Ginnie Mae (Government National Mortgage Association) home loan programs that resulted in losses of $30 million. The Justice Department convicted the president of First Beneficial and six others. The court sentenced the president to twenty-one years in prison and ordered him to pay $23 million in restitution and forfeit about $8 million of property.

Swecker described another case in Charlotte, North Carolina, where the FBI identified thirty-five industry insiders involved in 380 fraudulent loans exceeding $70 million. He reported that in 2002, the FBI's Cleveland office had secured the indictment of ninety-four insiders, including two accountants, four title company employees, five appraisers, eight underwriters, and forty loan brokers.

These cases, he warned, were the tip of an enlarging iceberg of crime—partially visible, massive, and expanding. A 2004 FBI analysis identified twenty-six states as having problems. Presciently, Swecker warned,

> *If fraudulent practices become systemic within the mortgage industry and mortgage fraud is allowed to become unrestrained, it will ultimately place financial institutions at risk and have adverse effects on the stock market itself. . . . Mortgage fraud losses adversely affect loan loss reserves, profits, liquidity levels, and capitalization ratios, ultimately affecting the soundness of the financial institution.*

And it did become systemic. The Treasury Department, under the authority of the Bank Security Act, collects Suspicious Activity Reports (SARs), which financial institutions are required to file. In 2000, the Treasury received 3,515 reports of fraudulent mortgages. It received 18,000 SARs in 2004, 21,000 in 2006, 46,000 in 2007, and more than 63,000 in 2008. Viewed in relative terms, the number of reports on mortgage fraud in 2008 was seventeen times greater than in 2000.

Though mortgage fraud was escalating rapidly during the housing bubble of that era, and though the FBI kept Congress and the Bush administration fully briefed, the bureau was forced to reassign 2,400 agents to counterterrorism duty after the 9/11 attacks, leaving the criminal division stretched very thin. At the same time, the SEC was uninterested in the issue, even ignoring persuasive evidence of the Bernard Madoff Ponzi scheme. Self-regulation was the Federal Reserve's policy under chairman Alan Greenspan's leadership.

Even with a reduced staff, the FBI got 560 indictments and 338 convictions in 2008. Plus, it had two thousand investigations under way by the end of the year. But as the SARs data suggest, most mortgage fraud, a particularly insidious crime, has gone uninvestigated.

The FBI divides mortgage fraud into two categories. Fraud

for property and housing entails misrepresentation by an applicant for a primary residence, but the usual intent is to repay the loan. Fraud for profit involves elaborate schemes to gain illicit proceeds from property sales. Swecker told Congress that each mortgage fraud scheme contains some type of "material misstatement, misrepresentation, or omission relied upon by an underwriter or lender to fund, purchase, or insure a loan." The Treasury reported in April 2008 that a sample of SARs revealed that 31 percent of the misrepresentation of income, assets, or debt was fraud for profit and that more than 60 percent of appraisal fraud was also for profit. This means that there were almost thirty-seven thousand reported cases of mortgage fraud for profit in 2008 alone.

According to William K. Black—a lead investigator in the savings and loan scandal of the 1980s and former director of the Institute for Fraud Prevention who now teaches economics and law at the University of Missouri, Kansas City—the current wave of mortgage fraud eventually involved America's largest banks and their top officials. Some firms, such as the failed IndyMac, specialized in subprime mortgage loans and were notorious for nonverification of loan applications. Thus, they were knowingly making loans to people without the capacity to pay and charging extra fees, making such business highly profitable.

Once a loan was closed, it would be sold to other financial institutions or it would be packaged with other loans and sold to Fannie Mae, Ginnie Mae, or another of the major financial players, which would in turn add their fees and push what was then termed a collateralized package onto the world market. Often the seller would purchase a derivative from AIG or some other bank to guarantee the package and with that acquire a AAA rating. Buyers assumed that they were getting prime collateral.

At each stage there was deception, which means fraud. Throughout the nation, local brokers and local banks knew the mortgages were unserviceable. The banks and investment houses that packaged many mortgages into a bundle, which they sold, knew that as well. But as Black points out, the worse the mortgage, the more the bank and the investment house could charge in extra fees, thus the greater the annual profits and the higher the corporate bonuses. In large measure, this explains how so many financial officials involved with subpar mortgages made so much money earlier in this decade: They were profiting from fraudulent activities on a massive scale.

The important point is that virtually all the participants knew they were involved in a massive scheme. The FBI's Swecker testified in 2004 that "based upon existing investigations and mortgage fraud reporting, 80 percent of all reported fraud losses involve collaboration or collusion by industry insiders."

The systemic failure that followed involved virtually all the largest banks and investment houses in America. While the public most often blames the CEOs of these organizations for these corporate failures, others share the responsibility, notably members of boards of directors. In American capitalism, a member of a private corporate board of directors has major duties: to provide continuity; select, appoint, and if need be fire a chief executive; govern the organization by broad policies; acquire the resources needed for operation; and account to the public for the corporation's products and services and for the expenditure of its funds.

One of a board's principal responsibilities is to "provide for fiscal accountability and accept responsibility for all conditions and policies aligned with new or experimental programs." In American corporations, the buck stops with its board.

In a fair world where justice is impartial, unearned bonuses, high salaries, and lavish corporate indulgences would be recouped from the executives of failed financial organizations, particularly those that took federal bailouts. But in reality, that will be difficult.

The more important issue is how stop a repeat. How does the nation ensure that the same executives and potted-plant directors do not reemerge elsewhere in a revived financial industry? And how do we ensure that those who receive public funds from the Treasury's new public–private toxic assets program are not the same people who participated in the fraud that created the financial collapse in the first place? Fortunately, a legal and long-used means exists: a ban on working in the securities and financial industry.

The experience of Henry Blodget illustrates how the process works. Blodget was a star financial analyst at Oppenheimer & Co. and then at Merrill Lynch. In 2000, he was voted the number one Internet/e-commerce analyst on Wall Street by *Institutional Investor* and *Greenwich Associates.* After the dot-com bust, the SEC and other law enforcement agencies examined copies of Blodget's e-mails, which revealed that his real assessments were other than what he published for clients. The SEC charged him with securities fraud. He settled without admitting or denying the allegations, and the Securities and Exchange Commission barred him from working in the securities industry for life. Hundreds of other people from the money industry need to be put on the sidelines along with Blodget.

A LIFETIME BAN

The CEOs and compliant board members of far too many financial institutions facilitated an economic disaster that did far greater economic damage than Blodget and harmed far more people. Under the prevailing self-regulation ethos, they were particularly responsible for the actions of the institutions they headed. With responsibility comes accountability. The most elementary step is to impose a lifetime ban on people responsible for this crisis from working in the securities and financial industries. Those who would automatically qualify are the CEOs and all board members from every bank, insurance company, and investment house of that era that failed because of the corporation's overexposure to subprime mortgages. Their companies were involved in deceit and thus fraud, and those responsible for self-regulating their corporation failed in their duty, costing their equity holders, customers, and the nation trillions of dollars. Never again for them is a minimal response.

Others who merit the same ban include leadership (CEOs and boards) of all the major banks that had to take federal bailout monies to prevent failure because of their subprime mortgage activities. The list of CEOs and corporate boards that should be banned include those who led Washington Mutual, Wachovia, Bear Stearns, Lehman Brothers, Goldman Sachs, Citigroup, and Bank of America. This, of course, is only a partial list. Fortunately, America has more than enough competent people to replace them.

The ban would tell the world that market capitalism is about responsibility and that the United States is dead serious about restoring the soundness and integrity of its money industry. Nothing can send that message better than banning the prominent people who so deceived the nation and the world. Think of President Obama firing Rick Wagoner, General Motors' long-term CEO, as the signal to fire about two thousand more.

A corresponding noncompete clause for some long period, such as five to ten years, should be imposed on the employment contracts of all those in the federal government who are managing, or responsible in any way, for this bailout. Too many come from Wall Street and intend to return there. As events have amply illustrated, Wall Street is corrupt and its ways and means of bribery and influence are seemingly limitless. We need those who manage the public's money in this bailout to have not just the appearance but the actual quality of propriety. America has many skilled, smart, financially savvy people who are incorruptible and would love to help their government clean up America's financial system.

RESTITUTION AND SHAME

One of the conspicuous features of this financial meltdown is the apparent absence of any feeling of guilt, shortcoming, or impropriety by leaders of the money industry. Though the working people of America had to provide hundreds of billions of dollars to keep their corporations out of bankruptcy, virtually all of these organizations still operating under their own management paid out high bonuses for work done in 2008 and surely will try to do the same in 2009.

Most of the corporations receiving bailouts still pay their executives very high salaries; continue to own corporate jets; and have private chefs, executive dining rooms, unlimited expense accounts, corporate art collections, and all the other privileges enjoyed before the crash of 2008. Although the net wealth of these executives may have dropped by half or more, their remaining wherewithal is more than enough to ensure them and their families a comfortable and worry-free financial situation for the rest of their lives. While the Obama administration fired the CEO and board of federal bailout money recipient General Motors in March 2009, the president met that same month with the CEOs of a number of the largest banks, many also bailout beneficiaries, at the White House for tea, cookies, and polite conversation.

Shame is a potent cultural force for defining what is and is not considered proper in a society. Apparently, the people who created this crisis are not ashamed of what they did and the harm they created. Yet much of the money they received and still possess came from paper profits generated by fraudulent activities. They must be made to return those funds. Such a process would have the added benefit of shaming them for what they did. Standing in front of a jury composed of their fellow citizens would be a bracing experience for them and a strong example for others.

The message the president must send is that acting recklessly or stealing other people's money, regardless of how cleverly the violator rationalizes it, is shameful and will not be tolerated. A big step in that direction would be for President Obama and Congress to expand funding of the financial crimes division of the FBI. The expertise and resources of that division will allow the tracking of the loot wherever the thieves stashed it.

Because the financial crimes involved in this economic collapse are so vast and complicated, Congress should lift any statutes of limitations for these wrongdoings. If criminals like Bernard Madoff, for instance, and other Wall Street miscreants had accomplices, no time limit should be placed on the authorities' ability to prosecute such individuals and search for and retrieve any funds they stole.

STRENGTHEN THE FDIC'S LEADERSHIP POSITION

The FDIC has the expertise, staff, statutory mandate, and resources to restore the economic health and integrity of America's wayward banks and holding companies. The Treasury Department has amply demonstrated that it does not. The Treasury's ad hoc efforts may ensure the survival of stockholder and bondholder interests in these large institutions, but this risks creating a half decade or more of impaired banking.

America needs its major banks to be dynamic and sound, sooner rather than later. Quick, decisive repairs are required, and a lead agency is essential. Relying on those who got the country into this mess to get it out is not the wisest approach. Thus, the president and Congress should rely on the FDIC to lead efforts to heal the money industry—with the support of the Treasury and the Federal Reserve.

The FDIC staff and leadership are astute and experienced enough to recognize that while taking over and reorganizing virtually any U.S. bank, including large ones, is possible, there may be a handful that are too large to fail, too large to ignore, and too large to nationalize.

William M. Isaac, when chairman of the FDIC, nationalized Continental Illinois Bank in 1984. Continental was then the seventh-largest U.S. bank and held 2 percent of the country's banking assets. After seven years, the FDIC was able to put the bank on a solid foundation and sell it to Bank of America. But Isaac says that nationalizing any of the top ten U.S. banks, which collectively hold two-thirds of America's banking assets, would be a nightmare for several major reasons. First, once this happened to one or two banks, there would be massive political and financial pressure to take over some or all of the others. Second, he notes, an exit strategy would be limited because these banks are so huge that a large number of potential buyers will be foreign governments and their sovereign wealth funds. Washington, for instance, is unlikely to allow a Middle Eastern or Asian country to buy and control any of America's major banks. Finally, these big banks are enormously complex, and the talent required to run them is scarce.

A backdoor way of reducing their excesses is for the federal government to put public directors on the boards of those top ten banks in proportion to the equity and loans provided by the nation's taxpayers. The process would shrink the equity of the existing shareholders accordingly and perhaps even eliminate it. The appointment of such directors should be highly scrutinized, to prevent a repeat of the cronyism that afflicted the boards of Fannie Mae and Freddie Mac, and accompanied by mandatory public hearings and confirmation by Congress.

These new public directors could work with new private directors to change management where needed, set new compensation rules, alter operational policies, and dispose of problem assets on an orderly basis. Ideally, the FDIC and the public directors would remain involved with these institutions for enough time, at least four or five years, to restaff them properly and impose a culture of responsibility. Far better than nationalizing the banks and failed financial institutions, such a shift of control should adhere to conservative banking principles, act quickly, guarantee honest oversight, and, hopefully, eliminate political pressure from the right and left for more radical solutions. For all other banks, the existing FDIC approach is appropriate.

REGULATE THE MONEY INDUSTRY IN ITS ENTIRETY

The financial regulatory regimes created during the New Deal need modernization and reinstitution. This recommendation means separating, once again, commercial banking from brokerage activities and bringing all forms of financial activities, including banks, derivatives, hedge funds, investment banks, credit rating agencies, mortgage lenders, private-equity funds, asset managers, and insurance, under a regulatory regime that allows the federal takeover of any financial organization whose failure risks the national economy.

On June 17, 2009, the Obama administration released its proposed package of financial reforms. It is comprehensive. Among its many features, the proposed new regulatory regime would:

1. Transform the president's Working Group into a Financial Services Oversight Council.
2. Establish the Federal Reserve as the systemic risk regulator, overseer of too-big-to-fail institutions, and financial monitor of all U.S. financial firms of a certain size and above.
3. Provide authority and process for the federal government to take over any large nonbank institution whose imminent failure would threaten the economy.

4. Require hedge funds, private-equity funds, and venture-capital funds to register with the SEC.
5. Establish capital reserve requirements for financial institutions.
6. Create a new Consumer Financial Protection Agency that would protect consumers from predatory financial practices.

The problem with these proposals is that the Obama administration moved too slowly to secure congressional enactment of any meaningful provisions. The financial industry is no longer as desperate as it was in early 2009. Many banks that took bailout loans have now made repayments. Others will follow their example to escape reporting requirements and limiting executive pay. Inevitably, the big banks that have repaid their loans will pay out massive bonuses in late 2009 and early 2010. The lesson for the next financial crisis is this: Enact financial regulation laws before providing the money industry any bailout monies.

European leaders are asking President Obama and the 111th Congress to join them in devising a global financial regulatory regime. The last time the United States entered into such an arrangement was in 1994, when the nation joined the World Trade Organization (WTO). As subsequent chapters will discuss, this arrangement has had marginal results and has entailed great costs both financially and in the loss of sovereignty. As to global financial regulation, FDR adopted a policy in 1933 of "first things first," and that meant putting America's financial house in order first. The same course is prudent now. While we can join efforts to eliminate banking havens for tax cheats and improve transparency, the United States should first take on the task of putting its house in order and only then consider various worldwide regulatory proposals.

INVESTMENT OVER SPECULATION

Some speculation is essential in any capitalist market to constantly update and define values and hedge the future. But short-term speculation is now rampant in the American money industry and is favored over long-term investment.

If American entrepreneurs and corporations are to make the investments capitalism requires, they need an economic environment that permits and encourages long-term action. The creation of such a background hinges on a reduction in the demands of Wall Street for immediate returns regardless of longer-term consequences.

In turn, this requires a recognition that control of America's major corporations has steadily shifted from individual investors to financial institutions—pension funds, hedge funds, insurance companies, foundations, investment companies, educational endowments, trust funds, and banks. This shift has far-reaching consequences, because individuals and institutions invest in the stock market for different reasons: Individuals are primarily investors looking for long-term performance; institutions are pursuing short-term profits. Thus, at a time when U.S. companies need to be making long-term investments to meet global competition, those in control—the institutions—are pressing for quick results.

Institutions now hold so much equity and are such a powerful presence in stock markets that most corporations must respond to their demands. Specifically, institutions hold half of all equities listed on the New York Stock Exchange (NYSE).

Yet their biggest impact comes not through mere ownership but through the growing pace of their transactions. In 1953, when institutions controlled about 15 percent of the equities on the NYSE, their trades constituted a quarter of stock market transactions. Today institutional trades constitute more than 90 percent of transactions.

Because of such hyperactive trading, the fundamental focus of the stock market has been transformed from long-term investing to short-term speculation. The quickening pace at which the entire value of stocks listed on the NYSE is traded gauges this shift.

In 1960, the turnover rate was 12 percent a year, which meant it took more than eight years for the entire value of the stock market to turn over. By 1970, it was up to 19 percent, which meant it took five years. By 1980, it was 36 percent (a three-year turnover). It was 46 percent in 1990 (two-year turnover) and 88 percent in 2000 (thirteen-month turnover). But as of February 2009, it was 145 percent, or barely an eight-month turnover. This is speculation, not investing.

In the speculative, short-term-oriented equity markets that now exist, only a few American entrepreneurs' firms have sufficient profits and assets to make the commitments that long-term competitiveness requires without sacrificing shorter-term earnings. Most companies are obliged to focus their efforts and resources on results that can bolster the price of their stock. The pursuit of these objectives diverts resources from investment in modern plant and equipment, research, technology, and training to clever financial manipulations. It sacrifices market share to high quarterly earnings. And it discourages workers from making long-term commitments to companies.

The solution is relatively simple. Federal regulators can create an economic environment that will encourage institutional investors to think and act long-term rather than speculate. Two changes are desirable:

A first step is for federal regulations to mandate that institutional managers be compensated on the basis of some measure of long-term financial performance, rather than on a simple percentage of the funds managed and a major portion of any profits. A fund manager's billion-dollar paycheck for a year's work, which often consists of little more than being in the right place when the economy is booming, is nothing more than looting other people's pensions and assets. The existing structure encourages speculation with other people's money.

A second viable means of creating an environment for long-term investment is to impose either a transaction tax on each corporate stock trade or a tax on short-term trades. Wall Street, of course, will oppose this as vigorously as its hedge fund managers oppose paying the same taxes as all other Americans. Alternatively, a high capital gains tax on short-term trades that is reduced over some period of time to zero could be imposed. The goal is to change the rules of the game in a way that will force fund managers to concentrate on a company's longer-term prospects—its capital management, research and development, worker training, management, and global competitiveness. In sum, America needs more investment and less speculation from the money industry. These actions will produce those results.

CONCLUSION

Restoring the financial health and integrity of the American financial system is essential to any effort to strengthen American capitalism. The following actions can help in that effort.

1. The U.S. government, working through the FDIC, should seize insolvent banks, as current law allows; inject cash in the form of Treasury notes; remove the banks' bad assets to the Treasury; hold those assets until it can be ascertained what they are really worth; and auction off the bank with a clean balance sheet.
2. Create an independent, modern-day "Pecora" commission to study the causes of the economic crash of 2008 and identify remedies.
3. Impose a federal lifetime ban on working in the securities

and financial industry upon the CEOs and board members of those financial institutions that failed because of their subprime mortgage portfolios or were forced to take federal bailout funds because of those portfolios.

4. Require a noncompete clause in the employment contracts of those public officials who manage the federal bailout program for banks and other financial institutions.
5. Provide the FBI financial crimes division sufficient funds to prosecute those in the mortgage industry who engaged in fraudulent for-profit activities.
6. Eliminate any statute of limitations for prosecution of fraudulent financial activities associated with the crash of 2008.
7. Regulate the money industry in its entirety.
8. Designate the FDIC as lead agency for federal financial salvage activities.
9. Reduce financial speculation and increase long-term investment by imposing either a sliding tax (which decreases over time) on trading profits or a tax on each stock transaction sufficient to favor the economics of longer-term investment.

CHAPTER TWO

TAXES

Massive debt, piling up at incomprehensible levels since 1981—and particularly since 2001—is a major cause of the current economic crisis and a formidable barrier to any recovery.

The math is staggering. The mind has great difficulty even imagining the dimensions of $1 trillion of national debt. When Jimmy Carter left the White House in January 1981, the United States' national debt was slightly less than $1 trillion. Put into context, in the almost two centuries between 1790 and 1981, the United States fought dozens of small wars, engaged in a brutal civil war, settled and populated the continent, endured the Depression, defeated the Axis powers, created the Great Society, sent Americans to the moon, built the Interstate Highway System, won the Cold War, and paid for thousands of other extraordinary accomplishments, and still had accumulated less than $1 trillion of federal debt.

A trillion dollars, of course, bought more then. But when inflation is factored out and that debt is expressed as a percentage of gross domestic product (GDP)—that is, our ability to pay—the national debt-to-GDP ratio was barely more than 33 percent in 1980. Now it is 69 percent.

That 33 percent ratio in 1980, moreover, steadily declined from its all-time high of 121 percent at the end of World War II, through the presidencies of Truman, Eisenhower, Kennedy, Johnson, Nixon, Ford, and Carter. As this suggests, before 1981, Americans taxed themselves to pay for the government services they received. "Tax and spend" was the mantra.

All that changed in 1981. "Borrow and spend" became the policy of Ronald Reagan, George H. W. Bush, and George W. Bush. While President Bill Clinton's administration returned to "tax and spend" and ended with budget surpluses, George W. Bush's swift reversion to a borrow-and-spend policy increased the gross federal debt from $5.7 trillion in 2001, when he became president, to more than $10.6 trillion when he left the presidency in 2009—a gain of almost $5 trillion.

American taxpayers accumulated almost $3.3 trillion of interest on the national debt during George W. Bush's eight-year tenure and paid much of it by borrowing even more money, a process akin to paying off one credit card by charging the balance to another. Now the Congressional Budget Office (CBO) estimates that the Obama administration's budget plans will add another $9.2 trillion over the next decade.

The assumption of so much debt has siphoned trillions of dollars from productive private investment and vital public expenditures, such as infrastructure improvements and education, in order to pay for current consumption. Just as high interest imposed by a loan shark can destroy a company or individual, the same is true of a nation.

The way we finance federal deficits poses its own threat to our national sovereignty and to global financial stability. Beginning with the Reagan administration, our government has increasingly financed its debt by selling national assets and borrowing money from the central banks of Japan and China, the oil-exporting nations, and Caribbean banking centers (probably drug and "hot" money).

Altogether, those foreign entities held almost $3.3 trillion of U.S. Treasury securities in April 2009. This debt, and a continuing dependence on those same sources to provide even more loans, gives them a powerful means of influencing American policy on everything from national security to what is taught about them in our schools.

The dangers of excessive debt—personal, corporate, and national—are well understood. It is crucial to state that America will be unable to surmount the current economic crisis until it again controls its debt and puts its economy on a lower debt-to-GDP ratio, as existed before 1981. The tough question is how.

The principal obstacles to solving America's debt crisis are ideological and political, not economic. The ideology that has taken over during the past three decades is the budgetary and political metaphor "starve the beast," which roughly translates into "lower government revenues will set a ceiling on government spending." The assumption, of course, is that the federal government will spend only what it collects in taxes—tax and spend—in order to starve the beast. But what has happened since 1981 is that most administrations borrow and spend, and thus we now have this huge national debt.

Over the past three decades, the ideological fervor coupled with the rabid partisanship of the Republican Party leadership to shrink the size and scope of the federal government—to undo FDR's New Deal—overcame traditional GOP concerns about debt and deficit financing of government. Indeed, many Republican theorists have argued that before government could cut federal programs it might be necessary to use most of the federal government's debt capacity to fiscally limit the scope of government. The more radical of these advocates seem willing to destroy the economy as a means of eliminating the New Deal programs; to them higher debt is merely a step toward their larger goal.

Grover Norquist, a prominent Republican activist, famously said, "My goal is to cut government in half in twenty-five years, to get it down to the size where we can drown it in the bathtub." To such absolutists, "drowning" the federal government, of course, means no Social Security, Medicare, or almost any other public program put into place since the early twentieth century.

Norquist and his allies have been devastatingly effective with their one-note advocacy of no new taxes, including their willingness to stalk any Republicans who hold an opposing view and deny them political money and support. George H. W. Bush famously promised in the 1988 election, "Read my lips: no new taxes." When budgetary and political circumstances led him to act otherwise, starve-the-beast advocates actively worked for his defeat in the 1992 election. Their message was absolutist: Always and in every circumstance refuse to raise taxes, or face our wrath in elections.

Since 1993, according to the *Congressional Record,* not a single Republican member of the House or Senate has voted to increase taxes, despite the necessity of doing so at times.

The politics of starve the beast are reinforced by what is known as "the Pledge." When the public elects Republicans to positions in the states or in Washington, D.C., the tax absolutists ask them to take two oaths. The first is the oath of office. The second is the Taxpayer Protection Pledge against taxes. Specifically, Norquist's advocacy group, Americans for Tax Reform, forcefully urges public officials and candidates for office to sign a pledge. For members of Congress, it says in full:

> I, __________, pledge to the taxpayers of __________, and to the American people that I will:
>
> ONE, oppose any and all efforts to increase the marginal income tax rates for individuals and/or businesses; and
>
> TWO, oppose any net reduction or elimination of deductions and credits, unless matched dollar for dollar by further reducing tax rates.

By signing this pledge, officeholders are putting themselves into straitjackets—they can vote for unlimited credits and deductions to corporations, bail out Wall Street, spend lavishly, and bribe taxpayers with cash rebates, as long as they do it with borrowed money and not by raising taxes. Once a deduction or credit is given, Pledge signers can never take it away without making corresponding cuts in other areas. It is political emasculation of the federal government by a thousand cuts.

If officeholders eliminate a corporate or personal tax deduction, Norquist's site explains, more tax would have to be paid and, therefore, those who voted to get rid of the tax deduction would be in violation of their pledge. The only way to eliminate a deduction and avoid violating the Pledge is to also reduce tax rates overall or increase deductions and credits for some other taxpayers enough to ensure that the net tax remains neutral.

One of the obvious economic effects of the Pledge has been to shift the burden of taxes from the wealthy and corporations onto the present-day middle class and future middle-class generations of taxpayers, who will have to pay for today's deficits. The Pledge instantly converts its signers into servants of those interests that seek a free ride tax-wise from society.

The Pledge and its signers are, more than any other factor, responsible for America's huge federal debt. The political power of the no-new-tax movement is reflected in those who sign the Pledge. As of May 2009, 172 members of the House of Representatives and 34 senators had signed it and were listed on Norquist's Web site (http://www.atr.org). Also listed are 1,113 state legislators and six governors.

Put into context, as long as these thirty-four senators honor their pledge, the rest will not enact any tax for any purpose regardless of necessity, even to pay for national security or the cost of war. Accordingly, Congress is financing the wars in Iraq and Afghanistan with borrowed monies. Also, no bill can be passed in the Senate that cuts any deduction or credit for a special interest unless the Senate also reduces overall tax rates or increases someone else's deduction or credit. The Pledge is absolute and its demand on officeholders is unyielding. Fiscal impasse is the result.

In the House of Representatives, where a majority of 218 out of 435 members is required to enact legislation, any bill to cut special-interest tax deductions or credits or raise taxes must secure 87 percent of the votes of those who refused to take the Pledge, an almost impossible barrier to overcome.

That, of course, is the goal of the Pledge's creators; they have created a trap in which officeholders must cut federal programs or leave their positions. In 2005, starve-the-beast advocates tried to spring that trap and eliminate the social program they detest most, Social Security. After GOP House and Senate victories in the 2004 elections, and with solid control of Congress, President George W. Bush aggressively moved to privatize Social Security. But he and the other Pledgers could not close their trap, and their attempt was so politically toxic that the GOP lost control of both the House and Senate in the 2006 elections.

The result of the Pledgers' unsuccessful starve-the-beast gambit over the past thirty years is an additional almost $11 trillion of national debt as of May 2009.

We are now at an in-between moment. The Pledgers lack the power to achieve their dream of "drowning" the federal government yet retain sufficient power to prevent others from putting the nation on a pay-as-you-go policy. It is a political Gordian knot. Yet, if anything is clear after three decades of starve-the-beast economic policies, it is that the beast will not be starved—American voters want Social Security, Medicare, and other federal programs.

As Alexander the Great dealt with the challenge of untying the real Gordian knot by cutting through it with his sword, the president needs to take similar decisive action on financing the U.S. government. America is quickly approaching the limits on loans provided by foreign governments. Under present policies, the next step will be the printing of money, which will lead to an inflationary cycle like the one that occurred in the late 1970s and early 1980s.

Since the crash of 2008, China's leaders have repeatedly expressed their concern about the health of the American dollar and the value of China's large holdings. Exporting nations that long used the dollar as the global reserve currency are increasingly demanding payment in other currencies and are openly arguing that the time has come to end the dollar's central role in global finance.

Global economic collapse is now a real possibility, and the harmful effects will be much greater in today's interconnected world economy than they were during the Great Depression of the 1930s. Most significantly, the contemporary politics surrounding taxes are in such gridlock that the present income tax system is incapable of providing the federal government the funds it needs. If program cuts, more foreign loans, and the inflationary printing of more money are not long-term options, America's only choice is to return to its traditional pay-as-you-go policies—all else is worthless palaver. To make this happen, America needs a true economic and political game changer—a new tax system.

One of the few things most Americans—liberal, conservative, moderate, or indifferent—agree upon is that the federal income tax system is terrible.

It consists of five types of taxes: (1) personal income taxes; (2) corporate income taxes; (3) social insurance taxes such as Social Security, Medicare, and unemployment compensation; (4) estate and gift taxes; and (5) excise taxes on selected goods such as fuel, alcohol, and tobacco.

The principal of these is the income tax. Congress created the personal income tax in 1913. The rate was 1 percent on all income up to $20,000 and 7 percent for those with more than $500,000.

Less than 1 percent of Americans were eligible to pay income taxes. Then the tax code was so simple that the original 1040 filing document of 1913 was only three pages in length and had a one-page instruction sheet. Now the U.S. Tax Code is a twenty-four-megabyte download that fills 7,500 letter-size pages at sixty lines per page.

The administrative costs to the American economy of complying with this code are enormous, with the Government Accountability Office (GAO) estimating that compliance consumes approximately 1 percent of the GDP annually ($140 billion in 2008). The Cato Institute, a Washington-based think tank, estimates that the U.S. "tax army" of accountants, lawyers, and computer experts includes more than 1.2 million tax preparers and processors.

Keeping up with changes in the code is difficult because it is in constant flux, with Congress making four hundred or more alterations each year. The complexity of the code is so great that Treasury Department auditors report that even IRS-assisted guidance provides incorrect answers about 33 percent of the time.

The present system also has vast noncompliance. The IRS estimates the difference between what taxpayers paid and what they should have paid in 2001 was $345 billion, which was 17 percent of federal revenue that year. Put another way, cheaters evade paying one of every six dollars of taxes due the federal government. The administration of George W. Bush cut the number of IRS examiners who audited the very rich, ensuring that the tax collection gap is even larger now. In September 2008, an official of UBS, Switzerland's largest bank, testified before a Senate investigating committee that the bank had the names of forty-seven thousand American depositors who paid no U.S. taxes on their accounts. The bank refuses to give the names to the IRS.

The existing system is also vastly unfair. Wall Street's billion-dollar-a-year hedge fund owners pay only 15 percent on their profits, about half the tax rate of most Americans. When Congress looked into this disparity in early 2008, an invading army of Wall Street executives and their lobbyists rushed to Capitol Hill. The issue soon disappeared, and the fund owners still have their low tax rates.

The current corporate and income tax system has huge administrative costs and large compliance losses, and is open to widespread manipulation. It is the product of a system long shaped and dominated by corporate and political insiders, bonded in a politically incestuous relationship. Almost a century ago, president-elect Woodrow Wilson wrote a campaign book titled *The New Freedom* that brilliantly described those ties. With undisguised revulsion, he wrote:

> *There has been substituted for the unschooled body of citizens that used to clamor at the doors of the Finance Committee and the Committee on Ways and Means, one of the most interesting and able bodies of expert lobbyists that has ever been developed in the experience of any country. They so overwhelm you with their familiarity with detail that you cannot discover wherein their scheme lies. Thus, the relation between business and government becomes, not a matter of the exposure of all the sensitive parts of the government to all the active parts of the people, but the special impression upon them of a particular organized force in the business world. Furthermore, every expedient and device of secrecy is brought into use to keep the public unaware of the arguments, ignorant of the facts which refute them, and uninformed of the intentions of the framers of the proposed legislation.*

A century later little has changed. On its Web site, OpenSecrets .org, the Center for Responsive Politics tracks and publishes the activity reports registered lobbyists must file with Congress. In

2009, it identified 1,779 corporations and organizations that filed 8,691 reports on their tax lobbying.

The House and Senate tax committees are the preserves of Washington's congressional and lobbying elite. The members expect those seeking favors to fill their campaign chests, and they do. Most members, as well as many of their staff, expect to be offered high-paying jobs as advisors or lobbyists when they return to private life, and many are.

These insiders, both public and private, have every financial and professional incentive to keep the tax system as it is, for they are among the few who can successfully and profitably traverse it. Thus, they are likely to fiercely oppose any idea so radical as instituting a new, not yet corrupted, tax system for corporate and individual income taxes. Such a change, however, is essential if America is to avoid fiscal and even social ruin.

PRINCIPLED CHANGE

The last time America made a systemic change in financing the federal government was a century ago. Any new change of such magnitude will likely last many decades and thus needs to be well thought out and publicly debated.

In testimony before the Senate Committee on Finance in 2006, David Walker, then Comptroller General of the United States, identified five basic principles that should guide any business tax reform. They are equally applicable to any broader change in America's tax system.

The first principle is that "any new system should raise sufficient revenue to fund America's current and future expected expenditures." The radical Pledgers are sure to oppose such a commonsense principle, since their real goal is to "drown" federal programs, even at the risk of ruining the nation. Yet when the Pledgers and their allies had absolute control of the federal government during the administrations of Ronald Reagan and George W. Bush, they actually raised spending and increased federal employment. Many of them now claim that they "came to change Washington and Washington changed them." The reality is that they failed to persuade Americans to accept their agenda to do away with federal programs.

The real question now is how the country will pay for future public services, plus finance the debt legacy the Pledgers created. Thus, return to pay-as-you-go fiscal policies is an immutable principle for any future tax reform.

Walker's second principle is that "the tax base should be as broad as possible, which helps to minimize overall tax rates." This is a matter of fairness, because all Americans benefit from a strong and prosperous nation and all should contribute to paying the financial costs, even if that contribution is minuscule.

The third principle is that the proposed system "should improve compliance rates by reducing tax preferences and complexity and increasing transparency." Reducing loopholes and simplifying the code—even condensing the 1040 to three pages, its length a century ago—will make collecting easier and cheating more difficult. It will also reduce a good part of the cost of compliance now imposed on taxpayers.

The fourth principle is a bit more complex: "To the extent that other goals, such as equity and simplicity, allow, the tax system should aim for neutrality by not favoring some business activities over others." The present income tax system is anything but neutral. As discussed in chapter one, Congress began favoring finance over manufacturing four decades ago, with the result that America is deindustrializing. The present tax code also favors the rich over the middle class, which widens the disparity in wealth and income and reduces the overall standard of living. Tax neutrality is essential in any new approach to raising federal revenue.

Wisely, Walker imposed a nontraditional fifth principle, that "transition rules must be an integral part of any reform proposal." Other nations have shifted from an income tax to some other tax system in a matter of a few years. When other nations have made such changes, though, many companies and individuals waited until the last moment to do whatever was required of them, thereby creating chaos. Transition rules that establish interim steps, instead of one giant leap, will ease that shift. Ministeps can also be used to educate the public about whatever approach is used.

There should be a sixth principle, that "any new tax system be trade compatible." It should qualify American manufacturers and service providers in accordance with World Trade Organization agreements for export rebates by the U.S. government and for foreign government credits for U.S. taxes paid on American-made goods and services that other nations import.

The idea behind the sixth principle is little understood in the United States because the government does not use a value-added tax (VAT), even though 153 other nations do. Because the United States is the only industrial country that does not have a VAT, other countries "game" global tax treaties by employing the VAT to subsidize their exports to the United States, simultaneously (and purposely) pricing U.S. imports out of the other countries' markets. Some explanation seems appropriate at this point about how they game the system and about the VAT, which is actually a very simple tax system.

A VAT is a consumption tax. It greatly encourages savings by not taxing money saved or the interest generated. A 2008 report by the GAO illustrates, with an example of a furniture sale, how a VAT works. First, a lumber company cuts trees and mills the wood, which is sold to a furniture maker for $50. With a 10 percent VAT, the lumber company adds $5 to the price, remits $5 to the government, and puts on its invoice $50 for the milled wood and $5 of VAT.

If the furniture maker sells a finished table to a retail store for

$120, its invoice would add $12 of VAT for a total price of $132. The furniture maker would subtract the $5 already paid by the lumber company and remit the balance, $7, to the government.

If the retailer sold the table to a customer for $150, it would add $15 to the final price and charge $165. It would then subtract the $12 of VAT paid by the lumber and furniture companies and remit $3 to the government. In this example, the government would get 10 percent of the final price, or $15 for a product that sold for $150. The payments would come at each stage from raw materials to final sale with each participant paying the tax only on its value added.

In practice, firms in most countries either pay the tax instantly or accrue the amounts owed and pay the government monthly or quarterly. The system is simple, perfect for modern computerized accounting, and allows taxpayers to know their tax liability and the government to better anticipate revenue. Cheating is difficult with a VAT, easily spotted, and thus limited. Best of all, taxpayers have no compliance burdens. None. There are no IRS penalties. The VAT is paid automatically when someone buys something. Business does the paperwork. There is no April 15 tax day.

But simplicity and ease of compliance—that is, making the U.S. tax system more user-friendly—are not the reasons for this sixth principle. It is added because of the long-standing WTO policy of discriminating against direct taxes (such as income taxes) in favor of indirect taxes (VAT), a policy bias that puts U.S. producers and workers at a more than $355 billion annual disadvantage in international trade (see table 1 in the appendix). This WTO policy allows other nations to rebate the VAT, thereby subsidizing their exports sold in the United States, while imposing a tariff-like VAT on U.S. imports into their countries.

The income tax used by the United States is a direct tax; the VAT is an indirect tax. According to WTO rules, a government's rebate of indirect taxes on exports is considered trade-neutral, while rebate of a direct tax on exports is treated as a trade subsidy. As global trade expands and economies become ever more entwined, the discrimination against the United States increases proportionately. The $355 billion trade disadvantage in 2007, for example, was almost triple what it was in 1995 ($137 billion). Of the total disadvantage in 2007, almost $230 billion was from other governments' rebate of the VAT to their companies that exported goods and services into the United States.

These governments also created another $125 billion disadvantage when they imposed VAT-equivalent taxes on American goods and services imported into their countries, taxes that were not rebated. This discrimination is a major cause of our large and ongoing trade deficit and costs the United States millions of jobs. A country-by-country breakdown of the VAT disadvantage is provided in table 1 in the appendix.

Changing the U.S. tax system presents a historic opportunity to eliminate this discriminatory foreign tax treatment, thereby helping reduce the huge U.S. trade deficit and recapturing millions of American jobs. This may seem almost too good to be true. But it is.

This inequitable system has its origins in the aftermath of World War II, when the United States was trying to speed Europe's economic recovery. As part of those efforts, the United States accepted a tax loophole in postwar trade agreements that allowed other governments to rebate to their producers any indirect taxes paid on their exported goods and impose an equal tax on any imports, including those from the United States. It was a great idea at the time and contributed in a major way to the rebuilding of Europe.

Europe recuperated decades ago; however, the tax loophole remains. In order to compete in international trade, European countries over the years negotiated away their import tariffs, but as they reduced the tariff rate, they increased their VAT. France, for example, had a combination VAT and tariff rate of about 22 percent in the early 1960s. While the tariff rate was cut heavily, the VAT was increased, and the combination VAT and tariff on

U.S. imports is still about 22 percent today. The same is true across the world.

The use of the VAT means, for example, that a German manufacturer of a car exported into the United States gets a rebate on that product from the German government equal to the indirect taxes paid on the production of the vehicle in Germany. Since the German VAT is 19 percent, this amounts to a rebate of 19 percent to the manufacturer on its exports to the United States, a major export subsidy by any measure. If the vehicle is priced at $50,000, the German government will rebate $9,500 to the manufacturer, allowing the base price of the vehicle to be slightly less than $40,500 in the United States.

Conversely, any U.S. carmaker, or other producer, exporting to Germany must pay that government a VAT-equivalent tax of 19 percent of the price of the product imported into that nation, plus another 19 percent tax on the cost of all transport, insurance, docking, and duties involved in getting the product into Germany. Thus, a $50,000 Cadillac exported to Germany has more than $10,000 added to its price by the VAT, for a total of over $60,000.

Worse, the American company gets no offsetting tax credit in Germany for the corporate taxes it pays in the United States, which also must be factored into the price of a product. Consequently, the VAT equivalent imposed on U.S. imports into Germany is, in effect, a giant German import tariff. The VAT allows German producers to cut their price in America by 19 percent and simultaneously increases the price of any U.S.-made products imported into Germany by the same percentage. American producers, therefore, are at a disadvantage in both domestic and German markets.

Today a VAT is applied to almost 95 percent of all American exports. The resulting discrimination is a major reason U.S. products are increasingly noncompetitive both at home and abroad. Thousands of American manufacturers are responding to this situation by moving their production to countries where they too can get the VAT advantage, sending tens of thousands of U.S. jobs overseas as well.

Congress repeatedly has tried to eliminate the VAT disadvantage. In 1974, for instance, it directed the Nixon administration to negotiate America's VAT handicap away at the Tokyo Round of global trade talks. The other nations, however, ignored the U.S. demand and refused to deal with the issue. The same thing happened in subsequent trade negotiations initiated in 1986 and again in 2002. Even today foreign governments refuse to consider the issue.

In 1972 and again in 1984, Congress confronted this stonewalling by changing the tax system so that U.S. exporters could exempt between 15 percent and 30 percent of their export income from U.S. taxes, thereby creating a VAT offset. In 1998, the European Union (EU) lodged a complaint with the newly created WTO, claiming the tax benefit was an export subsidy that violated the WTO agreement.

The WTO formed a panel to hear the case. The panel met in closed session with the media excluded and the proceedings sealed, as is the practice in all WTO dispute cases. In October 1999, the WTO panel upheld the European position. With that, the United States had one year to change its contested tax law or pay WTO-sanctioned tariffs as compensation to Europe.

Congress enacted replacement legislation in November 2000, which was again unsatisfactory to the Europeans, who filed another WTO case against the United States. In August 2001, a new panel upheld the European position, and in January 2002, the WTO's appellate body affirmed the panel's decision.

Congress ignored the WTO decision, which caused the organization to authorize the EU to impose $4 billion of retaliatory tariffs per year on U.S. imports. This got the attention of the Bush administration, and it responded by persuading Congress to enact in October 2004 a substitute for its replacement bill of 2000. Meanwhile, the WTO sanctions were postponed.

Again the EU filed a case at the WTO, arguing that the new legislation still provided export subsidies. A panel formed in Geneva, Switzerland, in September 2005 issued a thirty-four-page decision that concluded the U.S. law enacted in 2004 indeed constituted an illegal subsidy that violated the United States' WTO obligations. The Europeans again threatened to impose sanctions. In 2006, President Bush and Congress gave up and stripped from U.S. law the offending tax provisions.

Throughout this almost eight-year trade battle, the Europeans, like all other VAT-using countries, continued to provide full VAT rebates on their exports and impose a VAT-equivalent tax on all U.S. imports.

The United States could instantly eliminate this export-import disadvantage by shifting from a direct to a VAT tax system. Negotiations with other nations would not be required, since the United States has treaty rights with them to get these advantages if it adopts the VAT.

Not surprisingly, major U.S. and foreign corporations that serve the American market from countries with VAT systems are likely to oppose this shift. They are now invested abroad and will try to keep their existing VAT-based competitive advantage over U.S. domestic competitors. Most foreign governments that maintain major lobbying efforts in Washington will likely try to sabotage any efforts to shift the United States from an income tax to a VAT.

But this is a historic economic crisis, and in such times impossible things can be accomplished.

CHOOSING A NEW TAX SYSTEM

There are other tax systems to consider as well. Which is best able to meet David Walker's five principles and the additional one, even after the inevitable political tinkering? Two additional contenders could be game changers—the flat tax and the fair tax. There's also a third, the value-added tax, as already discussed.

The flat tax, as defined by former House majority leader Dick Armey (R-TX), who is a professional economist, would eliminate the current tax code and treat all taxpayers the same. Everyone would pay a specific rate, such as 17 percent, of what is left of their annual income from all sources—wages, pensions, dividends, capital gains, rents, etc.—after subtracting from that total a personal allowance. Social Security and Medicare payroll deductions would not be taxed. The Armey version of the flat tax would have only four allowances: (1) $23,200 for married couples filing jointly, (2) $14,850 for single heads of households, (3) $11,600 for nonmarried individuals, and (4) $5,300 for each dependent child.

The entire tax form would be a single postcard.

Armey estimates that with these exemptions, a family of four earning $25,000 would owe nothing. If it made $50,000, it would owe 6 percent; at $200,000, it would owe a tax of 14 percent.

Taxes on business would be equally simple. A company would subtract all expenses from all income, and if income exceeded expenses, it would pay a tax of 17 percent on that residual.

While this flat tax would significantly simplify the tax code, much of the current system would remain, from wage withholding to income tax–related record keeping for business. As now, many people would continue to hide income and cheat on their taxes.

The leading alternative to the flat tax is the fair tax. As advocated by the late representative Daniel Schaefer (R-CO), it would be a 15 percent sales tax on the gross receipts from the sale of any taxable property or service sold in the United States. Under this plan, income, estate, gift, and non–trust fund dedicated excise taxes would all be repealed.

The IRS would be abolished.

A consumption tax, the 15 percent levy would be collected on all goods and services sold at retail. Also, utility, legal, accounting, and other service-related activities would be taxed at the same rate. Federal taxes would not be withheld from paychecks, and individuals would have no forms to fill out. Only Social Security deductions would remain. The fair tax would not be collected on goods or services bought for resale or used to produce other goods or services, or on those that would be exported.

The value-added tax, also a broad-based consumption tax, avoids many problems associated with an income tax, including the need to define and calculate depreciation and capital gains. Since VAT is collected by business, individual taxpayers are relieved of virtually all burdens, including filing any returns. The General Accountability Office reported to Congress in 2008 that the compliance costs for the VAT would be about 0.55 percent of revenue collected versus 1.27 percent for an income tax. The savings would be between .5 percent to 1 percent of the GDP. In 2008, that would have been between $70 billion and $140 billion, an enormous savings by any measure.

The two principal criticisms of the VAT are (1) that it is inequitable, imposing proportionately greater burdens on low-income individuals than upon the rich, and (2) because it is hidden from taxpayers inside the costs of production, it would be too politically easy to increase.

Many nations that use the VAT have eliminated its inequities by imposing zero or low rates on food, health care, and religious and cultural services. Anyway, nothing could be more inequitable than today's U.S. income tax, with billionaires often paying less in both relative and absolute terms than their secretaries.

The second criticism, the political ease in increasing it, is actually one of the VAT's major advantages. Indeed, the VAT is the most powerful and efficient way ever invented to raise government revenue. It is precisely what America needs now.

An analysis by the Tax Foundation of the fair and flat taxes is that both would favor savings over consumption and could generate large amounts of revenue. The VAT would also do the same.

The flat tax would require taxpayers to file a return as they do now, but an enormously simplified one. The fair tax would rely on merchants to collect sales taxes, as they do now for most state and local governments. The VAT would also rely on businesses to remit it at each stage of production. Individual taxpayers would be relieved of any compliance burdens or penalties by the fair tax and VAT.

All three tax systems would eliminate estate and capital gains taxes, and all three are single-tax systems that eliminate double taxation, as now happens with corporate and income taxes. All three plans would reduce the tax system's "dead-weight" loss to the economy and encourage private investment.

Simplicity further improves the performance of all these tax systems. The GAO study of the VAT concluded that "adding complexity through exemptions, exclusions, and reduced rates . . . decreases revenues and increases compliance risks, administrative costs, and compliance burden." The lesson is that any new tax system would benefit greatly by keeping it simple and streamlined.

All three taxes meet the test of being able to raise sufficient revenue to finance the federal government's operations on a pay-as-you-go basis. All are broad based and would minimize tax rates, lower the amount of taxes paid by the overwhelming majority of individuals, improve compliance, cut cheating, and reduce administrative costs. All are industry-neutral, neither favoring nor disadvantaging any one industry over another.

Many other nations have made the transition from income taxes to a flat tax, fair tax, or VAT, which means we can learn from their experiences and design working rules for such a change that would be relatively simple, even for a large and complex economy such as ours. Many nations have both a VAT and an income tax system.

The major difference between the three tax systems is that only the VAT would be instantly compatible with WTO treaties. Overnight, the tariff-like VAT barriers to U.S. exports that now exist in 153 nations would disappear. Also, foreign government VAT rebates (subsidies) on goods and services exported into the United States would be instantly neutralized.

Since the fair and flat taxes are consumption based, they arguably should be recognized by the WTO, but the reality is they would not be. The United States would face years of litigation and negotiations at the WTO in Geneva, and the final outcome would be determined by the votes of other nations that now enjoy their VAT advantage. The global political deck is stacked against America's adoption of those two types of taxes.

Replacing corporate and personal income taxes with the VAT would provide America the game changer it needs to put its fiscal house in order. As the budgets of every president since 1981, including Barack Obama, reveal, the people of the United States and their elected representatives have chosen to have a bigger government. The time has come to pay for it. The VAT can provide enough revenue—at lower tax rates and with a decreased burden on taxpayers, greater fairness, and far lower compliance costs—to balance the federal budget annually and to begin paying down the national debt. A VAT would also make a major contribution toward reducing the huge U.S. trade deficit.

Replacing U.S. corporate and income taxes with a VAT is totally within the treaty commitments this country has with other nations and can be accomplished by the president and Congress through legislation. The decision is ours alone.

Most important, shifting to a VAT will help heal the current economic crisis and greatly strengthen American capitalism by favoring savings and investment over consumption.

CHAPTER THREE

TRADE

"A chance to turn a 'once in a century' Depression into a golden opportunity" is how one Japanese business publication describes the current world economic crisis. Well-financed foreign corporations, owned or backed by their governments, see the crisis as a historic opportunity to seize markets now served by U.S. companies, which basically operate on their own without U.S. government support. The *Financial Times* observed in 2007, before the present crisis, that "globalization was supposed to mean the worldwide triumph of the market economy. Yet some of the most influential players are turning out to be states, not private actors. States play a dominant role in ownership and production of raw materials, notably oil and gas. Now states are also emerging as owners of wealth."

Indeed, the global economic crisis has brought into sharp focus the fact that many foreign nations possess enormous riches that are managed in accounts informally known as sovereign wealth funds, and are creating or backing transnational corporations that supply everything the world needs from financing to diapers. The national interests of these countries are not the same as those of the United States, nor are the structures of their economies.

While China is the most visible of these state-capitalist economies, variations exist in Japan, Taiwan, South Korea, and many European countries. In Japan, corporations often operate as part of huge conglomerates that are highly regulated by the central government. Airbus, the European aeronautical consortium, is a multigovernment-supported enterprise that has lost money for more than thirty years but nonetheless holds half the global airplane market. Corporations in Germany are part of a complex, largely invisible but entwined national system that controls everything from bank financing through distribution of products and services.

State capitalism, whether supported or directly controlled by the state, flexes the power of the national government over the market. Corporations and their employees, in effect, work with the state as a national team in the pursuit of set goals. In contrast, corporations and entrepreneurs working in America's market capitalism are on their own and often have no real relationship with the federal government. The collapse of General Motors and Chrysler are stark examples.

Economic "warriors" from other nations, such as Germany and countries in Asia, closely monitor international business cycles. When the global economy embarks on a downslide, these corporations, backed by their governments, expand their R&D, increase their marketing, and go after U.S. domestic and foreign markets. With each downturn, these foreign corporations know their American competition, operating without the deep pockets of government support and without a protected domestic market that can guarantee profits, will reduce R&D, cut production, lay off workers, and, consequently, lose market share and not be prepared for an upturn when and if it arrives.

America's market capitalism cannot compete against state capitalism, particularly when the competitors' sophisticated national industrial policies are backed by government-owned sovereign wealth funds that can buy entire industries. If the present economic crisis deepens and continues for several years, both of which are likely, the United States is certain to lose dozens of its remaining manufacturing industries, a good portion of its high-end business services, and millions of additional jobs. Ultimately, the contest is a clash of private companies against national governments.

Unlike state-capitalist nations, the United States generally has eschewed the idea of a formal industrial policy. The United States has adopted, however, ad hoc policies in, among many other areas, finance, housing, aerospace, health care, agriculture, and aircraft military weapon production. Often partially hidden and always politically motivated, these U.S. policies have usually proven to be inefficient, ineffective, and of benefit to a handful of private interests at the expense of the general good. The most recent ad hoc addition to this list is the automobile industry, which automatically includes dozens of related supplier industries. Prospectively, the energy industry is next.

Despite the obviousness of state capitalism, the United States does not even recognize its rise, let alone have a grounded, coherent approach for confronting it. Without such recognition and some corresponding action, the trade warriors from state-capitalist nations will strip what remains of the U.S. economy as surely as a conquering army would.

We must act immediately to prevent such economic devastation during the chaos of this crisis. Like more opportunistic nations, we can use this financial crash and depression as a golden opportunity to modernize our approach to state capitalism, reignite our economy, and in the process create millions of new and better jobs.

The first step is to understand the nature of state capitalism and the dangers it poses for America. We start with Japan and then move to China, the most obvious illustration. They are just two of many state-capitalist national economies against which American firms compete.

THE RISE OF STATE CAPITALISM

Twenty-five years ago one of the prominent points of contention among economists was whether or not the Japanese economy was guided by a national industrial policy. At that time an effective U.S. response to Japanese attacks on the U.S. consumer electronics, machine tool, and auto industries, among many others, was not forthcoming because American policy makers were paralyzed by this difference of opinion.

Subsequently, most of those who have studied this issue have concluded that the Japanese government did indeed use formal industrial policies that sanctioned the formation of cartels, guided the cartels, forced technology sharing among Japanese corporations, and closed Japanese markets to outsiders. Under these policies, Japanese corporations had access to capital from a bank system that supported national export drives, and the primary objective of Japanese diplomacy was the advancement of Japan's national economic interests.

By the early 1980s, China was imitating Japan's approach and then began improving on it. China is now actively creating a hybrid economy the Chinese define as a "socialist-market system" (SMS). While to many outsiders this system appears to be market oriented and largely controlled by the private sector, it is neither. China is creating a system of state capitalism in which the government owns and controls all strategic industries, while secondary and service industries are left to private ownership, which the government also controls.

The principal differences between the Chinese and U.S. systems are that the United States does not own the major enterprises on which its economy depends, as does the Chinese government, and the United States operates under a two-party democratic system, while China is governed by one party. The ownership difference between the United States and China is fundamental. In China the government sets the economic agenda and controls all resources.

The Chinese government announced in December 2006 that seven industries were critical to the nation's economic security and would remain under strict government control. They are defense, power, oil, telecommunications, mineral resources, civil aviation, and shipping. This list, moreover, is not exclusive. Chinese officials have noted that the government intends to expand the volume and structure of these industries so that they will become leading world businesses.

Unlike when Mao Tse-tung and communist political ideologues governed the nation, China's development planning now reflects leadership by a techno-elite. In a nation of 1.3 billion people, about 63 million Chinese are members of the Communist Party. The real control of the government resides in the Politburo Standing Committee (PSC), which since 2002 has consisted of nine members drawn from the twenty-two-member Politburo. One of these nine serves as head of state (president) and another as head of government (premier). The number is kept uneven to prevent deadlocks.

All nine members of the Sixteenth Politburo Standing Committee (2002–7) were trained engineers, experienced in various national development disciplines. Eight of the nine members of the Seventeenth Politburo Standing Committee (2008–13) are also engineers; the other one holds both a law degree and a Ph.D. in economics. They are the techno-elite. All have extensive development experience; they began at the bottom of organizations and worked their way up.

In China's state capitalism, major projects are phased. Industries are clustered to gain efficiencies of colocation. Transport is built from local industrial areas to seaports. Basic infrastructure, such as electric generating power, is given priority in planning and the allocation of resources. Foreigners are involved when they can bring something China lacks, but their actions are controlled.

The point is that competent and experienced people lead

China's government and they proceed systematically, as engineers do. To close the industrial development gap with other nations, China began reconstituting its state-owned industries in the 1980s. In the process, the government has encouraged foreign direct investment, joint ventures, the elimination of redundant production, the transformation of state industries into joint-stock ventures, the outright sale of some operations, and the liquidation of tens of thousands of failing ventures.

In 2002, China's central government placed the responsibility for overseeing almost two hundred thousand enterprises in the State-owned Assets Supervision and Administration Commission (SASAC). Imagine SASAC as the world's largest equity fund, whose sole owner is the Chinese government. The chairman is Li Rongrong, born in 1944 and trained as an engineer, who began his career in 1968 as a factory worker in a plant he eventually came to manage.

At the first SASAC working conference in August 2003, Li Rongrong identified five priority sectors for future development: (1) national security, (2) monopolies for natural resources, (3) provision of key public goods and services, (4) critical resources, and (5) core enterprises of pillars and high-tech industries. He also announced that China would create thirty to fifty large corporations with international competitive power before 2010. These companies would be national champions on the scale of Microsoft, Motorola, GE, General Motors, and Pfizer.

A cluster of state-owned enterprises (SOEs)—what the Chinese call the "lifeline" sectors, including oil, coal, petrochemicals, metallurgy, power, telecommunications, defense, ocean shipping, air transport, defense, scientific instruments, and related industries—will remain under absolute control of the government.

State capitalism in China has developed to the point that Chinese producers have a price advantage over foreign competitors in virtually every product they make in almost every market in the world. In 2006, the Merage School of Business at the University of California-Irvine released an important study titled *A Report of 'The China Price Project.'* Professor Peter Navarro identified eight factors that gave China a price advantage in global competition and calculated their relative contributions to that advantage.

1. *Low wages for high-quality work.* Chinese wages are not the lowest in the world, but their workers are very productive and do high-quality work. Adjusting China's wages to account for the productivity of Chinese workers, Navarro found that the cost of an hour's work by a Chinese employee is about 18 percent that of a comparable American worker. What this means, of course, is that a company can hire five Chinese workers for the same price as one American. On a 100-point scale, low wages constituted 39.4 percent of China's price advantage.

2. *Piracy and counterfeiting.* China is the center of world piracy and counterfeiting. Sophisticated Western investors realize that if they take their technology to China it will be ripped off. Japan has asked its leading technology corporations to keep their most advanced work inside Japan and not even patent it out of fear the patent applications themselves might give away that nation's most vital technological secrets. Navarro calculates that more than 8.6 percent of the Chinese price advantage can be attributed to the piracy and counterfeiting factor.

3. *Minimal worker health and safety regulations.* The World Health Organization and the International Labor Organization jointly report a growth of workplace accidents in China. One of the attractions to foreign investors is that they can eliminate investments in occupational safety equipment and training in Chinese factories and escape virtually any obligation when workers are killed or injured. Laws exist but are not enforced. Navarro estimates that factory owners in China spend a third of what their counterparts in the United States do on health and safety. This contributes 2.4 percent to the China price advantage.

4. *Lax environmental regulations and enforcement.* China is

the world's top polluter. Companies that operate in China are not required to meet the environmental obligations they are in Japan and the West. Navarro calculates the absence of environmental regulations makes up 2.4 percent of the price advantage.

5. *Export subsidies.* The government, as well as provincial and local regimes, heavily subsidizes both domestic and foreign-based corporations in a variety of ways. The China Development Bank and the Export and Import Bank of China provide Chinese enterprises massive credit lines for global expansion. Tax exemptions are used extensively, particularly to lure foreign companies into China. A new foreign company gets two full years of income-tax exemption and a 50 percent reduction for the next three years. Foreign companies also get a full refund of the income tax paid on reinvestment in China for export businesses or for companies that make advanced technologies. Overall, Professor Navarro calculates government subsidies contribute 16.7 percent of the China price advantage.

6. *Industrial network clustering.* Think of River Rouge, the automobile factory Henry Ford built between 1917 and 1928 in Dearborn, Michigan, a one-thousand-acre site where raw materials arrived on the docks and, ultimately, finished automobiles were driven out of the factory. China has built similar complexes that specialize in the production of specific items. The city of Huizo makes DVDs and laser diodes. Ingrid produces computers. Leilu turns out bicycles. Yanbun manufactures underwear. Dozens of these clusters, involving millions of workers, now exist, and great efficiencies are achieved. Navarro estimates such clustering adds 16 percent to the China price advantage, almost as much as government subsidies.

7. *Foreign direct investment.* China is the world's principal destination for foreign direct investment (FDI). Foreign technology, managerial expertise, and global distribution networks accompany these funds. Navarro concludes that FDI adds a bit more than 3 percent to China's price advantage.

8. *Undervalued currency.* In 1994, China pegged the value of

its currency to the dollar and has since kept it undervalued. Navarro, taking a very conservative approach to his calculations, estimates the Chinese currency is undervalued by only 20 percent. Even then, the currency factor contributes 11.4 percent to the China price advantage.

The China price advantage, coupled with open access to the U.S. market, has enabled Chinese-based producers to overwhelm their U.S.-based competitors. The arithmetic of this trade is daunting. In 1990, China had a $10 billion trade surplus with the United States. In 2008, the surplus exceeded $268 billion, a growth of 2,680 percent over 18 years. Significantly, the composition of that trade ranges from the simplest to the most complex goods the United States consumes.

In 2003, the Chinese government announced that foreign investment would be permitted in banking, telecommunications, education, medical services, the auto industry, civilian satellite production, large equipment manufacturing, and large-scale integrated circuit production. While foreigners can own a minority position, the Chinese make the major decisions. In the end, foreigners get a toehold in China, and China gets their capital and expert help in becoming world-class competitors.

In March 2007, Intel Corporation announced it would build a massive $2.5 billion chip factory in China and have it operational by 2010. Intel will receive a package of subsidies worth as much as $1 billion. Paul Otellini, CEO of Intel, said at the announcement ceremony in Beijing at the Great Hall of the People that Intel's goal in China "is to support a transition from 'manufactured in China' to 'innovated in China.' " Otellini and some of the Chinese officials present also expressed their hope that the Intel operations would draw other high-tech business to Dalian, China, and nurture other supporting industries.

The Intel decision to build is consistent with China's eleventh five-year guideline (2006–10) to invigorate the nation with science and education. As transnational corporations transfer their

R&D and high-tech production to China and other nations, the United States is losing its preeminent position as the world's leading producer of advanced technology products (ATP), that is, leading-edge technologies that require research and development and whose benefits extend into other areas and often result in new products, such as improved materials, which in turn create more spin-offs. ATP production also matters greatly because the work generally requires higher-skilled, better-educated, and better-paid participants.

The Commerce Department has identified approximately five hundred items out of twenty-two thousand possibilities that it divides into ten fields and classifies as "advanced technology" goods:

1. biotechnology
2. life sciences
3. opto-electronics
4. information and communications
5. electronics
6. flexible manufacturing
7. advanced materials
8. aerospace
9. weapons
10. nuclear technology

For decades, the United States was the global epicenter of such advanced technology production. No longer. In 2008, the United States exported $275 billion of such goods but imported more than $329 billion. Of those imports, almost $91 billion (27 percent) came from China. Overall, the United States had a $72 billion ATP trade deficit with China in 2008, up from $11 billion in 2000.

The U.S. economy depends on these technologies, yet we are outsourcing their production. More significant, the Defense

Department's policy of using commercial technologies in military goods means that many of our most advanced weapons are dependent on ATP production from China. The possibilities for compromising American weapons systems are limitless.

China's state capitalism is backed by that country's sovereign wealth investment fund. It exceeds $1.8 trillion even after the global economic crash. China is secretive about how these funds are used. We do know, for instance, that the Chinese used investments to persuade Costa Rica to break diplomatic relations with Taiwan. The fund also has large investments in U.S. stocks.

China's deployment of those monies to advance its state capitalism promises to shift global economics at least as much as its quick emergence as a world-class manufacturing and exporting powerhouse. The fastest way for China's many state-owned national champions to become global companies is to buy all or a majority of the stock of well-positioned transnational corporations, much as it bought IBM's personal computer division to instantly make the Chinese company Lenovo a major worldwide enterprise.

The government of Japan will never permit such foreign control of major Japanese corporations. Germany put new investment controls into place in 2009. U.S. free-market absolutists have been willing to allow the sale of anything in America.

To avoid political fallout—such as in 2006, when Dubai's sovereign wealth fund attempted to take over a corporation that managed several U.S. ports—the Chinese have enlisted Wall Street investment bankers for help. The Chinese government also has allowed several state-owned banks to sell a small portion of their equity in public stock offerings to Western investors. The Western financial firms granted such privileges are ones with which China wishes to establish long-term strategic relationships.

Goldman Sachs was permitted to invest $2.6 billion for 5 percent of the Industrial & Commercial Bank of China in 2005, a deal put together by Goldman Sachs CEO Henry Paulson, who later became U.S. treasury secretary. Within six months, the value of Goldman's stock in that bank grew by almost $4 billion. Germany's largest insurer, Allianz SE of Munich, and American Express invested $1.24 billion together; they doubled their money in six months. Also, Bank of America doubled its investment in the China Construction Bank Corporation, and Royal Bank of Scotland Group made a quick $1 billion profit on its investment in the Bank of China.

As these examples suggest, China has now put into place the relationships it needs to discreetly buy assets and commodities around the world. The United States is thus on the verge of state-owned Chinese corporations trying to buy significant portions of the U.S. economy. Often, these purchases will be made secretly through private investment groups and foreign banks, whose owners frequently are undeclared.

The Chinese government is under no obligation to be a passive investor. Current U.S. law and World Trade Organization (WTO) trade rules allow the new owners of corporate assets to move production and R&D to China and leave only distribution networks in the United States. A basic point about the rise of Chinese state capitalism is the impossibility of confronting it through the rules-based system embodied by the WTO.

No private company, no matter how strong, advanced, or clever, can compete in global markets for long against the government of China. Ideally, the United States would closely monitor who is buying and taking control of America's productive assets, but it does not. Thus, China or any other foreign government could buy control of a significant portion of the companies listed on the New York Stock Exchange and no U.S. officials would know.

Chinese wages are rising, but they should remain far lower than those paid American workers. This cheap but competent labor, combined with the global mobility of technology and capital, means that China either already has or can create an unbreakable absolute global price advantage in virtually any industry, present or future.

Even if all foreign direct investment were stopped; even if the Chinese currency were adjusted to its real value; even if U.S.- and European-type health, safety, and environmental measures were imposed; even if China stopped its tax subsidies; and even if all its piracy and counterfeiting were eliminated, China would still have an absolute economic advantage because of the high efficiencies derived from clustering its production and the economic staying power provided by its many other government subsidies.

In sum, not only does America lack a strategy to deal with state capitalism, we even lack a lexicon. The terms we use, such as *free trade, fair trade,* and *protectionism,* are as outdated as *Marxism, proletariat, labor theory of value,* and *base superstructure.*

The state of global trade today is just as precarious as global finance was before its 2008 collapse, largely because the same proponents of free-market absolutism who deregulated the money industry also deregulated global trade over the past two decades.

Their goal was the unhindered movement of capital, technology, goods, and services across national borders, with most workers and all unions remaining where they were. The result, however, has been a massive outsourcing of jobs from the United States and a surge of imports from low-wage nations that have few or no health, safety, environmental, or social regulations.

This deindustrialization of America has created a great economic imbalance—in 2008 the United States imported $58 billion a month more than it exported, paying for that consumption by selling assets and borrowing from foreign central banks and other sources. The trade deficit more than offsets any U.S. economic stimulus currently at work. See Chart.

U.S. TRADE IN GOODS AND SERVICES—BALANCE OF PAYMENTS (BOP) BASIS

VALUE IN MILLIONS OF DOLLARS 1960 THROUGH 1973

	Balance			Exports			Imports		
Period	Total	Goods BOP	Services	Total	Goods BOP	Services	Total	Goods BOP	Services
1960	3,508	4,892	−1,384	25,940	19,650	6,290	22,432	14,758	7,674
1961	4,195	5,571	−1,376	26,403	20,108	6,295	22,208	14,537	7,671
1962	3,370	4,521	−1,151	27,722	20,781	6,941	24,352	16,260	8,092
1963	4,210	5,224	−1,014	29,620	22,272	7,348	25,410	17,048	8,362
1964	6,022	6,801	−779	33,341	25,501	7,840	27,319	18,700	8,619
1965	4,664	4,951	−287	35,285	26,461	8,824	30,621	21,510	9,111
1966	2,939	3,817	−878	38,926	29,310	9,616	35,987	25,493	10,494
1967	2,604	3,800	−1,196	41,333	30,666	10,667	38,729	26,866	11,863
1968	250	635	−385	45,543	33,626	11,917	45,293	32,991	12,302
1969	91	607	−516	49,220	36,414	12,806	49,129	35,807	13,322
1970	2,254	2,603	−349	56,640	42,469	14,171	54,386	39,866	14,520
1971	−1,302	−2,260	958	59,677	43,319	16,358	60,979	45,579	15,400
1972	−5,443	−6,416	973	67,222	49,381	17,841	72,665	55,797	16,868
1973	1,900	911	989	91,242	71,410	19,832	89,342	70,499	18,843

U.S. TRADE IN GOODS AND SERVICES—BALANCE OF PAYMENTS (BOP) BASIS (*continued*)

VALUE IN MILLIONS OF DOLLARS 1974 THROUGH 2008

	Balance			Exports			Imports		
Period	Total	Goods BOP	Services	Total	Goods BOP	Services	Total	Goods BOP	Services
1974	−4,293	−5,505	1,212	120,897	98,306	22,591	125,190	103,811	21,379
1975	12,404	8,903	3,501	132,585	107,088	25,497	120,181	98,185	21,996
1976	−6,082	−9,483	3,401	142,716	114,745	27,971	148,798	124,228	24,570
1977	−27,246	−31,091	3,845	152,301	120,816	31,485	179,547	151,907	27,640
1978	−29,763	−33,927	4,164	178,428	142,075	36,353	208,191	176,002	32,189
1979	−24,565	−27,568	3,003	224,131	184,439	39,692	248,696	212,007	36,689
1980	−19,407	−25,500	6,093	271,834	224,250	47,584	291,241	249,750	41,491
1981	−16,172	−28,023	11,851	294,398	237,044	57,354	310,570	265,067	45,503
1982	−24,156	−36,485	12,329	275,236	211,157	64,079	299,391	247,642	51,749
1983	−57,767	−67,102	9,335	266,106	201,799	64,307	323,874	268,901	54,973
1984	−109,072	−112,492	3,420	291,094	219,926	71,168	400,166	332,418	67,748
1985	−121,880	−122,173	294	289,070	215,915	73,155	410,950	338,088	72,862
1986	−138,538	−145,081	6,543	310,033	223,344	86,689	448,572	368,425	80,147
1987	−151,684	−159,557	7,874	348,869	250,208	98,661	500,552	409,765	90,787
1988	−114,566	−126,959	12,393	431,149	320,230	110,919	545,715	447,189	98,526
1989	−93,141	−117,749	24,607	487,003	359,916	127,087	580,144	477,665	102,479

1990	−80,864	−111,037	30,173	535,233	387,401	147,832	616,097	498,438	117,659
1991	−31,135	−76,937	45,802	578,344	414,083	164,261	609,479	491,020	118,459
1992	−39,212	−96,897	57,685	616,882	439,631	177,251	656,094	536,528	119,566
1993	−70,311	−132,451	62,141	642,863	456,943	185,920	713,174	589,394	123,780
1994	−98,493	−165,831	67,338	703,254	502,859	200,395	801,747	668,690	133,057
1995	−96,384	−174,170	77,786	794,387	575,204	219,183	890,771	749,374	141,397
1996	−104,065	−191,000	86,935	851,602	612,113	239,489	955,667	803,113	152,554
1997	−108,273	−198,428	90,155	934,453	678,366	256,087	1,042,726	876,794	165,932
1998	−166,140	−248,221	82,081	933,174	670,416	262,758	1,099,314	918,637	180,677
1999	−265,090	−347,819	82,729	965,884	683,965	281,919	1,230,974	1,031,784	199,190
2000	−379,835	−454,690	74,855	1,070,597	771,994	298,603	1,450,432	1,226,684	223,748
2001	−365,505	−429,898	64,393	1,004,896	718,711	286,184	1,370,400	1,148,609	221,791
2002	−421,601	−482,831	61,230	977,470	685,170	292,299	1,399,071	1,168,002	231,069
2003	−495,035	−549,012	53,977	1,020,190	715,848	304,342	1,515,225	1,264,860	250,365
2004	−609,987	−671,835	61,848	1,159,233	806,161	353,072	1,769,220	1,477,996	291,224
2005	−715,269	−790,851	75,582	1,281,459	892,337	389,122	1,996,728	1,683,188	313,540
2006	−760,359	−847,260	86,901	1,451,685	1,015,812	435,873	2,212,044	1,863,072	348,972
2007	−701,423	−830,992	129,569	1,643,168	1,138,384	504,784	2,344,590	1,969,375	375,215
2008	−695,937	−840,252	144,315	1,826,596	1,276,994	549,602	2,522,532	2,117,245	405,287

Source: U.S. Census Bureau, Foreign Trade Division.

NOTE: (1) Data presented on a Balance of Payment (BOP) basis. Information on data sources and methodology are available at www.census.gov/foreign-trade/www/press.html.

Fixing this unbalanced trade relationship in an orderly way is as vital to global economic stability as are the current efforts to repair the world financial system. Simply put, nothing can repair the economy of the United States or that of the world until U.S. trade is balanced—anything less is akin to trying to fill with water a bucket whose bottom is mostly missing. Simply put, Americans cannot continue for much longer to consume more than the country produces. Left unchecked, this imbalance will produce economic and political chaos here and around the world—a replay of the 1930s. Our consumption will decrease as we become poorer. Our suppliers from abroad will be unable to sell us goods and services. When nations cannot purchase the goods and raw materials their people need or want, or cannot sell what they make, war becomes thinkable.

Inexplicably, reducing America's massive trade deficits seems to be off the Obama administration's economic agenda, and consequently, the United States is ill prepared to manage the issue at home, let alone in the world.

Long-term U.S. trade policy is managed by the Office of the United States Trade Representative (USTR), often with what seems like an invisible hand. This small organization has fewer than 150 employees and a newly appointed leader, the former mayor of Dallas, a lawyer-lobbyist for a major Houston law firm who has no trade experience whatsoever and is new to Washington. Significantly, President Obama has prohibited the USTR from dealing with China. Only the president, secretary of state, and treasury secretary have that portfolio, with the central aspects of dealing with China being foreign policy and keeping Chinese loans coming to finance our national debt, just as during the George W. Bush administration.

THE ANGLO-SAXON VIEW

In a way, we can think of the past two hundred years as centuries of the English-speaking peoples, for Great Britain and its empire dominated the nineteenth-century world and the United States the twentieth. The two nations are bound by much more than blood and language; they also share religion, history, economic ideology, culture, and English common law. Liberty, guaranteed by English common law and the U.S. Constitution, is of paramount importance to the people of both countries.

With government in the English-speaking world there are rules and there are rights, and there are courts that provide government and people the means to enforce those rules and assert their rights. These rules (laws) of democracy have evolved over hundreds of years and are deeply embedded in the culture. Though their governments differ in many ways, the British and Americans each naturally view their system as superior to all others and have tried, even with missionary zeal, to proselytize, even force, others to adopt their type of democracy.

Because Britain and the United States, among others, were victorious in World War II, they had the power to impose their will, their values, and their systems of governance and economics on the vanquished, as well as on some members of the Allies whose systems had been destroyed. Nations that resisted such sweeping cultural implantation—notably the Soviet Union, its satellites, and China—were isolated.

Thus, the United States and Britain created the post–World War II global trade regime in their own image, and those who voluntarily participated were expected at least to pretend to follow the rules. Participation by many developing nations was forced. They were required to adopt a set of policies unofficially termed the "Washington Consensus." This really was not a consensus, but rather what Moisés Naím, editor of *Foreign Policy* magazine, termed in a 1999 article "the views of an influential majority of academics and high-level staff of the IMF, World Bank, U.S. Treasury, and think tanks, along with assorted editorialists."

Among the prescriptions advocated by this elite group was for the United States, working through the World Bank and the IMF, to withhold financial aid to developing nations until they agreed to take the following actions:

1. Privatize every publicly owned industry, public utility, public port, government-owned mine, or any other revenue-generating function then controlled by government.
2. Deregulate the private sector, permit unrestricted direct foreign investment, and strengthen property rights.
3. Cut domestic spending and raise taxes until the government's budget is balanced or in surplus, while redirecting public expenditures to education, health, and infrastructure.
4. Produce more exports than imports through a variety of steps to increase the global competitiveness of local products, including cutting wages and benefits and becoming a low-wage, low-cost export platform for foreign companies.
5. Adopt an absolutist open-market trade policy.

The stated goal of these requirements was to transform the developing countries into market-oriented regimes with economies like that of the United States. An offer of aid usually came when a financially distressed nation had few if any alternatives. Thus, a carrot was held out: If this harsh economic agenda were adopted, the country would be given expanded access to the rich U.S. market, making the country attractive for direct American investment in factories and other productive activities.

To make the carrot real, advocates of the Washington Consensus also championed changing U.S. trade laws in a way that would encourage the relocation of American manufacturing facilities to foreign sites and then allow those companies to import their products into the U.S. market duty-free. By using low-wage labor in countries with fewer environmental, health, social, and worker safety regulations than in the United States, companies could sharply increase profitability and the expanded economic activity in the developing nations could generate local taxes those governments could use to pay their U.S. bank loans.

Large U.S. and international banks were hardly disinterested players in this ideological push. To ensure repayment of their loans, the banks required U.S. manufacturers to have a "China strategy," one that forced loan applicants to prove their domestic production could beat the low prices of Chinese competitors or, if not, outsource their production and jobs in order to do so. Few American manufacturers could resist such pressure.

For decades after World War II, few noncommunist nations openly criticized the Anglo-Saxon economic model. That is, until it collapsed spectacularly in 2008. French president Nicolas Sarkozy, who previously posed as an open-market reformer, now denounces the lack of safety nets and automatic stabilizers in the Anglo-Saxon approach and praises the virtues of the French socialist model.

Such criticism, moreover, does not come just from observers in developed nations. On a visit to Brazil in March 2009, British prime minister Gordon Brown found himself at a joint press conference with Brazilian president Luiz Inácio Lula da Silva, who charged that the present economic crisis was due to the "irrational behavior of some people that are white, blue-eyed . . . and have demonstrated they know nothing about economics." Presumably, the prime minister was not offended, as his eyes are brown.

As this criticism suggests, the world economy contains several economic models other than the Anglo-Saxon one, and their differences are often great. American trade policies, however, remain bound by three immutable Anglo-Saxon principles:

1. Open markets and trade are the most efficient means to expand global trade and, therefore, will eventually become the economic model that guides world commerce.
2. The United States has a primary responsibility among nations to advance open trade and equal commercial access.
3. Multilateral negotiations are the best means to open markets and expand trade.

The basic flaw in these assumptions is that most other nations' economies are not like that of the United States, nor will they be, nor should they be. Other countries compete in the world marketplace using vastly different assumptions that aim for vastly different ends. Economic systems differ in ways both manifest and subtle, reflecting basic differences in history, culture, national aspirations, finance, and politics.

Three types of economic systems compete with the Anglo-Saxon model used by the United States, Great Britain, Canada, Australia, Ireland, New Zealand, and others. None of these three is based on open trade and equal commercial access.

One of these is the centrally planned economy found in Cuba, North Korea, and, previously, the former Soviet Union. Theirs has proven to be a failed approach and exists today only in the last of the old communist dictatorships.

A second is the mixed model prevalent in most of Europe.

The third is the plan-driven model as practiced in most of Asia, notably Japan, China, South Korea, and Taiwan.

Within these three frameworks are many variations. The mixed economy of France differs in many ways from the mixed economy of Sweden; Japan's version of a plan-driven system differs from China's plan-driven economy; and even between

Canada, Great Britain, and the United States there are clear distinctions.

It is possible to sketch the differences among the systems by comparing them along four dimensions: the role of government in the economy, the ownership of industry, the relationship between processes and results in the system, and the way trade is conducted.

In the rule-driven, market-oriented Anglo-Saxon economic model, government sets the economic backdrop with fiscal, monetary, exchange rate, and trade policies but takes few overt positions on which industries should exist, grow, or decline. In contrast, plan-driven economies such as China's and Japan's pointedly identify industries that are a national priority and arrange resources and a host of policies to back them, including trade protectionism of the home market. Japan's steady takeover of the global auto industry is one such example. Mixed economies such as France's skillfully blend the strength of the government with the flexibility of the marketplace to achieve specific outcomes. Who but the French, for example, now drive French-made automobiles?

In Anglo-Saxon economies, private ownership of business and industry is the standard. Planned economies are based on a combination of state and private ownership, with the state making market and nonmarket decisions. Major industries are either owned by the state, as in China, or tightly regulated, as in Japan. Major enterprises in the centrally planned economies are, of course, state-owned.

Anglo-Saxon economies are process oriented; once rules are established, market processes dominate. Plan-driven economies are results oriented; business and government shape a national "vision" that often includes targeting certain industries, such as automobiles or advanced technology. To guide the economy toward desired results, governments of plan-driven economies provide financing, research, and training. Mixed economies rely on a combination of market processes and government planning. Command economies are dominated by state planning.

Economists, lawyers, and politicians who make, interpret, and enforce the rules under which market processes work heavily influence the process-oriented Anglo-Saxon economies. Because plan-driven economies are results oriented, they have far less need for lawyers and economists to make and enforce rules. Instead, politicians, bureaucrats, and business leaders direct the results-oriented economies. The same is true of mixed economies.

In trade negotiations, all have different views. Americans tend to focus on rules that will facilitate market processes, while the Japanese, Chinese, and Koreans focus on measures that will advance their national economic vision—that is, will lead to specific results.

American policy makers, devoted to open markets and equal commercial access, often tend to ignore the vast differences between U.S. and foreign economic systems. Rather, they operate on the premise that policies that don't harm American industry will produce the same benefits globally. They do not, of course. Consequently, these shortsighted trade policies are doing enormous harm to the U.S. economy and the American people.

The math of America's trade imbalance is daunting. In 2008, the United States imported $2.5 trillion of goods and services while exporting only $1.8 trillion, thereby creating a net trade deficit of nearly $700 billion—almost $2 billion a day. During the twentieth century, the United States ran an annual trade surplus until 1971, when for the first time there was a deficit. The last year the United States ran a trade surplus with the rest of the world was 1975. Between 1976 and 2008, the United States accumulated a trade deficit of $6.9 trillion, which represents the largest transfer of wealth from one nation to others in world history.

Another way to view this wealth shift is to look at it as reparations paid by the loser in global trade wars to the victor, such as Germany did after World War I.

The overwhelming majority of America's trade deficit comes

from trade in goods, not crude oil. In 2008, for example, while America imported $453 billion in crude oil, it also imported $1.64 trillion in nonpetroleum goods. Put another way, of the $2.1 trillion total of imported goods and crude oil, nonpetroleum goods constituted 72 percent and oil 28 percent. During the same year, the United States exported $1.2 trillion in nonpetroleum goods. Again, to put these figures in context, for every seven dollars' worth of nonpetroleum goods the U.S. exported, it imported ten dollars' worth. This trade imbalance is impoverishing the American economy and its workers.

This imbalance partially reflects the mass outsourcing of manufacturing overseas during the past three decades. It also reflects the many protectionist barriers American producers face when they export into foreign markets. Getting foreign goods into the U.S. market is easy; getting U.S. goods into many foreign markets is difficult, if not impossible.

Since the mid-1980s, the USTR has issued an annual report that identifies this protectionism country by country. The 547-page *2009 National Trade Estimate Report on Foreign Trade Barriers* covers the practices of sixty-three nations. This inventory classifies ten different categories of obstacles to the U.S. export of goods and services, foreign direct investment by U.S. nationals, and protection of intellectual property rights:

1. Import policies such as tariffs, import charges, quantitative restrictions, import licensing, and customs barriers.
2. Standards, testing, labeling, and certification, including unnecessarily restrictive application of sanitary and phytosanitary standards and environmental measures.
3. Nationalistic government procurement policies and closed bidding.
4. Export subsidies, including export financing and subsidies that displace competitive U.S. exports in third-country markets.
5. Ineffective patent, copyright, and trademark protections.

6. Service barriers, including limits on the range of financial services that can be offered, regulation of international data flow, and restrictions on the use of foreign data processing.
7. Investment barriers, including limitations on foreign equity participation and on access to foreign-government-funded research and development programs, local content and export performance requirements, and restrictions on transferring earnings and capital.
8. Anticompetitive activities tolerated by foreign governments, and by both state-owned and private firms, that apply to services or to goods and that restrict the sale of U.S. products to any firm, not just to foreign firms that perpetuate the practices.
9. Restrictions on electronic commerce, including tariff and nontariff obstacles, discriminatory regulations, standards, and taxation.
10. Bribery and corruption.

As this list suggests, the ways, means, and combinations foreign governments use to thwart the import of U.S. goods, services, and investments are varied and numerous. The list of barriers for China took up fifty-six pages of the USTR document. Korea and India each required fourteen pages, and Japan twenty-two pages.

Clearly, the U.S. government is well aware of these protectionist tools, as the *2009 National Trade Estimate Report* was the twenty-fourth in the series. Strikingly, these barriers still exist despite more than sixty years of intensive postwar trade negotiations with other countries beginning in 1947.

Despite America's spirited urging of other nations to adopt the Anglo-Saxon economic model—open markets and deregulation—this system has enjoyed little appeal abroad. It suits the United States, but it would not fit most other countries. Most countries tolerate the United States' championing of open-market absolutism just as they would the rants of a diminished relative: They ignore it. Yet as long as the United States remains ideologically blinded and does nothing about the imbalance of trade, the transfer of wealth and power will continue unimpeded. After all, it is not the responsibility of other nations to inform us of our arrogance and stupidity.

Again, numbers reveal the shape of the U.S. trade position. Of the world's 6.7 billion people, only 427 million (6.4 percent) live and work in nations that use the Anglo-Saxon model. Of the world's $78 trillion GDP in 2008, the Anglo-Saxon model accounted for $20 trillion (25 percent) and other models $58 trillion (75 percent).

Since we have failed for decades to persuade others to adopt our model, our choice now is simple: We can either continue to urge other nations to be like us and continue to suffer trade losses, or we can change U.S. trade policy to deal with other nations as they are rather than as we wish they would be and balance our accounts. It could be called a "tailored" trade policy.

Clearly, only the second course makes sense. It is pure folly to presume we can somehow convince other countries to abandon economic systems that have served them well and change to a system that serves us. Nor can we continue to blindly look the other way. Indeed, America can no longer afford its missionary work on behalf of the Anglo-Saxon economic model.

When the United States had huge trade surpluses and was the world's largest creditor, it had enough money to grant other countries special trade concessions as a means of influencing their foreign and economic policies. But now that we have accumulated a $6 trillion trade deficit over the past three decades and are the world's largest debtor, a continuation of this "beggar thyself" policy is so impractical it is madness.

America needs an economic strategy that deals with other countries as they are—a tailored approach.

A TAILORED APPROACH

The World Trade Organization is the principal global trade regime. The United States led in its creation, and unsurprisingly, it is constructed on Anglo-Saxon assumptions and rules. Established in 1995, the WTO now has 153 member nations. It has acquired a bureaucracy in Geneva that is change averse.

A round of multilateral trade negotiations began at the WTO in 2002, stalled in 2007, and then failed in the last months of George W. Bush's administration. One reason for the failure was that one of the key American goals was deregulation of the global financial system, as had been done in the United States. That idea is not attractive to other countries and, accordingly, has been abandoned by the Obama administration.

Multilateral negotiations under the WTO and its predecessor, the General Agreement on Tariffs and Trade (GATT), are distinguished by a growing time lag between each: 1947, 1949, 1951, 1956, 1960–62, 1962–67, 1973–79, 1986–94, and 2002–unfinished.

These negotiations have been unable to deal with the trade imbalance to the satisfaction of the United States mainly because they largely reflect flaws in U.S. policies. As the imbalance gets ever more out of kilter, so do the risks for a global trade meltdown, as happened in the 1930s when the U.S. economy collapsed. These foreign trade dependencies on U.S. consumption are traps that are as much a problem for other countries as they are for the United States. Imagine, for instance, what would happen to China without the American market.

Drastic action is appropriate to escape this trade trap. Congress should exercise its constitutional authority under Article I, Section 8, to regulate commerce with foreign nations, declare that a trade emergency exists, and temporarily suspend U.S. obligations under the WTO until the crisis passes. To prevent a trade panic, Congress and the Obama administration should announce that the United States intends to voluntarily follow existing agreements, except for an agenda of emergency negotiations and measures.

The United States should ask other nations to share more fully the burdens of expanding global trade. Until now, the United States has been expected to be the locomotive of world economic recovery, taking in during global economic downturns more goods and services than it exports. The country has gone far beyond any sensible limits with imports, and the moment has come for Europe and Asia to share those responsibilities by stimulating their economies and taking more. Trade and prosperity are presumably as important to them as they are to America.

A tailored trade strategy would elevate a handful of ongoing bilateral and plurilateral (involving several countries) negotiations from secondary to primary roles, importantly allowing American representatives to match their negotiations to the other countries' economies. For example, trade negotiations with planned, results-oriented economies, such as those of China and Japan, would focus on results-oriented agreements. Trade talks with Europe's mixed economies would center on a combination of both results and process. Negotiations with the command economies will still be unlikely, since they are generally economically irrelevant and largely based on domestic politics.

Ironically, the trade deficit that compels the United States to reform its trade policies also generates enormous negotiating leverage. Since America is the largest market for dozens of nations, the possibility of limited access to or loss of that market by nations unwilling to seek a balanced trade relationship is the best, if not only, negotiating chip the United States possesses.

TAILORED TRADE NEGOTIATIONS

One hopes that policy makers, politicians, and commentators realize the difference between limiting U.S. market access to avoid foreign competition and limiting it as a device to expand

U.S. exports and balance trade. The former shrinks trade and the latter expands it. America's long-term interests lie with expanded, but balanced, trade.

Interestingly, the United States is fortunate in that more than two-thirds of its trade deficit in goods is with only five nations: China, Japan, Mexico, Canada, and Germany. When the imports of oil and natural gas from Canada and Mexico are factored out, the ratio is close to 80 percent.

In 2008, the United States imported $1.1 trillion in goods from those five countries. Of this, almost $155 billion was in imports of oil and gas and $971 billion was in nonpetroleum goods. Since the worldwide total goods deficit for the United States in 2008 was $799 billion, if American negotiators can reduce the goods imported from those five countries, or get them to take more exports of U.S.-made goods and services, or some combination of the above, major progress can be made in rebalancing U.S. trade.

Rather than negotiating with 153 countries at the WTO in Geneva, the United States can resolve many of its existing trade problems with bilateral negotiations in Tokyo, Berlin, Beijing, Mexico City, and Ottawa. Ideally, negotiations with Mexico and Canada would be conducted under the auspices of the North American Free Trade Agreement (NAFTA). In the 2008 presidential campaign, candidate Barack Obama repeatedly promised voters that he would reopen NAFTA negotiations; now he says he will not. But that could change.

The goal of all this is to lower America's trade deficit by reducing imports, moving production of certain goods back into the United States, exporting more U.S. goods, or some combination of these methods. Ideally, this would be done by reaching agreements at the WTO with individual nations or with groups of nations. If not, the United States can make other choices and proceed accordingly.

In these negotiations, America should deal with both the

instant problem of trade imbalance and structural changes to avoid its recurrence. An obvious step toward accomplishing this would be eliminating the economic discrimination created by the value-added tax. As explained in chapter two, WTO rules allow nations that use the VAT to provide rebates on their exports and impose a VAT-equivalent tax on imports from nations that do not use the VAT. Under this unfair system, U.S. producers get no credit for corporate income taxes they pay on goods they export, plus they must pay the VAT-equivalent taxes.

One early agreement the United States should seek in any negotiations is elimination of the VAT distortion in trade with its five largest trading partners. The arithmetic suggests just how economically important this would be. The nearly $171 billion in 2007 for those five was 48 percent of the nearly $356 billion VAT distortion the United States had with all other member countries of the WTO.

VAT RATES AND THE RESULTING TAX DISTORTION ON U.S. TRADE 2007 TRADE DATA
(Billions of Dollars)

Country	VAT Rate (Percent)	Rebates on Exports to the U.S.	VAT on Imports from the U.S.	Total VAT Distortion
China	17	$42,001.1	$10,372.2	$52,373.3
Japan	5	7,246.4	2,904.8	10,151.2
Mexico	15	31,523.8	17,907.2	49,431.0
Canada	7	21,875.3	14,918.3	36,793.6
Germany	16	15,106.6	7,087.1	22,193.7
Total		$117,753.2	$53,189.6	$170,942.8

Source: See appendix 1, table 1

The VAT in these five nations, in effect, gives them an export subsidy for goods and services exported to the United States. The imposition of the VAT on U.S. imports is, in effect, a protectionist tariff. If the United States were to shift to a VAT-based approach in raising revenues, as recommended in chapter two, this distortion of trade would be automatically eliminated in accordance with the existing WTO agreement. Agreements with these five countries would rebalance trade between them and the United States.

Bilateral negotiations with China, Japan, and Germany would deal directly with numerous additional barriers to trade that are identified in the USTR's annual reports.

Among the key U.S.–China issues, for instance, are China's many restrictions on importing U.S. agricultural products and its local content requirements on imports from the U.S. automobile sector. China uses an array of policies to promote and protect what it calls its "pillar" industries, it promotes Chinese brands worldwide by giving them prohibited export subsidies, and it limits foreign imports in those same industries.

These Chinese actions, while illegal under WTO rules, are precisely what a planned economic model does. Growth through planning is far more important to the Chinese government than complying with the WTO's Anglo-Saxon rules. A tailored response is the logical response from the United States.

Japan restricts agricultural imports from the United States through a variety of quotas, tariffs, and nontariff barriers, and refuses to allow the sale of American rice to Japanese consumers, though they clearly would buy it if available. The Japanese government buys American wheat and then resells it in Japan at an exorbitant rate that raises the price of wheat-based foods and thus limits demand. Contract rigging in Japan against outsider corporations also is common.

Since the mid-1950s, Japan has created an array of nontariff barriers to exclude U.S. car and auto parts from the Japanese market. Though Japan annually exports millions of vehicles to the United States (2.2 million in 2007), it imports virtually none

(16.5 thousand in 2007). And the issue is not that U.S. automakers refuse to produce right-hand drives—the Big Three produce forty different such models that are sold throughout the world. Because of Japanese protectionism, almost all U.S automakers and parts makers have given up trying to penetrate Japan's closed market and have sold their holdings in Japanese automobile manufacturers. Tailored trade, focusing on results, not process, is ideal for U.S.–Japan trade talks.

Canada and the United States have the world's largest bilateral trade relationship, with total trade between the two nations reaching almost $600 billion in 2008. Although Canada operates on an Anglo-Saxon economic model, problems remain.

The Canadian government, for instance, has a monopoly on Canadian wheat, which it uses to undercut U.S. sales. Canada alone of the three NAFTA partners imposes mandatory container sizes, all of which are unique to Canada, on a wide range of fruits and vegetables, thereby imposing additional costs on U.S. and Mexican producers. The Canadian government provides special funding for its aerospace, space, and security industries, subsidies that improve their competitiveness against U.S. and other foreign competitors.

Canada regulates foreign investment, and in several instances its government has prohibited U.S. takeovers of Canadian firms. Canada also bans U.S. and other foreign investors from buying existing Canadian-owned book publishing and distribution businesses and film distribution firms.

Mexico is a poor, developing country used by foreign corporations as a low-wage, low-regulation production platform for goods sold in the United States. Drug cartels threaten the government's stability, and U.S. exporters face an array of corrupt officials and inefficient barriers to sales there. Mexican importers, trying to bring more than four hundred different U.S. products into their market, must apply to their government for registration and permission. The Mexican government has created seven hundred technical regulations that are issued by several agencies. Some agencies keep their regulations secret, which makes meeting requirements difficult.

Mexico is a special situation. It is our immediate neighbor. Its people on average earn less than 10 percent of what their American counterparts earn. Illegal Mexican immigration into the United States is rampant, and U.S. employers exploit Mexican workers in both Mexico and the United States. NAFTA merely locked in that abuse.

A new approach is required. Though defining such an approach is not the purpose of this book, bringing Mexico, its people's lives, and its economy up to developed-world standards is a mission the United States and Canada have delayed for too long. Ultimately, a strong, prosperous Mexico is the solution to a host of problems concerning our three countries.

Germany is a highly competitive nation that strives to pay high wages, maintain a clean environment, and fulfill a host of social obligations. The VAT burden is a major obstacle for U.S. producers who wish to export to Germany, and its elimination would go far in bringing U.S.–German trade more into balance.

Germany has an economic addiction to cartels and industry-bank relationships that often operate in the shadows and impede foreign participation in the local economy. Ideally, negotiations with Germany could be a springboard for similar talks with the European Union as a whole. Germany and the EU nations have mixed economies, and a mixed trade agenda could be tailored to the benefit of all parties.

CHANGE AT THE WTO

The WTO is the world's principal institution for international trade. However, because it was built on an Anglo-Saxon economic model, it is hampered in its mission to facilitate global commerce. Corrective actions are now appropriate.

The WTO provides a forum for governments to negotiate trade agreements that provide legal rules for global commerce. It is also a place where nations can settle trade disputes with each other.

One of the claimed benefits of the WTO is that it shields member governments from lobbying by their own narrow domestic interest groups, that is, their workers, industries, and citizens. According to WTO literature, membership allows governments "to focus on trade-offs that are made in interests of everyone in the economy." By joining the World Trade Organization in 1995, the United States agreed to:

- Ensure the conformity of U.S. laws, regulations, and administrative procedures with its obligations as provided in the WTO agreement.
- Make no reservations in respect of any provision of the agreement.
- Subject all federal, state, and local laws and practices that affect trade to international review by the WTO.
- Allow any WTO member to challenge a federal, state, or local law as trade impeding.
- Agree that all interpretations of WTO provisions require a three-quarters majority vote and the rejection of a WTO judicial decision on a trade dispute requires a consensus vote by all members of the WTO, including the affected party nations.
- Take all trade disputes with other nations to the WTO for resolution.
- Give the WTO judicial process final jurisdiction over all trade disputes.
- Agree that the proceedings of WTO judicial panels will be kept secret. All documents used shall remain secret. Opinions in the final report shall be secret. Votes of panelists shall be secret. No appeal exists outside of the WTO.
- Agree that the WTO is empowered to enforce its rulings by

imposing fines on the United States until the nation complies, to deny national trading rights, and to authorize cross-retaliation on any U.S. export, thereby allowing fines to be collected from any industry, even those not involved in the trade dispute.

- Agree that all trade policies and practices of the United States are subject to international review by the WTO.
- Agree that when the European Communities exercise their right to vote, they shall have a number of votes equal to their number of member states.
- Agree that the United States shall have only one vote in WTO proceedings.

Because American proponents of WTO membership feared they could not get the two-thirds majority of votes in the U.S. Senate the Constitution requires for ratification of a treaty, the United States joined the WTO by way of an executive agreement that required a simple majority vote in both the House and the Senate. As an executive agreement, the authorizing legislation provides the president authority to withdraw from WTO membership simply by notifying the organization by letter. Six months later, U.S. membership would end. The president is not mandated to consult with other nations or secure approval from Congress for such a drastic step. This gives President Obama enormous leverage in any negotiations to strengthen the global trade system.

Fortunately, U.S history provides a model of how to deal with important, but dysfunctional, institutions. After Washington, Jefferson, Madison, Franklin, and other founding fathers concluded that the Articles of Confederation were inadequate for the needs of the nascent United States, they were wise enough to replace them with the Constitution. Today the WTO, as now structured, is also a failing institution that requires major reform.

A principal problem is that the WTO is operated in an exclusionary and autocratic manner. Votes by members, for instance, carry equal weight, although individual nations may be unequally affected by WTO decisions. The vote of the tiny nation of Antigua (population 69,000), as an example, carries the same weight at the WTO as that of China (1.3 billion) or the United States (301 million). This would be insignificant were it not for the fact that WTO practice is to seek unanimity in voting, which gives the greatest power to those with the least stake.

When it joined the WTO, the United States agreed not to take unilateral or bilateral action against nations that violate their trade obligations to America, instead agreeing to take such disputes to the WTO for resolution. This process, however, has proven far from satisfactory.

Judges, who are often not impartial, are chosen by the WTO and may come from any member nation. They often are current or former trade officials or experts, and they serve on an ad hoc basis. Many are U.S. lawyers, academics, and former officials who were principal champions for U.S. membership in the WTO in the first place. While their decisions can be of enormous consequence, the Congress does not vet them for conflicts of interest, as they do U.S. judges. Altogether, this pool of panelists is a global club of open-market advocates. In a world of high-stakes trade issues amid corruption, this is naive and dangerous to U.S. interests.

Unlike U.S. judicial proceedings, WTO dispute settlement panels operate in total secrecy. The U.S. government cannot reveal detailed complaints from litigating nations to the American people, representatives from affected industries and unions cannot attend deliberations, panel votes are kept anonymous, amicus briefs are classified, and the rationales for decisions remain confidential. Decisions are final, and the only appeal is to another WTO panel.

Since the founding of the WTO, other nations have named the United States a defendant in far more cases than any other nation. Worse, the United States has lost an overwhelming majority of those cases. Former deputy U.S. trade representative Robert Lighthizer testified in August 2007 before the House Ways and Means Trade Subcommittee that the WTO ruled against the United States in forty of forty-seven cases in which it was a defendant. This is highly significant because most of these losses forced the United States to change its laws and administrative rules. Lighthizer told Congress, "Clearly, one of the biggest threats to our trade laws is from the dispute settlement system at the WTO. The system is fundamentally flawed, and the decisions being issued by the WTO are gutting our [fair] trade laws."

One ruling prohibited the United States from distributing money from fines collected on imported goods that were dumped on the U.S. market back to the companies and workers victimized by such predatory trade practices. Another ruling penalized America for prohibiting Internet gambling. Yet another ruling required the United States to weaken its environmental rules to allow the import of polluting fuels from Venezuela.

Foreign governments, flagrantly disobeying existing global trade rules, use the WTO to eliminate restrictions on dumping and subsidies and, by extension, force the United States to change its domestic laws in order to comply with WTO decisions. Repeatedly, according to Lighthizer, WTO judges have "exceeded their mandate by inventing new legal obligations that were never agreed to by the United States . . . allowing our trading partners to achieve through litigation what they could never achieve through negotiation." WTO panels and the WTO Appellate Body are "creating new WTO obligations out of whole cloth."

Among the least discussed and understood characteristics of the WTO is that member nations are obligated to accept common industrial standards promulgated by the International Organization for Standardization (ISO) and the standards for food, additives, residues, and contaminants set by the Codex Alimentarius Commission, a United Nations organization. Both the ISO and the Codex rely on private companies and associations to develop the standards they promulgate. The Codex deliberations, like the WTO's, are closed to the public. Companies and trade associations that have been unable to weaken U.S. standards through legislation and open rule-making processes can do so by working with other nations to set lower ISO and Codex standards that are then enforced by the WTO on the United States.

The time has long come for the United States government to review its experiences at the World Trade Organization and think about changes that are appropriate to a tailored trade approach. The failed Doha Round of negotiations and the massive U.S. trade deficit are compelling reasons to redefine the WTO's role overall and its relationship to U.S. trade policy making specifically.

The WTO charter provides for decisions being made by vote. At an absolute minimum, the United States should insist the WTO voting structure be altered to reflect the stakes each individual nation has in global trade. If the United States has 22 percent of global trade, it should have 22 percent of the WTO votes. After some period, such as five or ten years, the stakes and votes should be recalculated and apportioned to ensure fairness. While the consensus model was appropriate for the GATT, the WTO predecessor, because it was a weak negotiating forum only, the WTO is a global regulatory body empowered to impose heavy penalties. Apportioned voting would provide fairness and vigor to its decisions.

Also, the United States should insist on open procedures at the WTO, its dispute panels, and in the work of the ISO and the Codex. The American people should have full transparency from any quasi-governmental body that can compel the United States to revoke its health, safety, environmental, or food standards or force the payment of financial penalties to other nations. As a simple standard, the United States should refuse to participate in any panel or obey any decisions unless the proceedings are open.

The United States needs to require that all WTO panelists judging any American interests be thoroughly screened for conflicts of interest and that sitting government officials should be barred from WTO panels. Lighthizer rightly advised Congress that it should hold hearings on the WTO's judicial activism, form an expert body to advise Congress and U.S. trade negotiators on WTO dispute settlement decisions, and allow private lawyers to participate in WTO dispute proceedings.

When American trade lawyers represent a foreign government at the WTO, they can participate in all proceedings. Yet WTO rules prohibit attorneys for U.S. companies and unions involved in these cases from observing the proceedings or reading documents concerning their cases. Only attorneys for the U.S. government can participate. The process requires transparency.

Finally, before the United States accepts them, all WTO decisions that necessitate changes to U.S. laws should require a simple majority vote of approval in both houses of Congress through normal legislative procedures. This congressional scrutiny would focus attention on foreign governments that try to change U.S. trade laws through WTO judicial activism. Such scrutiny will constantly remind other governments that U.S. membership at the WTO is a choice, not an obligation.

The deregulation of trade during the past three decades, the absence of effective enforcement of the trade agreements that have been made, and our complete lack of a strategy to deal with state capitalism have put at risk not just our economy but the larger global economic stability. Before the world economy completely collapses, the Obama administration and Congress need to recognize the dimensions of the calamity America faces—the trade trap—and balance America's trade in a way that is neither protectionist nor mercantilist.

Because of the great interdependence created by globalization policies of recent years, America and the world face a global trade meltdown far worse than what occurred in the early 1930s. It is imperative to remember that now, as at the beginning of the worldwide Great Depression, the closing of world markets could lead to massive political instability, even war.

CHAPTER FOUR

INNOVATION

Imagine that Ian Fleming's James Bond novels were true chronicles of a secret agent's battles against SPECTRE, Fleming's organization dedicated to world domination. If SPECTRE decided to destroy America, what would be its quickest and most likely plan of action?

Placing enough of "their" people in federal leadership positions to deregulate the U.S. financial system would certainly be one way to cause great damage and chaos. Instructing the same people to undermine America's energy independence efforts and deepen U.S. dependence on imported crude oil would be another, as would be the expansion of already massive federal budget deficits.

The ultimate strategy for dominating the United States, however, would be to wreck its economy by strangling American innovation—that is, slow or stop the invention, development, and implementation of new and altered products, services, and processes.

The strategic element in innovation is invention. Stop invention, even drastically slow it, and the entire dynamic will collapse and with it will go the American economy, for a long time, perhaps forever.

A real SPECTRE would target the U.S. patent system. The heart of invention, now as always, is the patent. The Constitution of the United States grants inventors the *right* to a patent for the exclusive use of a creation for a limited time set by Congress in exchange for revealing to society all the knowledge behind the invention, including the inventor's best mode to reproduce it. The patent system motivates creativity by rewarding exclusive use—and the possibility of fame and wealth. It facilitates the invention process because inventors know they are protected by exclusive use and their patent rights are backed by access to the federal courts and the right of private action against those who use their creations without permission.

SPECTRE, of course, does not exist, but other powerful forces interested in their own selfish interests do. In their pursuit of higher profits, greater market share, and ego gratification for some high executives, some giant corporations are attempting to alter to their narrow advantage the U.S. system of innovation. The governments of Japan, China, and other nations whose societies lack the ethos of creativity found in America have joined them.

The solution chosen by these corporations and nations is not to change themselves and spur more individual creativity, but to try to slow innovation in America by rendering the U.S. patent system inoperable, that is, by making it more like the systems of other nations, a process of change called "harmonization."

This very real threat to American innovation is far greater than any plot Ian Fleming invented for SPECTRE.

President Obama and Congress have only a few major tools they can use to bring the country out of the current meltdown. One is fiscal policy that, with our current and projected massive budget deficits, is at its limits. The second is monetary policy, which at today's virtually zero rediscount rates is at its limit. The third is exchange-rate policy, whose power is now constrained by the United States' extraordinary status as the world's largest debtor nation and its dependence on foreign borrowing. The fourth is trade policy, which is also mostly inoperable because of the large deficits we are running with other nations.

The only macroeconomic tool for which the United States still has almost total freedom of use is innovation policy. America came out of the economic lethargy of the 1970s, for example, with a wave of computer-based inventions that hit the market in the late 1970s and early 1980s and created an economic revolution and millions of new and better jobs.

Eventually, the president, Congress, and our other national leaders will realize that the current stimulus program is focused almost exclusively on stopping the global economic power dive. Even if it begins to succeed, the present recovery program cannot make the U.S. and world economies soar again. But innovation on a massive scale can.

For that to happen, our leaders need to make the American patent system a facilitator of innovation rather than the inhibitor it is becoming. This chapter presents ideas on some strategic actions that can help the United States reach that goal.

THE FOUNTAINHEAD OF PROGRESS

The world's largest exporter of manufactured goods has a declining population of 83 million people whose average age is forty-four. That country, roughly the size of Montana, has few national resources other than low-grade coal, water, some arable land, and the skills of its people. The nation is Germany. For more than a century and a half, big business and big banks—tightly entwined and often operating as either real or de facto cartels—have dominated Germany's economy. Germany is prosperous because Germans are innovative.

The world's second-largest economy is located on a chain of mostly barren islands off the eastern coast of Asia and has virtually no energy or other natural resources. Only 11 percent of this California-size nation is arable, forcing the country to import most of the food consumed by its 127 million people, whose average age is more than forty-four. This nation is Japan. Truly, virtually all Japan has are the Japanese. Like Germany, Japan is a cartelized economy dominated by influential industries and large banks and governed by officials chosen from the best and brightest graduates of the country's top universities. Japan also is prosperous because the Japanese are innovative.

While innovation is the open secret to success in both nations, they operate under a state- and corporate-driven system in which individual creativity is subordinate to the needs of society and its corporations.

America is different. It relies heavily on independent inventors, small companies, research institutes, and universities for its major innovations. The United States Patent and Trademark Office (USPTO) annually awards these inventors 30 percent of all U.S. patents. This difference is of vital importance because what large and small firms create is startlingly different. Germany and Japan rely on large firms, also called "large entities," for innovations; the United States relies on what are termed "small-entity" inventors.

Small-entity inventors are America's innovators. The Small Business Administration reports that they receive thirteen times more patents per employee than larger enterprises. Their patents are more significant as measured by citations, originality, and generality and are more likely to create "breakthrough" or "pioneer" patents that originate an entire file of technology. Far more so than large entities, small entities are prolific in their creativity and in the twentieth century created more than half of the most important inventions. Many are serial inventors. Equally significant, small and medium-size businesses produce approximately 75 percent of the U.S. GDP, making them also America's major job creators.

A partial list of breakthrough innovations by small firms includes biosynthetic insulin, electronic spreadsheets, personal computers, digital recording and sound, WebTV, high-resolution

CAT scanners, microprocessors, optical scanners, pacemakers, portable computers, and soft contact lenses, among thousands of others. These innovations changed our lives for the better, expanded our national wealth, and created millions of new jobs. Many of their inventors, moreover, are still actively creating.

According to the National Science Foundation, of the thirty thousand firms with R&D expenditures in 2000, almost half of the expenditures came from 167 giant corporations with twenty-five thousand employees or more. The results produced by these giant corporations were greatly different from those of the small-entity inventors. The big corporations focused on modest, predictable product improvements and new uses for their existing products, while small firms focused on breakthroughs. Greatly simplified, small firms make breakthroughs and large firms produce incremental improvements.

Consequently, a pattern has emerged indicating that once entrepreneurial firms become big, they often tend to create less-significant technologies. They also depend more on the purchase of small innovative firms in order to gain breakthrough inventions.

Herein lies the problem for large corporations everywhere, what economists call "creative destruction." For leaders of most large entities, creative people working either independently or at small firms, private research institutes, or universities are their worst nightmare.

"Innovation is a hostile act as it threatens the status quo and those who benefit from it," wrote Paul Heckel, an inventor and a cofounder of Intellectual Property Creators, an independent inventors' group. That threat, Heckel claims, explains the difference between the U.S. patent system and the systems of Japan and nations in Europe. Those nations developed systems to minimize outside threats to entrenched interests, while the U.S. system was created after the American Revolution, when the entrenched interests—the British—had been overthrown and those in power had the future of the new nation to develop.

The American experience suggests that an independent inventor can devastate an entrenched interest almost overnight.

Some recent examples include Apple cofounders Steve Jobs and Steve Wozniak's invention of the personal computer in the late 1970s, which basically destroyed IBM's typewriter business, as well as dozens of other industries. Michael Dell, working out of his room at the University of Texas with a girlfriend assembling computers, invented a business model that enabled his tiny company to overtake IBM and Compaq as the world's largest computer maker, becoming a multibillionaire in the process. A college student named Fred Smith wrote a thesis on how to create a spoke-and-hub overnight distribution system that was faster and more reliable than the U.S. Postal Service, raised financing, created Federal Express, and also became a billionaire. Invention is the magic of which dreams are made.

Is it any surprise, therefore, that governments in Japan and Europe and large corporations have long sought to weaken U.S. patent protections for small-entity inventors?

A QUICK AND ESSENTIAL HISTORY

The idea behind the U.S. patent system is very simple: Society agrees to give an inventor of something useful, nonobvious, and unique the right (a patent) to its exclusive use for a set period, and the inventor can defend that right in the federal courts. In exchange, the inventor agrees to share with society all knowledge about this creation and provide the best mode to replicate it. Sharing knowledge is the price of exclusive use.

Patent rights in America flow from the original imperative to industrialize the fledgling nation for reasons of national security. When the thirteen British colonies revolted in 1776 and declared independence, they had virtually no means to produce the weapons and goods needed to fight what was then the world's superpower. Ninety-four percent of Americans lived and worked on farms, and England prohibited the colonies from manufacturing even the most basic goods. Imports came from England, and the colonists paid for them with exports of natural resources, tobacco, fish, timber, and other basic commodities.

The revolutionaries' and the colonies' desperate lack of manufacturing capacity is illustrated by the list of prospective purchases Benjamin Franklin carried with him to France in 1777. It included 80,000 shirts, 80,000 blankets, 100 tons of powder, 100 tons of saltpeter, 8 ships of the line, 10,000 muskets, and 100 fieldpieces—all to be purchased on credit.

Amazingly, he succeeded on his shopping expedition, but then he had to arrange shipping across the Atlantic Ocean, where the goods had to pass a British naval blockade in a 4,000-mile, three-month journey to St. Eustatius, a Dutch island in the Caribbean. Then smugglers received the goods, put them into small boats, and slipped them past the blockade into the colonies, a 1,400-mile trip that consumed another five to six weeks.

Needless to say, industrial self-sufficiency was foremost on the minds of American leaders after the war as a matter of national security as much as economics. The Constitutional Convention in the summer of 1787 adopted a noncontroversial provision, later known as the Progress Clause, stating that "the Congress shall have power to promote the progress of science and useful arts, by securing for limited times to authors and inventors the exclusive right to their respective writings and discoveries."

Innovation, based on patents and copyrights, was the new nation's first development strategy. It cost the government nothing, potentially involved anyone with a creative idea, and relied on individuals to implement it. President George Washington, in his first report to the first U.S. Congress, asked it to expeditiously create a patent system, which Congress did in April 1790. The importance of patents and innovation is highlighted by the structure of the first three-person patent board. The chairman was the secretary of state (Thomas Jefferson), plus the attorney general (Edmund Randolph) and the secretary of war (Henry Knox).

Early protectionist trade policies gave Americans a fast-growing domestic market all their own. Patents, with their right of exclusive use, gave inventors the means to attract investors and satisfy the market. Basically, this American innovation policy allowed a nation of farmers to become the world's foremost industrial power within one average lifetime.

DANGEROUS VICTORIES

Until the 1930s, the American people held inventors and their patents in the highest esteem, but that changed during the Great Depression and the early years of World War II, when economic and social reformers accused monopolistic sellers and cartels of selfishly holding back economic recovery.

In one instance early in the war, the nation learned that Standard Oil of New Jersey had colluded with I.G. Farben, the giant German chemical cartel, to hold back from the U.S. military their joint secrets on producing synthetic rubber, just as natural rubber supplies were cut off by the Japanese. Other investigations revealed that General Electric was using its patents to maintain a monopoly in the electric lamp industry and the Hartford-Empire Company was doing the same in the glass container business.

Antitrust proponents felt the exclusive right to a patent was a monopolistic threat to competition. To stop anticompetitive behavior, the Federal Trade Commission (FTC) broke open corporate patent portfolios and forced companies to license patents to other parties at giveaway royalty rates, often zero.

In their book *The Invisible Edge,* Mark Blaxill and Ralph Eckardt recount one of the most devastating examples of these attacks, the Xerox case.

The inventor was physicist Chester Carlson, who in the midst of the Depression (1934–38) showed twenty different corporations his invention, but none were interested. Finally, he reached an agreement with the Battelle Memorial Institute. Battelle scientists and engineers made additional improvements to Carlson's technology, but ultimately the commercialization of xerography was also beyond their means.

In 1946, Battelle found a company willing to take on the challenge, Haloid, a $6 million-a-year Rochester, New York, corporation. Haloid later changed its name to Xerox, and eventually Battelle received $3.5 million in cash and 1.1 million shares of stock.

To raise capital, Xerox borrowed heavily and sold stock. Corporate executives cut their pay, and many mortgaged their homes and lent money to the company, a story that was later often repeated in technology circles.

Beginning in the early 1960s, Xerox finally became an extraordinary commercial and financial success. The company continued to invest heavily in R&D and created a world-class research center in Palo Alto, California, where Xerox scientists and engineers invented the next generations of Xerox high-tech magic. As Blaxill and Eckardt document, Xerox invented the mouse, the local area network, the text editor, Ethernet, the laser printer, and much more. Much of what eventually became the Apple Macintosh and Microsoft Windows originated at Xerox.

In the mid-1970s, the FTC brought Xerox and its innovation to a screeching halt. The FTC decided in 1973 that the public interest would best be served by breaking Xerox's hold on the copying industry that it had created. Explaining the FTC position twenty years later, F. M. Scherer, who had been the lead FTC economist, said that by 1973 Xerox "had enjoyed monopoly sales for fourteen years . . . and the time had come for therapeutic intervention." The FTC staff believed that Kodak and IBM would enter the market if the federal government imposed a mandatory licensing decree on Xerox, and that would lower the price of plain-paper copying.

Xerox executives, self-confident in success, believed they could defeat both Kodak and IBM on the open market, and they probably could have. Accordingly, in 1975 Xerox entered a consent decree with the FTC. The key provision was that

> *Xerox would grant non-exclusive compulsory licenses to its existing patents, domestic and foreign, and any applied for during the three years following the decree. The first three patents chosen by the applicant for license were to be royalty-free; each additional patent bore a 0.5 percent royalty rate up to a maximum royalty rate of 1.5 percent. Other provisions called for know-how transfer, a ban on multi-model lease price discounts, the publication of toner quality specifications, and a mechanism for resolving disputes over whether a rival toner was unsuitable for use.*

With that, potential Xerox rivals got instant and free access to billions of dollars of research, development, and experience, and if Xerox held back anything, the federal government would prosecute its corporate leaders.

Kodak and IBM were not the competitors that emerged. The Japanese government had long before created an imaging cartel among its own corporations, illegally using Xerox technology. When the FTC forced Xerox into compulsory licensing, the Japanese took the licenses and its cartel entered the market. With lightning speed, Canon, Toshiba, Sharp, Panasonic, Konica, and Minolta took over the U.S. and then the world paper copier market.

Xerox had 100 percent of the plain-paper copying market in 1973, but by 1979 it had only 14 percent. Without those sales and profits, the corporation collapsed and its innovative R&D efforts ceased.

The FTC justified its actions with the claim that the American public benefited by getting less expensive plain-paper copying.

Even if that were true, what the FTC did not acknowledge were the hidden costs—America lost all the innovation, wealth, and jobs Xerox had created and, more important, would have created in the future. Instead, Japan got it all.

The amazing aspect of the Xerox story is that it is neither unique nor extreme. In the thirty years between the end of World War II and 1975, the FTC, a somewhat little-known independent federal agency headed by even lesser-known political appointees, forced almost one hundred similar compulsory licensing decrees upon other American companies, including American Air Filter, AT&T, Bausch & Lomb, Bendix, Bristol-Myers, Carrier, Chrysler, Cincinnati Milacron, Corning, DuPont, Eastman Kodak, Exxon, Ford, General Motors, Hughes Tool, IBM, Merck, Minnesota Mining, NCR, Owens-Corning, Pfizer, Phelps-Dodge, Rohm & Haas, and Westinghouse Electric.

Rather than breaking up a corporation, as the federal government did with Standard Oil, or imposing fines and jail terms on executives convicted of violations of antitrust laws, thus forcing changes in business practices, the FTC attacked the patents. It imposed compulsory patent licensing on those companies and forced them to share their technology—their crown jewels, if you will—with the rest of the world for virtually no compensation. The FTC decrees led to the issuance of more than forty thousand compulsory patent licenses, unwittingly catapulting "Japan Inc." into the high-tech stratosphere, all the while discouraging new U.S. corporate investment in innovation.

After a 1956 FTC decree that forced the compulsory licensing of 8,600 AT&T patents, the *Wall Street Journal* editorialized:

> *So it may turn out that these are dangerous victories the Government boasts about. The settlements in these cases indicate a belief that everybody's patents should be everybody else's. But this is a philosophy that strikes at incentive; new ideas and new inventions may be lost. Such Govern-*

ment victories may turn out to be far more costly for the nation than for the companies.

The *Wall Street Journal* editors were never more prescient.

In the late 1970s, the United States was in great economic trouble. In 1978, President Jimmy Carter appointed the Advisory Committee on Industrial Innovation to investigate and report on why innovation in America seemed in decline. As one committee member noted, "Investment in basic research had disappeared . . . U.S. production was no longer competitive . . . old technologies were stagnant . . . New technologies were dormant." Members attributed this, among other conditions, to a "diminished patent incentive."

The unacknowledged elephant in the room was the FTC's compulsory license decrees, which gave away forty thousand patents. Why would corporations and capitalists invest in innovation if the government would force them to issue royalty-free, compulsory patent licenses to their global rivals? Even worse, as the Xerox case illustrated, the more successful a company was with a new patented technology, the more likely the FTC was to force the corporation to give it away.

After due consideration, the Carter advisory committee recommended more federal investment in R&D, the creation of a specialized appellate court for patent cases, and establishment in the Patent Office of a simplified, inexpensive patent reexamination process. Congress enacted those recommendations, plus other legislation that encouraged more entrepreneurial activities by American colleges and universities, early in the first Reagan administration.

Simultaneously, more than one hundred government-industry study groups on U.S. competitiveness were formed in the early 1980s. Compulsory licensing quickly became passé,

R&D expanded, and America enjoyed a burst of innovation that lasted the next twenty years.

The intriguing question is, why did the FTC impose the licensing decrees in the first place?

What happened at the FTC in those three decades after World War II is very much akin to what happened at the Securities and Exchange Commission between 1998 and 2008 that has led us into our current economic problems. Little-known but powerful federal agencies, led by political appointees operating with scant congressional oversight, pursued absolutist ideological agendas: The FTC's was a twisted New Deal liberalism, and the SEC's was an equally perverse Reagan conservatism. One gave away many of America's most essential technologies, and the other left Wall Street to its own devices and created a global financial collapse.

The FTC's patent history is virtually unknown among contemporary policy makers. Frighteningly, President Obama and Congress are on the verge of repeating the FTC's antipatent mistakes, but in a new way through new laws that will do to innovation in this century what the FTC decrees did to it in the last.

PATENT WAR I

Of all nations, Japan most eagerly scooped up the free technology thanks to the FTC's compulsory licensing, using it from 1954 to 1975 to create an advanced industrial base. By the time the U.S. patents underpinning those compulsory licenses had expired, Japan's industries needed the next generation of American technology. They obtained some of this technology by extorting companies like IBM to share innovations as a condition of gaining market access inside Japan. Not surprisingly, when these companies developed new technologies in Japan, the Japanese government prohibited them from sending the innovations to their U.S.-based facilities. Many foreign corporations entered similar agreements.

The Japanese also used their patent system as a tool of technology extortion. Once an American patent owner filed for a Japanese patent, local corporations, who could access the patent, would soon submit a host of related patents that challenged or limited the original creation. The Japanese companies would eventually suggest a cross-licensing arrangement in which neither side paid royalties. The goal of the Japanese, of course, was to use the American innovation for free. All the Americans received was access to Japan's closed market, if that.

At the same time Japanese companies, with the tacit support of their government, were using economic espionage to steal U.S.-owned technologies inside the United States. In the early 1980s, the FBI successfully ran sting operations that caught some of those thieves. By then, some American patent owners were suing Japanese companies for infringement and winning in American courts. The Japanese government responded by mounting a political campaign to weaken U.S. patent laws.

In the 1980s, Japan created a powerful political machine inside the United States, a topic examined in my book *Agents of Influence.* In brief, the Japanese mission was to deflect U.S. criticism, lawsuits, and political actions directed against their business practices, most notably trade, investment, and patent infringement.

The Japanese campaign provided subsidies to leading U.S. policy institutes (think tanks) and universities, planted newspaper and magazine articles, paid for advertising to advance "correct" editorial positions, and subsidized pro-Japan programs in public educational institutions. It also employed an army of lobbyists drawn from the ranks of former high officials in the White House; the Office of the U.S. Trade Representative; the State, Defense, Justice, Treasury, and Commerce departments; and Congress.

By the late 1980s, Japan was operating a sort of shadow U.S. government composed of former officials drawn from both Republican and Democratic administrations. At one point, the chairman of the Republican National Committee (RNC) was a registered foreign agent of the Japanese auto industry, and the chairman of the Democratic National Committee (DNC) was a registered foreign agent of the Japanese electronics industry.

Japan's political investment paid off spectacularly during the Clinton administration largely because the Japanese had hired Ron Brown. In 1989, Brown was a candidate for chairman of the DNC, and his twenty-one Japanese electronic industry clients raised more than $100,000, then an enormous contribution, to help finance his campaign. Brown won the chairmanship and subsequently led a reinvigorated Democratic Party to win control of the White House in the 1992 elections, even as he continued to work as Japan's top lobbyist in America.

Once elected president, Bill Clinton appointed Brown commerce secretary, and later Brown invited Clinton to a private preinaugural dinner with the heads of the twenty-one Japanese companies. Brown cancelled the event after the *Washington Post* reported it, causing a public uproar.

One of President Clinton's first moves was to establish a U.S.–Japan working group, with Brown leading the U.S. team. High on the group's agenda were intellectual property matters. Brown's first overseas trip as commerce secretary was to Tokyo, where Akio Morita, founder of Sony, hosted a welcoming lunch. Among the other guests were Brown's former Japanese clients.

The Japanese agenda was to transform the U.S. patent system so it would be more like Japan's; that is, it would favor large-entity corporations over small-entity inventors. The U.S. Patent and Trademark Office defines individual inventors, independent research institutions, small businesses with fewer than five hundred employees, and universities as small entities. Big corporations are known as large entities.

As part of their agenda, the Japanese wanted the United States to shift from its two-century-long practice of awarding a patent to the first person to invent to the first person to file for a patent. They also wanted the United States to limit patents to a fixed twenty-year term that begins when a patent application is filed, not when the patent is granted, and publish all the details in a patent application at eighteen months from filing. Finally, they wanted the United States to allow third parties, especially Japanese corporations and their American lawyers, to participate in the Patent Office review of patent applications. All these proposals were and are antipatent.

Japan's requests were brazen. By common consent, the U.S. patent system is the finest in the world. Individual (small-entity) inventors in Israel, Denmark, Sweden, Switzerland, Norway, and most other large European nations rely on their U.S. patents to provide protection against infringers. For example, Teva, a large Israeli-owned pharmaceutical company, sues infringers of its patents from India in New Jersey because those protections are real.

In effect, Japan's agenda was a move to persuade American officials to sacrifice the broader economic future of the United States to that of the Japanese. Japan's plan, moreover, was backed by many European patent officials and by many large corporations in the United States. The real battle was between those large-entity advocates and America's small-entity inventors.

Without congressional authorization, Brown and Bruce Lehman, the Clinton administration's new patent commissioner, made an agreement with the Japanese government that supposedly bound the Clinton administration to secure congressional approval of the Japanese proposals on first-to-invent, early publication, the twenty-year patent term, and third-party inspections.

When the Tokyo bureau of the *New York Times* reported on the agreement, members of Congress from both parties exploded in anger. Over the next five years, a patent war was fought in Congress between the supporters of large- and small-entity inventors, an intense fight I documented in my book *Hot Property.*

By the end of the Clinton administration, Congress had agreed to a fixed twenty-year patent and to publishing all patent applications at eighteen months after filing, with the exception of those applications whose inventors agreed not to file for a foreign patent and petition the USPTO for nonpublication. The other items on the agenda of the foreign governments and large-entity corporations were rejected.

The two victories, however, are very significant. Prior to 1999, the U.S. patent term was seventeen years, regardless of how long it took the Patent Office to process the application. Sometimes complicated patent applications take many years to process and involve numerous clarifications between patent examiner and inventor, and in rare instances involving breakthrough technologies, the process can consume twenty years or more. But in the end, regardless of the delay, once a patent was issued, the inventor received seventeen years of exclusive use.

The new fixed twenty-year system does not make allowance for time consumed in processing by the Patent Office. If five or ten years pass, which is now common, the life of the patent once granted is reduced accordingly. One U.S. chemical patent application in Japan took nineteen years and eleven months to process. The applicant got one month of patent protection in Japan.

In 1993, as part of NAFTA, the United States changed the U.S. patent to a term of seventeen years after being granted or twenty years, whichever was longer. Later the Clinton administration and Congress shifted the term to a twenty-year fixed life, creating a situation in which competitors aggressively look for ways to consume some or all of the twenty years of a rival's patent.

The easiest way to slow down the patent process is to cut funding for the Patent Office, which the Clinton and Bush administrations did for other reasons. To no one's surprise, the average time to process a patent jumped from eighteen months in the early 1990s to thirty-three months today. If a patent's validity is challenged, which increasingly happens, another five to seven years of the twenty-year patent life can be consumed.

While long patent lives matter greatly in some industries such as pharmaceuticals, the life of many technology patents can be very short. In fast-changing areas such as electronics, a five-year delay in processing often means the technology will be obsolete by the time a patent is granted. This works for competitors who game the patent system.

The publication requirement is also significant. In 1999, Congress began requiring the Patent Office to publish all patent applications eighteen months after filing, the only exception being when inventors agree not to file a foreign patent and specifically request nonpublication. The rationale is that all other nations require such publication and U.S. patent applications in those nations are made public anyway. Missing in that argument is a key fact: 64 percent of U.S. patent applicants do not file for foreign patents. What large-entity inventors, the Japanese, European governments, and now the Chinese government want is an advance look at the secrets of small-entity inventors before U.S. patents are issued.

This new publication rule adopted by Congress is pernicious, because while it takes the Patent Office an average of thirty-three months to process an application, it reveals an inventor's secrets to the world at eighteen months. During the fifteen months between publication and the average patent decision, an inventor has no protection. Rivals who have access to the patent information can use that knowledge to work around the proposed patent and create similar, but different, innovations and begin using them with or without patents in their race to dominate global markets. In China and elsewhere, infringers take U.S. applications, modify them slightly, and file them as new patents at China's patent office.

A recent Japanese experience, ironically, illustrates the danger of premature publication. The Japan External Trade Organization (JETRO) maintains dozens of offices throughout the world, including six in the United States, and provides Japanese industries with timely foreign market intelligence and business development support. In the summer of 2004, Yoichi Gotani, director of JETRO's intellectual property office in Beijing, visited the head office of Haier Group, China's largest consumer-electronics maker, where he met the executive in charge of the company's intellectual property activities.

When Gotani asked about Haier's research, a corporate executive told him the company "spends only a small amount on research." Instead, the Haier executive said, "using several dozen computers, we search for patent applications submitted to patent offices in Japan, the United States, and European countries to obtain useful information to develop our products . . . Most of those foreign inventors and companies won't apply for patent rights in China; there's nothing legally wrong in us using them."

After Gotani reported his findings, the Japanese Patent Office (JPO) examined how often people inside China, as well as South Korea, entered the Japanese computer system to look at patent applications. JPO officials were stunned to learn there were seventeen thousand inquiries a *day* from China and fifty-five thousand a *day* from South Korea. The conclusion was obvious: Chinese and South Korean companies were systematically trolling for information they could incorporate into their products from the most advanced research and development under way in Japan. Surely those countries were also searching computers at U.S. and European patent offices.

Yomiuri Shimbun, one of Japan's largest newspapers, in July 2005 used the Gotani story to illustrate the technological vulnerability created in Japan by the premature publication of information in Japanese patent applications. The newspaper concluded editorially that Japan's intellectual property competitiveness, a foundation of that nation's economic strength, was widely threatened. Publishing patent applications at the eighteen-month point was a major factor in that threat.

Prior to the 1999 legislation requiring eighteen-month publication, the U.S. Patent Office was required to keep details of applications secret and destroy all applications that were rejected. This allowed inventors to rework their applications and try again or use a creation as a trade secret. Coca-Cola does this with its secret formula. Now, once they are published by the Patent Office, all details in an application are automatically classified as "prior art," which means they are public property and can be accessed by anybody. Thus, an inventor gets no second chance to rework an application.

Today the Patent Office rejects 58 percent of all patent applications. This means an inventor now takes the great risk of losing control of a creation simply by seeking a patent.

In the politics of Washington, no battle is ever really over, particularly when big corporations and governments want something. Thus, as World War I was a prelude to World War II, Patent War I was a prologue to Patent War II.

PATENT WAR II

By 2001, the international competitiveness of Japanese industry was in serious condition. The real growth of Japan's GDP, for instance, declined from 3.8 percent in the 1980s to 1.4 percent in the late 1990s. Japanese labor productivity was falling while that of the United States and other industrial countries was increasing. The three top Japanese universities filed 73 patent applications in 2000, while their three American counterparts filed 1,239—seventeen times more.

The Japanese government noted that, though Japan led technological competitiveness in many fields, the United States was regaining the lead in many others, especially new areas thought to define the future.

The Japanese government did in 2001 what President Carter

had done a quarter century earlier: It formed an advisory committee composed of leading academics, industrialists, and financiers. Ironically, the principal recommendations the group made in its 2002 report were the same ones the U.S. committee made in the late 1970s—establish a pro-patent policy and encourage more innovation by individual inventors, small businesses, research institutes, and universities, plus seek stronger patent protections globally. The committee encouraged Japan to adopt a small-entity innovation strategy.

The Japanese, who own hundreds of thousands of advanced technology patents, have turned their principal concern from rigging the U.S. patent system to their advantage to protecting what they have from infringers, notably their Asian neighbors, who are now a true economic threat.

As the Japanese were rethinking their patent policy, the FTC was also reexamining the proper balance between competition (antitrust) and patent law in the United States. In October 2003, the agency issued a major report, *To Promote Innovation,* which gave a long list of recommendations, virtually all of which are antipatent. They include:

- Shift to a first-to-file patent system.
- Eliminate the publication exemption given to those who file for a patent only in the United States.
- Tighten examination at the Patent Office to eliminate questionable patents.
- Create a new process at the Patent Office to allow postgrant opposition to issued patents.
- Reduce the legal standard on defending infringement from "clear and convincing" evidence to the weaker "preponderance of evidence."
- Tighten legal standards in evaluating whether a patent is "obvious."
- Tighten legal standards so as to strengthen requirements for

proving "willful" infringement and thus liability for treble damages.

These recommendations would weaken patent applications, weaken patents granted, increase patent processing time, raise the bar for getting a patent, lower the bar for challenging a patent, cut the life of patents, eliminate the presumption of validity of issued patents, and offer new processes to challenge the validity of a patent. The FTC gave the role of patents in our national innovation strategy a negligible consideration. And all these recommendations favor large-entity over small-entity interests.

The FTC report represents a brew of antitrust intellectual predilections and large-entity thinking. Of the five FTC commissioners who signed off on the report, all came from or would have links to major law firms representing large-entity corporations such as General Motors, General Electric, Cisco, and Microsoft.

Former White House counsel and longtime Washington lobbyist Harry McPherson has best explained the resulting dynamic: "Most advocates are not born with a position on catalytic converters. In developing the argument for their client's position, they often convince themselves of its truth." Often it is an honest self-deception on issues that many carry with them if and when they enter public office.

Equally significant, the three hundred witnesses the FTC heard in its hearings overwhelmingly came from large-entity corporations, their trade associations, their law firms, or law schools supported by the big entities. While 30 percent of U.S. patents go to small-entity inventors, only a tiny fraction of those consulted by the FTC were in that category. One of the notable characteristics of all the recent study commissions and congressional hearings on patent reform is that virtually no inventors were asked to give their views. Finally, the staff that developed the report was primarily drawn from the FTC's general counsel staff—that is, antitrust lawyers. Not surprisingly, the report is strongly pro-antitrust and equally robustly antipatent.

The report has exerted an enormous influence on U.S. patent policy since its issuance in 2003. It gave legitimacy to arguments that the patent system is broken, that it is biased against large-entity inventors, that it is abused by nonpracticing entities (trolls), that a patent litigation crisis exists, that patent lawsuits are diverting massive amounts of corporate monies from badly needed R&D, and other charges. These arguments all are factually wrong, as documented in several studies cited in the end-notes to this book.

Most important of all, the FTC report gave legitimacy to a legal and lobbying campaign that has been financed and led by Apple, Cisco, Dell, HP, Intel, Micron, Oracle, Palm, RIM, Symantec, SAP, Google, AutoDesk, Microsoft, and IBM. This group will be referred to hereafter as the 15.

These corporations use aggressive business practices that test the limits of the law and repeatedly bring them into conflict with inventors, other companies, universities, independent research organizations, and domestic and foreign governments. From 1996 to 2008, the 15 were defendants in 730 patent infringement cases and paid out almost $4 billion in infringement judgments and settlements for the unauthorized use of technology owned by others (see tables 2 and 4 in the appendix). Their payments are an estimated half or more of all patent infringement settlements made by all companies in the United States during that period.

During that same thirteen-year period, the 15 were defendants in 641 antitrust actions and other legal proceedings for their anticompetitive behavior. Following are some examples:

- The European Commission (EC) has fined Microsoft almost $2.5 billion for its anticompetitive acts over the past decade.

PATENTS GRANTED, LAWSUITS COMMENCED, PATENT CASES TRIED

(FY 1979–2008)

Fiscal Year	USPTO Patents Granted	Patent Lawsuits Commenced	Lawsuits as a Percent of Patents Granted	Patent Cases Tried
2008	182,556	2,817	1.54%	109
2007	184,376	2,712	1.47%	94
2006	183,000	2,830	1.55%	106
2005	165,000	2,720	1.64%	104
2004	187,000	3,075	1.64%	98
2003	190,000	2,814	1.48%	83
2002	177,000	2,700	1.52%	86
2001	188,000	2,520	1.32%	83
2000	182,000	2,484	1.36%	85
1999	159,000	2,318	1.45%	98
1998	155,000	2,218	1.43%	103
1997	123,000	2,112	1.71%	103
1996	117,000	1,840	1.57%	101
1995	114,000	1,723	1.51%	87
1994	113,000	1,617	1.43%	86
1993	107,332	1,553	1.45%	87
1992	109,728	1,474	1.34%	52
1991	101,860	1,171	1.14%	86
1990	96,727	1,238	1.27%	96
1989	102,712	1,155	1.12%	105
1988	83,584	1,226	1.46%	108
1987	88,793	1,129	1.27%	89
1986	76,993	1,105	1.43%	89
1985	75,302	1,155	1.53%	85
1984	72,149	1,057	1.46%	90
1983	59,715	1,017	1.70%	112
1982	65,152	811	1.24%	108
1981	71,010	805	1.13%	92
1980	61,227	811	1.32%	99
1979	55,418	829	1.49%	73

Sources: Data on Patents Granted is from USPTO Annual Reports. Data for lawsuits commenced is from the Federal Judicial Statistics, Table C-4. *U.S. District Courts—Civil Cases Terminated, by Nature of Suit and Action* for the respective years.

In 2004, Microsoft settled a class-action lawsuit with California for $1.1 billion, plus $258 million in legal fees, for overcharging customers. In 2008, a federal court ruled that Microsoft owed Alcatel-Lucent $512 million for patent infringement.

- The EC fined Intel more than $1.4 billion in 2009 for monopoly abuse; the corporation settled a similar charge privately with Japan in 2005. South Korea also fined Intel $25 million in 2007 for similar anticompetitive practices.
- Micron Technology Inc. participated in a long-running conspiracy with Asian and European producers in a Dram price-fixing and bid-rigging scheme. Several participants went to prison, and the Justice Department imposed $731 million in fines, the second-highest total ever obtained in a criminal antitrust investigation.
- Brazil charged Cisco in 2007 with tax fraud and evasion of $845 million in import duties and other taxes.

Despite being defendants in 1,371 antitrust and patent infringement cases, or perhaps because of it, between 1996 and 2008, these corporations tripled their collective revenues from $176 billion to $534 billion. Indictments, lawsuits, and even massive fines seem neither to deter them from anticompetitive behavior nor constrain their success. To a corporation with $30 billion to $50 billion of annual revenues and cash reserves often as large, a $1.5 billion fine can be largely irrelevant, even a bargain if it can suppress competitors and facilitate the unauthorized and uncompensated use of their best ideas.

In the past, the Justice Department would seek jail time for CEOs and other coconspirators in such anticompetitive crimes. The prospect of jail time might have a deterrent effect now.

Rather than change their business models to reduce infringement liabilities, the 15 have chosen to mount a multiyear campaign in the federal courts and Congress to weaken America's patent laws. They seek to make infringement easier and less expensive. The problem, of course, is that weakening barriers to infringement for them means weakening protections for everyone else.

The agenda of the 15 has succeeded spectacularly in the federal courts. One victory was a Supreme Court ruling in 2006 that diminished a patent owner's right to injunctive relief, a case titled *eBay Inc. v. MercExchange, L.L.C.* Before this decision, the general rule was that federal courts would almost automatically issue permanent injunctions to prohibit the use of a valid patent without the owner's permission. Property was property, with all the attendant rights for owners. The Supreme Court, however, ruled that there should be no general rule as to when a court would issue an injunction in a patent case. Rather, the court drew some guidelines for the lower courts. Now injunctions are to be used only as an extraordinary remedy strictly limited to a situation involving "irreparable harm"—a standard that is virtually impossible for small entities to meet, making them highly vulnerable to infringers with deep pockets.

This decision means an infringer can use someone else's patented invention without permission, continue using it until a jury or judge finds infringement, and then pay a royalty rate set by the court. This is self-initiated compulsory licensing of someone else's property. University inventors and researchers are particularly vulnerable because they seldom manufacture what they invent—they license. At a minimum, this decision locks a patent owner into long and expensive litigation. It also makes the licensing of patents difficult for owners. Why should infringers pay a license when they can steal with limited liability?

In the 2007 Seagate Technology, L.L.C., ruling, the appeals court for patent cases raised to virtually impossible heights the standards of proof a patent owner must meet to substantiate that an infringer negligently disregarded the owner's patent rights. For decades, the doctrine of "willfulness" protected patent owners by providing that if someone continued to infringe a patent after learning or being told about it, the court could treble the patent owner's entitlement to a reasonable royalty if the infringer was found guilty.

To avoid such willfulness, the 15 and other large-entity inventors pursue what is called "engineered ignorance," which means that these companies instruct their scientists and engineers to avoid by all means looking at any patents, research papers, or literature that might reveal details of someone else's patents. Their theory is that if they were "ignorant" of that information, they could claim any infringement was accidental and the court would be less likely to impose treble damages if they were found guilty of infringement.

Amazingly, the FTC report called upon the courts and Congress to make willfulness more difficult to prove, thereby discouraging efforts to make potential infringers take care not to violate patents. Even more disturbing, the FTC failed to take the next logical step and recommend that the courts automatically impose treble damages if an infringer was found guilty, *unless* the infringer's contemporaneous records could prove that the infringer had made a good-faith effort at due diligence. Once again, the FTC subordinated the interests of the inventor and economy to those of the infringer.

In yet another 2007 ruling, *Microsoft Corp. v. AT&T Corp.*, the Supreme Court found that Microsoft had used a key AT&T technology without permission and had to pay for its use in the United States. But the court also reversed a long-standing precedent and ruled that Microsoft did not have to pay AT&T when Microsoft sold the same purloined technology outside the United States. Instead, the court ruled that AT&T must bring lawsuits against Microsoft country by country to collect royalties and damages, a challenge AT&T can afford but one that is prohibitively expensive for small-entity inventors.

Also in 2007, in a case known as *KSR International Co. v. Tele-*

flex Inc., the Supreme Court lowered the standard of proof for a patent being "obvious." For decades, the invalidation of a patent required the infringer to find all elements of a patented invention in a single piece of work that was public before the filing of the application that resulted in the patent. But the KSR decision held that if one of each of, say, four elements of a patented invention could be found in four different publicly known works and they could be combined to show that the invention was "obvious," it was not patentable. The court did not impose a requirement that anyone, much less the inventor, ever combined the four works or even knew they existed. Again, this favors infringers by making it easier to invalidate an issued patent.

Defendants in patent infringement cases are abusing the USPTO program that permits anyone to challenge a patent's validity. An example is the experience of Avistar Communications Corp., a small San Mateo, California, company. Following Avistar's failed attempt to persuade Microsoft to license its technologies in 2008, the giant software corporation challenged the validity of Avistar's complete portfolio of twenty-nine patents at the Patent Office. While fighting the challenges, Avistar was unable to pursue other development strategies and had to cut its workforce by 25 percent. The company confronts a hard choice of submitting to Microsoft's demands or facing years of legal expenses and reexaminations at the Patent Office.

Big companies such as the 15 are willing to weaken the patent system because patents are increasingly unimportant to their own operations. Here is how Howard Markey, first chief judge of the Federal Circuit, the appellate court that hears patent cases exclusively, explains it:

> *Many giant corporations have no need of a patent system. They may obtain patents, but only as a defense against some*

> *little machine shop operator who might otherwise invent and patent something the public would demand, and the big corporation would have to negotiate for, instead of adding the item to its product line. Many large corporations should be glad to compete on size, nationwide service, high volume, strong finance, and prompt delivery. They can kill off smaller competitors on any of these bases, unless the small competitor has a patent on a product somebody wants to buy.*

For small-entity inventors, however, patents are vital because they are the key to raising venture capital and protecting inventions against infringers.

In 2005, the 15, minus IBM, formed a cleverly named lobbying group, the Coalition for Patent Fairness, and began a campaign to change U.S. patent laws. They have labeled their tough antipatent agenda patent "reform." The campaign has five goals:

1. Legislatively change the formula used to calculate patent damages so that they can pay less when found guilty of infringement.
2. Create new ways of challenging the validity of an issued patent.
3. Impose on the courts and Patent Office lengthier processing and reexaminations that will consume the life of the patents being challenged.
4. Limit the venue where they can be sued to places where they have major facilities and employment.
5. Embed the judicial decision on willfulness into legislation.

Virtually every other group dependent on patents is on the other side of this political fight, including organized labor, venture capitalists, environmentalists, the National Association of Manufacturers, the American Bar Association, independent inventors, small-business groups, universities, and thousands of individual companies. Both sides fought the patent battle in the 109th and 110th Congresses, and it is currently before the 111th Congress.

Amazingly, the 15 have convinced many in Congress that they are victims of the small-entity inventors and their lawyers who filed the 730 infringement lawsuits, and that they need legislation to protect them from the little guys. The FTC's somewhat Orwellian response has been to investigate the licensing and litigation activities of small-entity inventors.

RECOMMENDATIONS

America is deeply in debt. The principal way for the nation to revive the economy and avert a deeper and more prolonged depression is to innovate on a massive scale. A patent system is needed that encourages inventors to invent, investors to invest, and entrepreneurs to sell the new creations that flow from this process.

A stronger patent system will help all large-entity industries that depend on patents, including the pharmaceutical and biotech industries. Certainly, small entities will benefit. So too will the emerging green industries, for their inventors require patents to get financing and to have protection against infringers.

For America, a strong innovation agenda, backed by strong patents, is all gain, requiring few federal outlays and virtually no social costs. It is the principal means of ultimately restoring economic sovereignty.

Step one in this process would be for Congress to scrap the Federal Trade Commission's big-entity, antipatent agenda as embodied in the 15's proposed legislation. Congress needs to challenge the FTC to focus on its legislated mission—regulation of anticompetitive behavior. An FTC investigation into why the

15 are defendants in so many infringement and antitrust lawsuits and lose or settle so often would be a useful starting point.

Retaining America's first-to-invent approach to patents is also vital. The United States is the only country that uses a first-to-invent system, while all others use a first-to-file method. The first-to-invent approach is far more efficient and produces better-quality patents. Academy Award recipient Steve Perlman, who invented the computer-generated imaging for the movie *The Curious Case of Benjamin Button,* which starred Brad Pitt, says he went through more than one hundred experiments to develop the technology, many of which were failures. Had the United States used a first-to-file system, he notes, the only way he could have protected his innovations from infringement would have been to file almost one hundred patents on partially developed ideas.

With a first-to-invent system, he was able to wait until he perfected the technology, ultimately filing only seven patents that gave him complete protection. The difference, he says, is that between a "soft" and a "deep" patent. A soft patent is a work in progress; a deep patent is the finished product. The U.S. system encourages the filing of deep patents, and the consequences to an already overloaded Patent Office are obvious.

The United States is the only major nation whose constitution authorizes a patent system. The founding fathers intended, as noted in the language of the Constitution, for a patent to go to the inventor, not, by some gimmick, to the first inventor to file. The importance of granting a patent to the first to invent was enshrined when Washington, Jefferson, Randolph, and Knox established America's patent system.

A widely distributed business solicitation brochure from a California law firm that calls its patent reexamination specialists the Patent Assassins illustrates the dangers of weakened patent protections. These lawyers help infringers nullify others' patents through legal proceedings. Their "knockout" strategy is to challenge a patent at the USPTO, often anonymously, and they claim they can "create a simulated swell of opposition to the patent. This can hide your identity and even draw the patent owner's ire toward your competitors."

The brochure also claims they can use "an arsenal of tactics that can keep a problem patent in re-exam for a long, long time," thereby allowing infringers to "argue against paying royalties until the re-exam is complete or for lower rates until the uncertainty ends." Justice delayed, the Patent Assassins point out, is justice denied.

To stop such gaming of the patent system by clever litigants and their "assassin" lawyers, several recent Supreme Court patent decisions merit being revisited. This would:

- Encourage the courts to impose injunctions automatically on infringers of issued patents; a patent is property and the courts should defend its sanctity.
- Extend damages for infringement of U.S. patents by American infringers to again include foreign violations; if Microsoft is guilty of infringing AT&T's U.S. patent, the courts should hold it accountable for the same infringement of the same patent elsewhere.
- Revert the standard for "obviousness" to its pre-2007 definition in order to encourage innovation rather than making it more difficult to prove.
- Revert the standard for "willfulness" to its pre-2007 definition and mandate automatic treble damages unless a convicted infringer can convince the court a good-faith due diligence effort was made.

Challenges to a patent at the Patent Office should be limited to the *ex parte* process established in 1981, the inexpensive, nonadversarial, and relatively quick patent challenge performed by experienced examiners. Today nine out of ten patents survive such exams with at least one claim intact, and one-quarter emerge with all claims intact.

The *inter partes* process created in the 1999 American Inventors Protection Act is in effect a minitrial that now takes eight or more years, including appeal, to conclude. As these delays suggest, the Patent Office is not the place to operate an adversarial judicial system. They divert resources from patent examination, the office's true purpose. The remedy for Congress is obvious: eliminate the *inter partes* process and require that challenges to patents, other than through the *ex parte* process, be made through the courts.

Global publication of patent applications by the Patent Office needs to be limited to the abstract that accompanies the submission. Limited disclosure will both alert others to an innovation and protect an inventor's secrets. Full publication should be limited to granted patents. As previously discussed, the system introduced in the 1999 act foolishly distributes an inventor's most precious secrets worldwide before providing any patent protections.

Such premature publication is also a risk to national security. For the past decade, the State, Commerce, and Defense departments have forbidden the export of hundreds of technologies deemed vital to national defense, and the law prohibits patent owners from talking with foreign nationals about those technologies or sharing any materials. Violation of these restrictions is a criminal offense, carrying a heavy fine. Yet at eighteen months from the filing of a patent application on these same national defense technologies, the Patent Office is publishing the full documentation, including instructions on the best way to replicate the innovation.

As part of a new publication policy, the Patent Office should also, once again, be required to keep all denied applications secret and destroy the documentation under some time schedule, thereby allowing an inventor to use a creation as a trade secret or rework the idea into a new application.

Congress has starved the Patent Office of money. The world's greatest trove of unknown and unused innovations is stacked in USPTO warehouses in Virginia, where almost one million patent applications languish unexamined. There is a peculiar madness to providing hundreds of billions of federal dollars in grants and tax breaks annually to create innovations, but then put the resulting patent applications away in a warehouse for many years because the Patent Office is too underfunded to examine them.

Part of the funding problem at the USPTO is that it relies on patent and maintenance fees to fund its operations; these bring in about $2 billion annually. This is too little, as the backlog attests. For the president and Congress not to supplement this with one or two billion dollars of appropriated federal funds for an office so critical to the country's future is beyond foolish. President Obama needs to intervene quickly and urge Congress to supplement the budget of the United States Patent and Trademark Office with funds sufficient to ensure that it:

- Eliminates the existing patent application backlog of one million applications within some brief period, such as four years.
- Processes patent applications in six months or less. (The patent office processed Alexander Graham Bell's telephone patent application in three weeks, and it withstood six hundred court challenges. America is in a global technology race and needs its innovations deployed sooner rather than later.)
- Fully trains its examiners; quality patents require well-trained examiners.
- Provides examiners sufficient time to process applications; the average time allowed for examiners currently is about twenty-three hours, even for complex applications, which is far too little.
- Reduces the personnel turnover rate from 30 percent annually to a more reasonable 5 to 7 percent.
- Secures sufficient office space for its examiners and employ-

ees, many of whom must now work at home because of lack of office space.

- Provides examiners modern computers and search engines. (As of December 2008, almost 69 percent of the computer servers were more than five years old. Many should be in the Smithsonian rather than at the USPTO.)

Other changes in patent policy will stimulate more innovation. One recommendation for immediate action is to return the patent term to the traditional seventeen years from issuance or twenty years from filing, whichever is longer. Inventors and investors in many fields require the traditional seventeen-year life of a patent to make the economics of innovation positive. Congress should not continue to punish inventors by reducing the life of patents because of its failure to provide the USPTO enough resources to do its job in a timely way.

In some fields, such as medicine, a longer patent life, perhaps twenty-five to thirty years, is desirable. This would enable pharmaceutical companies to invest in treatments and cures for "niche" diseases that otherwise would generate insufficient client sales to pay for research. With other medical patents, accelerating the patent examination period to only two or three months would help innovators quickly join the rapidly changing world market. A longer patent term should be considered for "national interest" technologies such as those that will improve energy efficiencies, provide alternative energy sources, clean the environment, or deal with other priority problems.

Creative patent policies can raise far more money for national development than the federal government currently is capable of providing. Ironically, the situation now is an echo of that in 1790, when America wanted to stimulate innovation but the government lacked the required resources.

America faces the great economic danger that Congress and the president will immobilize the economy by unwittingly crippling the patent system. In reality, fostering innovation with strong patent protections and a well-run Patent Office is the surest, least expensive way to bring the nation out of the current depression and create long-term, noninflationary, self-sustaining economic growth.

The best way to keep America strong is to keep America innovating.

CHAPTER FIVE

INFRASTRUCTURE

If finance is the heart of America's economic system, infrastructure is the backbone.

This backbone—America's public facilities—is wearing out faster than it is being repaired, rehabilitated, or replaced. More than a quarter of American bridges are unsafe, urban highways are congested, wastewater pollutes our streams, parks are in disrepair, hundreds of small dams are unsafe, and the U.S. Internet system is the slowest of any advanced nation. This decline in America's infrastructure undermines all broader efforts to revitalize the economy. It threatens such basic public services as safety, fire protection, transportation, water, and sewage treatment in thousands of communities.

This situation exists because the United States has significantly underinvested in its domestic civil works for decades.

Math tells the story. While the United States devoted almost 2 percent of its GDP to public works in the 1960s, that amount dropped steadily over the intervening five decades to 1.1 percent by 2006, a decline of 43 percent. In the same period the U.S. population expanded by more than 120 million, a growth of 66 percent.

The American Society of Civil Engineers (ASCE) estimates the United States now has a backlog of more than $2.2 trillion in investment needed between 2009 and 2013 just to maintain present levels of service, let alone meet those of a growing nation in the future.

The missing element in American infrastructure strategy is a national capital budget—a plan to set priorities, financing, and time schedules. All state governments and major corporations have capital budgets that distinguish between expenditures for annual operations of programs and expenditures for long-term physical investments. This distinction is an elementary accounting method that does not exist in federal budgeting. The omission is no accident or oversight, as we shall examine.

Ironically, rebuilding and improving our deteriorated public infrastructure offers proven ways to get the American economy moving again, create millions of new jobs, revitalize manufacturing, and put budgeting on a sound foundation. What FDR and his administration did in the 1930s and early 1940s with public works investments, the Obama administration can do now.

THE ESSENTIALS

Despite several recent analyses, the precise condition of the nation's public works inventory—and future investment needs—is unclear. The American Society of Civil Engineers annually calculates how much governments and the private sector are spending and how much the nation needs to invest over the next five years to meet its stated standards of service. It then calculates the difference. The collected facts and data portray a disturbing situation:

- **Levees.** America has approximately one hundred thousand miles of levees—facilities designed to prevent flooding. Of federally inspected levees, almost 9 percent are expected to fail during a flood. The greatest levee failure in U.S. history happened in New Orleans in 2005, when waters pushed by Hurricane Katrina breached the city's levees in fifty-three places, forcing the evacuation of 80 percent of the population and causing more than seven hundred deaths and uncalculated billions in damage. The danger to New Orleans had long been known, and the Flood Control Act of 1965 authorized the Army Corps of Engineers to design and construct a modern levee system for the area, a project then estimated to take thirteen years to complete. Forty years later, in 2005, the project was between 60 and 90 percent finished, with an estimated completion date of 2015. This lag occurred because federal funds were not forthcoming in a timely manner. Today the total investment needed to bring all existing U.S. levees up to safe standards is $50 billion. Projected investments between 2009 and 2013 are $1.13 billion, creating a shortfall of more than $48 billion.

- **Dams.** America has 85,000 dams, of which more than 4,000 are rated as deficient, including 1,800 considered high hazards whose failure will cause loss of life. Between 2000 and 2008, 75 U.S. dams collapsed, including the 2004 failure of the Big Bay Lake dam in Purvis, Mississippi, which destroyed ninety-eight homes, two churches, and the local fire station. Another, the December 2008 failure of the Kingston Fossil Fuels Plant dam near Knoxville, Tennessee, flooded hundreds of acres with more than one billion gallons of toxic coal sludge. The federal government owns or regulates only 11 percent of these 85,000 dams. The states are in charge of regulating the balance, but actually spend little on them. America needs to invest a projected $12.5 billion to ensure that these dams remain safe. Yet the ASCE estimates these expenditures will be only $5.05 billion, leaving a $7.45 billion shortfall.

- **Drinking water and wastewater treatment.** The United States has fifty-three thousand community water systems, most of which need new investment. Most of Colorado's drinking water, for example, comes from systems that are more than fifty years old and beyond their engineered design life. The state's water control commission reported in 2008 that 292 drinking water and wastewater projects in Colorado urgently need more than $2.6 billion of investment. Roughly one-third of America's sixteen thousand publicly owned wastewater treatment systems are the subject of formal Environmental Protection Agency (EPA) enforcement action, because each year they pour more than 850 million gallons of storm water mixed with sewage onto beaches and into streams, lakes, and the oceans. The EPA reports that 5,500 people get sick annually from sewage overflow on beaches alone. Overall, the United States is projected to spend $146 billion on drinking water and wastewater systems between 2009 and 2013, roughly $108.6 billion short of the $255 billion required.

- **Solid waste disposal.** The average person in the United States generates about 1,700 pounds of solid waste of all types each year. The nation produced 254 million tons of such waste in 2007. To reduce groundwater contamination by hazardous materials disposed of in landfills, the federal government imposed stringent regulations on solid waste disposal in 1991. Licensed facilities dropped from 5,300 in 1992 to slightly more than 1,700 in 2007. These facilities can handle America's solid waste disposal for the next twenty years, but expansion of them for long-term use is essential. The total investment needed between 2009 and 2013 is an estimated $77 billion. The projected expenditure will be $33 billion, leaving a $44 billion deficit.

- **Bridges and roads.** America has slightly more than 601,000 bridges. Few fail as spectacularly as the I-35 bridge in Minnesota, which collapsed on August 1, 2007, killing 13 people and injuring 145. Yet more than 151,000 of America's bridges are too weak or out-of-date to function properly. Of America's 4 million miles of roads, about 160,000 are vital to America's economy, defense, and mobility. They include the Interstate Highway System, the other principal arterials, the strategic highway network that provides access between military installations, and the connectors between major intermodal facilities. Today a third of these roads are in poor or mediocre condition, and 36 percent of major urban highways are congested. About $930 billion of bridge and road investment is required between 2009 and 2013, but only an estimated $380 billion will be made, leaving a five-year investment shortfall of $549 billion.

- **Airports.** A goal of the Federal Aviation Administration (FAA) is that 93 percent of runways at major U.S. airports be maintained in good or fair condition. That goal was exceeded in 2007. The big challenge the FAA faces is modernizing its air traffic control system, many parts of which are up to four decades old. Delays caused by the antiquated system resulted in an on-time arrival record of 73 percent in 2007, a low second only to the 2000 rate of 72 percent. The next-generation system of air traffic control does not use radar, but a technology known as Automatic Dependent Surveillance-Broadcast (ADS-B). Canada began deploying the system in January 2009. The United States is a decade behind, a lag created in large part by the George W. Bush administration's failed efforts to persuade Congress to privatize the FAA. To install this new system and maintain quality facilities at major U.S. airports, approximately $87 billion needs to be invested between 2009 and 2013. The estimated spending, however, will be $46.3 billion, a gap of $40.7 billion.

- **Inland waterways.** A single barge on a waterway carries the equivalent load of 870 large trucks with trailers. The IRS guide to auditing inland waterway activities reports that the twenty-five-thousand-mile shallow-draft waterways system, twelve thousand miles of which are the taxable Inland Waterways, handles more than $100 billion in freight annually. The IRS notes that "barge shipping is by far the most energy-efficient freight mode, extremely safe, causes little congestion, produces little air/noise pollution and has minimal land/use social impact." The system saves an average of $10 per ton over alternative shipping modes, a savings of $7 billion annually. Half the locks in the system, however, are obsolete at more than fifty years of age, and of 257 locks in service, only 2 per year are now being modernized. The total investment required between 2009 and 2013 is $50 billion to bring this system to full performance. Almost $30 billion will be invested, leaving a deficit of $20 billion.

▪ **Rail.** America's Class I railroads own or operate more than 140,000 miles of track, carrying more than 40 percent by volume of all U.S. freight. These carriers are three times as fuel efficient as trucks. The private railroads that handle this profitable business project it to double over the next twenty years. Amtrak, a public corporation, is responsible for today's money-losing passenger rail service, whose volume of business is also likely to double. In April 2009, the Obama administration announced its intent to invest $8 billion immediately and $1 billion annually over the next several years to build in phases a high-speed passenger rail system. Trains use 20 percent less fuel per passenger than automobiles, making this an energy-saving project. The map for the Obama vision suggests the system will ultimately be nationwide, much like the Interstate Highway System. Excluding this new investment on passenger rail, the total expenditure (public and private) needed for America's rail system is $63 billion between 2009 and 2013. Anticipated investment will be $51 billion with a $12 billion shortfall.

▪ **Schools.** No federal agency has prepared comprehensive nationwide data on the physical condition of America's public schools over the past decade. A 2008 study by Parsons 3D/International of 184 schools across the nation found their mechanical, electrical, and plumbing systems antiquated and inefficient. More than two-thirds of the food service equipment was in poor condition and beyond its life expectancy. The buildings were on average thirty to fifty years old and show the wear and tear of old facilities. Most U.S. schools do not meet federal accessibility standards. Schools in the District of Columbia alone need $2 billion of reconstruction and new equipment. The projected five-year funding requirement for America's schools is $160 billion, of which $125 billion is likely to be made, leaving a $35 billion deficit.

▪ **Hazardous waste.** Hazardous waste contaminates soil in many parts of the United States and is toxic to human life. As of 2008, 1,255 sites were identified on the National Priorities List for cleanup. Between 1980 and 1995, corporations paid an environmental and excise tax on petroleum and other specific chemicals to be used to clean up hazardous areas. The tax expired in 1995 and has not been renewed. Before 2000, the EPA reported that seventy cleanups were completed annually. The Bush administration slowed the pace dramatically, finishing only twenty-four projects in 2007 and thirty in 2008. The total investment needed for hazardous waste work between 2009 and 2013 is $77 billion. Less than half that, $33.6 billion, will be expended, creating a deficit of more than $43 billion.

- **Public parks and recreation.** America's federal, state, and local parks have more than one billion visitors each year. Not surprisingly, the system requires substantial investment for operation and maintenance. Although they represent only a small portion of public budgets, these recreational facilities are always high on the agenda for budget cuts. Consequently, the National Park System faces a $7 billion maintenance backlog. State and local parks, which handle three times as many visitors as the federal parks, have an even greater, but largely undocumented, investment requirement. The American Society of Civil Engineers estimates the total investment need for public parks, beaches, and other recreation areas will be $85 billion between 2009 and 2013. It also estimates actual investments will be about $37 billion, or $48 billion less than what is required.

The problem of decaying and inadequate infrastructure is found everywhere in the United States. More than 44 percent of Maryland's major roads, for example, are in poor or mediocre condition. Nevada has 165 high-hazard dams whose failure would cause loss of life and significant property damage. In Texas, community drinking water facilities are so outdated and defective they need $28 billion of investment to meet existing standards. California, with hundreds of untreated polluted sites, ranks first in the number of hazardous waste producers.

Similar examples exist for every type of public works in every state and the District of Columbia. The problem is national in scope. Unless the issue is addressed, the United States will end 2020 with less of an infrastructure than it had in 2010.

THE MULTIPLIER EFFECT

In the early 1930s, a Russian-born Harvard University economist named Wassily Leontief developed a new analytical tool, the input-output model, which shows how changes in one economic sector affect other sectors. In a press conference following the announcement of his 1973 Nobel Prize in Economics, Leontief explained with a simple example how his model works: "When you make bread, you need eggs, flour, and milk. And if you want more bread, you must use more eggs. There are cooking recipes for all the industries in the economy."

As this suggests, Leontief's tool tracks dynamic relationships. Today the Bureau of Economic Analysis in the Commerce Department maintains an extensive input-output (I-O) database that charts these economic interrelationships nationally, by state, and even down to counties and regions. The I-O accounts, as they are commonly known, enable industries, governments, and communities to anticipate with much accuracy the effects of one set of investments or actions on other sectors of the economy.

David Swenson, a research scientist at Iowa State University's Department of Economics, has maintained an I-O model of the Iowa economy since the early 1990s. In March 2009, Swenson issued a report on the jobs that the federal stimulus investments in infrastructure would create in Iowa. He concluded that for every 100 new jobs that were created building roads, bridges, and other infrastructure, another 62 related positions would be created in other industries such as cement, steel, controls, transport, and business services.

Swenson also calculated that for every 100 new jobs in infrastructure maintenance and repair another 56 jobs would be produced in related activities such as new construction. Labor-intensive work, such as repair or maintenance, prompts more jobs per dollar invested. Swenson calculated that $100 million of investment in new construction would create 925 new jobs and another 570 in related work. Yet a similar $100 million invested in infrastructure maintenance and repair would create 1,116 new jobs and 627 related ones.

The national potential for job creation through infrastructure investment is again found in the math. Assuming the United States in general has an I-O relationship roughly similar to Iowa's, each $1 billion of investment in new infrastructure construction will create 14,950 jobs and each $1 billion investment in infrastructure repair and maintenance will create 17,430.

We currently have no details on how state and local governments are dividing the federal infrastructure funds they received from the $787 billion federal stimulus package (the American Recovery and Reinvestment Act of 2009). But a reasonable assumption is that they are dividing it fairly evenly between new construction and repairs/maintenance, thereby creating 16,000 new jobs for every $1 billion expended.

The federal stimulus program provided $51 billion for core investments in roads, bridges, railways, sewers, and other transportation. Another $29 billion for investment in government facilities includes monies for the Army Corps of Engineers; facility improvements for the National Guard, Coast Guard, public housing, and Job Corps; and $6 billion for water and wastewater state revolving funds.

In total, therefore, infrastructure needs got $86 billion, about 10 percent of the $787 billion provided in the economic stimulus. By contrast, the legislation furnishes $288 billion for corporate and individual tax relief—slightly more than 36 percent of the total.

The heartbreak of this division is that the $86 billion of infrastructure investment will create roughly 1.37 million new jobs (16,000 multiplied by 86), while only about 20 percent of the tax concessions ($58 billion) will go to the intended purpose of increasing consumption. Spending $288 billion to get a benefit of $58 billion is unlikely to bring America out of this economic crisis.

Of course, even though many of the 1.37 million new jobs will last for only one year, the money will ripple through the economy. About one-third of the funds will go to wages and salaries of workers and executives. About 7 percent will be used for lumber products, while another 7 percent will be spent on stone, clay, and glass. Heating, plumbing, and structural metal industries will receive more than 8 percent, and business services such as transport, insurance, accounting, and legal services will share another 6 percent. The steel, concrete, equipment, and other materials industries will get more than 21 percent. And, once completed, the nation will have the benefits of these new and rehabilitated facilities for decades.

The most important point about these infrastructure investments is that they should be the beginning of a much larger and longer effort to rebuild America, not a onetime limited response to the current economic crisis.

Thinking in grand terms, as is appropriate, America should mount a five-year effort to deal with the entire $2.2 trillion infrastructure backlog. In 2009 dollars, this would require an investment of $440 billion for each of the next five years. This would create 7 million new jobs; 4.6 million would be involved directly in rebuilding the nation, and 2.4 million would be in manufacturing and support industries.

Initially such boldness may seem stunning, yet it is comparable to the vision and audacity of Republican president Dwight D. Eisenhower and the Democratic Congress led by Senate Majority Leader Lyndon B. Johnson (D-TX) and House Speaker Sam Rayburn (D-TX) more than fifty years ago, when they decided to build the Interstate Highway System, the largest infrastructure project in world history, and to create NASA, the program that put Americans on the moon.

How would the country pay for such a major effort? Over time is the answer. Financing a project that will take years to complete and last a half century or more is very different from funding the annual operations of a government agency. This is why national capital budget investments need to be separated from annual operational expenses and handled differently.

The current practice of mixing capital and operational items in a unified budget reflects political decisions made in the latter part of the Johnson administration when the war in Vietnam was at its height and the president could not secure adequate money for what he envisioned as his legacy, the Great Society. As part of widespread budget change initiated in 1967, entitlements and trust accounts were put into a new "unified" budget, because some of those programs were collecting more funds than they were spending and would make the overall budget appear more nearly in balance. The federal government does not list capital investments separately for reasons explained almost thirty years ago in *Special Analysis: Budget of the United States Government—1981,* with a candor seldom found in budget statements:

> *The Federal Government has never produced a capital budget in the sense of one in which capital or investment type programs are financed separately from current expenditures. One major reason is that a capital budget could be misleading as a measure of the government's effect on the demand for economic resources. Another is that such a budget might favor programs with intensive expenditures for physical assets, such as construction, relative to other programs for which future benefits cannot be accurately capitalized, such as education or research. Likewise, physical assets might be favored relative to current operations in any given*

program, since deficit financing for capital would be easier to justify.

What LBJ did was alter the budget process so that his social programs were better able to compete for federal funding against proposed infrastructure projects. The system Johnson put in place continues more than forty years later. As anticipated, social expenditures have been favored over capital investments; therefore, our public infrastructure is now in a state of advanced decay.

A NATIONAL CAPITAL BUDGET

The idea of a national capital budget has been examined repeatedly since the end of World War II, beginning in 1947 with the Commission on Organization of the Executive Branch of the Government, headed by former president Herbert Hoover. It rejected the idea. The most recent national study was President Clinton's Commission to Study Capital Budgeting, which issued its report, very quietly, in February 1999. It made eleven major recommendations on improving national capital budgeting, none of which have been implemented.

The Hoover commission report came at a moment when federal aid programs were minuscule, and the Clinton commission was in response to a proposed 1996 constitutional amendment in the House of Representatives to balance the federal budget annually. The Clinton commission, which involved Republicans and Democrats, occurred at the contentious moment when GOP leaders had impeached the president and were attempting to remove him from office. Therefore, it received little attention.

In the fifty years between the Hoover commission and the Clinton report, the General Accountability Office has issued many reports on the topic, always urging the creation of this most fundamental of accounting and management tools. In 1981, I coauthored a book with Susan Walter on behalf of the National Governors Association, *America in Ruins: The Decaying Infrastructure.* The principal recommendation was for the federal government to create and use a national capital budget.

The least controversial way to begin a capital budgeting process is to keep it simple by limiting its scope to civilian public facilities. Military planning, budgeting, and capital investment are complex, and inevitably, advocates for more or less defense funding often corrupt the process. Therefore, military budgeting should be separate from capital budgeting. The real infrastructure challenge faced by the civilian economy, as we know, is the decline in public facilities.

The Clinton commission became bogged down by the question of whether to define education, training, scientific research, and other long-term investments that produce long-term results as capital items. In part, that debate was deeply affected by the ongoing battle between President Clinton and the Republican-controlled House on budgeting priorities and GOP attempts to cut the above items as annual expenditures. While those investments are critical, as will be discussed in the next chapter, they are not capital items in the traditional sense and should not be included in a national capital budget.

The basic purposes of such a budget would be those identified by Comptroller General Charles A. Bowsher in testimony before the Senate Committee on Governmental Affairs on September 14, 1983:

- provide budget projections for major federal capital investment programs and a summary of the most recent needs assessment for these programs;
- show the relationship of these needs to policy issues and economic variables;
- assist state and local governments in planning for major capital investment programs; and
- improve legislative oversight over federal capital investments.

A budget process that fulfills these purposes will provide a structured framework and visibility for capital investment decisions. The executive and legislative branches will have the basic information needed to set priorities and allocate funds for capital investment and related operations. A transparent federal capital investment strategy on both a program-by-program and an overall basis would make the current practice of ad hoc earmarking more difficult.

A national capital budget for federal investment in domestic civic works would create numerous benefits. Foremost, it would enable better capital planning, budgeting, and management by state and local governments. They do the majority of public work in the United States and are deeply affected by federal programs, grants, tax preferences, and regulations. The chaos we now have at the national level in such budgeting is felt immediately by state and local governments.

Such a budget would also produce the data, now missing, needed for the planning, budgeting, construction, and operation of our vast stock of civilian public works. This would include:

- Basic data. Despite progress over the past three decades, information on the national inventory of infrastructure is fragmented, and often comparisons cannot be made among the various data series. Little data exists on the fiscal capacities of state and local authorities.
- Replacement and repair. There are few standards for estimating the timing and costs required to maintain and operate existing and proposed facilities.
- New technology. Public works in general is a field averse to change and new technologies, even though the technology revolution of the past three decades has created new materials, tools, and techniques to cut costs and improve services. Major new programs of infrastructure investment must be accompanied by the adoption of new technologies by federal, state, and local officials.

- Funded projects. Part of the Obama administration's stimulus program is regular, systematic progress reports. Federal oversight of all federally sponsored projects is a significant improvement and should apply permanently to all public works projects that use federal funds. Such administrative oversight will identify problems that can then be addressed.
- Evaluation. Annually, the Federal Highway Administration inspects the nation's bridges, the Federal Aviation Administration reports on the condition of airports, and the Environmental Protection Agency advises on the state of America's water and wastewater treatment facilities. Their reports, as well as those of other regulatory agencies, should be standardized concerning time periods, methods, investment estimates, budget format, and publication of results, thereby providing both overall and program-specific information to policy makers.

Another important benefit of public works investment is that it can be timed to help stabilize the ups and downs of the economy—that is, serve as a countercyclical tool. Since 1960, Congress has enacted three countercyclical public works efforts: a $1.9 billion expenditure in 1961–62, a $130 million effort in 1972–73, and a $6 billion program in 1976–77. The problem with these efforts was resistance from the executive branch, where the preference was to rely on macro fiscal and monetary tools. Political paralysis set in, and the funding wasn't disbursed until after the bottom of each cycle had been reached.

For decades, most public works investments were made in a perverse procyclical pattern, increasing during expansionary phases of the economic cycle and decreasing as the economy contracted. Increasing construction during the expansionary phase of the cycle results in costs (materials, equipment, and labor) becoming artificially high and contributing to inflation. Decreasing public works investments during the contracting phase of the cycle leads to underutilization of labor and industrial facilities, worsening any recession.

The Obama administration's quick use of infrastructure investment to offset an economic downturn is the best timed of any such effort in modern history, including the New Deal.

A national capital budget would allow thousands of projects to be planned years in advance of funding. This would permit government at all levels to efficiently phase in design, engineering, land acquisition, bidding, and construction. During times of economic contraction, the nation could accelerate these projects for countercyclical purposes. Conversely, if the economy were heating up, we could delay construction.

The dangers of not having a vetted backlog of projects ready for such modulation of the economy will be more apparent in 2010 and 2011 as many projects funded under the economic stimulus plan become visible and problems appear. The selection standard was "Are they ready?" instead of "Are they the projects state and local governments most need?" Always in such chaos some purely political or just silly projects get funded. A multiyear backlog of projects, with public transparency, would help reduce future embarrassing mistakes.

A backlog would also reduce the lag between the beginning of a recession and the start of expanded infrastructure investment. The federal government could target investment to better accommodate regional differences, and improved fiscal stability would result for state and local capital investments.

FINANCING

The world has vast amounts of capital available to build a twenty-first-century American infrastructure. To engage that capital, a number of basic choices exist.

The most fundamental is the choice between public investment and public consumption. Today the United States invests about 1.4 percent of its GDP in public infrastructure, a reduction of 43 percent from a half century ago. An investment increase of .6 percent of the GDP, bringing the nation back to the levels of the 1960s, would produce roughly $84 billion of additional capital annually, enough to finance 20 percent of the grand strategy recommended earlier in this chapter.

A second choice is private versus public infrastructure investment. In the late 1960s and early 1970s, the federal government was unwilling to directly finance many of the infrastructure-related programs it created, such as cleaning the environment, and it mandated such expenditures onto the private sector and state and local governments. Also, private operation of public services such as telecommunications, electricity, natural gas, and waste removal became widespread. During the administration of George W. Bush, a further shift of public functions to private corporations was attempted.

The existing paradigm of public-private responsibilities is in flux. Many attempts, for instance, to privatize control of major highways and toll roads are floundering because of the weakened global financial system. In some instances, such as Texas's move to rely on toll roads as its main highway funding strategy, the costs are proving prohibitive. The expense for a private firm to operate a toll road would be about 30 percent more than for a public authority, simply because the private company must pay more for capital.

Ironically, Texas also provides a useful model on how to combine public-private financing to meet the huge investment needs of a growing state. In the 1950s, Texas authorized the construction of a toll road between Dallas and Fort Worth financed with private monies. When the bonds were paid, the state got possession of the facility.

A more extensive privatization approach may be attractive to many state and local governments. The private sector could work with the government to create a public authority that would construct, rehabilitate, maintain, or operate a city's water treatment plant, sewers, streets, or municipal buildings with debt that is privately raised and held. The local government would repay the debt over a fixed period, such as fifteen to twenty years, at the end of which the government would own the facility.

To further cut local costs, the federal government could create a national infrastructure bank. Ideally, it would use federal government borrowing power to secure long-term monies at low rates, a savings it would then pass on to state and local governments to finance projects, but only those that had a guaranteed stream of user fees, such as for water and sewers. The possibilities are many.

There are also some negative aspects. Unscrupulous Wall Street or other money interests could take advantage of state and local officials, particularly those who seek campaign funds, in order to influence infrastructure projects. Accordingly, sharp federal oversight over the financing of any project that involves federal funds is essential. Watchdogs perform a useful function in public life.

CORRUPTION

Historically, corruption has contaminated public works activities. A global association formed by major contractors estimates the costs associated with corruption at more than $250 billion annually worldwide.

Kessler International, a firm that specializes in corporate fraud investigations, notes that most construction frauds "go completely unseen and millions of dollars are embezzled from unwitting public and private organizations on a rather regular basis." This happens because construction fraud is easy to accomplish, hard to catch, and even more difficult to prosecute.

The ways to steal in construction, according to Kessler, are almost limitless. Fraudulent disbursements are one route, including shell corporations, ghost employees, falsified wages, phony worker compensation claims, fictitious expenses, fake invoices, altered contracts, or the purchase of excessive amounts of goods that are then sold. Using substandard materials, equipment, and labor is another technique often employed; a contractor obtains the cheapest resources possible and puts as little into the project as possible. Thus, bridges buckle, highways crumble, and streets develop potholes.

Old-fashioned bribery is another danger. Inspectors are slipped money to turn their heads or offer false reports, elected officials receive campaign donations in exchange for their support, and subcontractors are hired in exchange for kickbacks.

Tax fraud is often inevitable. Money received surreptitiously cannot be reported without incurring other liabilities, so it is hidden from taxes. Funds can be laundered through shell corporations or by coconspirators.

Bid rigging is common. A group of contractors will agree to bid much higher than in a competitive market, and a designated bidder will win with a slightly lower bid. Either the fraudulent difference in cost is split among the perpetrators or they wait their turn to take the next project.

Construction fraud is difficult to stop because the thieves are so experienced. Governments have tried to prevent such corruption by hiring public inspectors, an effective action in some cases but not all, because some inspectors have a knowledge of only one or two aspects of a project, such as foundations or plumbing, and know nothing of the other trades. And, of course, inspectors can be corrupted as well.

Public works corruption is part of the culture in many places. A special commission in Massachusetts, for instance, found that between 1968 and 1980 almost 60 percent of all public works built there were defective, including a new dormitory at the University of Massachusetts that was so poorly built it had to be abandoned after a toilet crashed through to the floor below. In another case, the Massachusetts attorney general demanded a repayment for "shoddy work" of more than $100 million from contractors that worked on Boston's Central Artery/Tunnel Project (the Big Dig). The consortium that oversaw the project agreed in 2008 to pay more than $400 million as restitution for lax oversight of the work of subcontractors, some of whom committed fraud.

Many of the largest U.S. construction firms have had extensive involvement with projects in Iraq and Afghanistan, and a number of government reports have documented endemic waste, fraud, and abuse in some of those projects. While U.S. officials have obtained about fifteen convictions in such cases, this probably involves only a portion of the fraud and contract breaches that exist. Unfortunately, many employees of these contractors bring this culture of corruption back to the United States. Some, perhaps many, of these individuals may become involved in national infrastructure investment programs. Caution must be accompanied by hard oversight and even harsher penalties, including prison, for those found guilty of corruption.

Kessler International recommends hiring independent inspectors who bring in a team of experts, none of whom have any association with local politicians and contractors, to inspect all phases of a project.

An excellent and most easily replicated example of effective agency oversight can be found in the Department of Commerce's Economic Development Administration (EDA), a small agency created in 1965 that has dispensed several billion dollars and has had no scandal due to fraudulent public works design, engineering, or construction practices.

- The agency permits recipients of its funds to use up to 6 percent to hire private architects and engineers. EDA engineers then perform expert reviews of all projects at every stage.

- At the prefunding stage, EDA engineers review proposed plans and cost estimates. If costs or designs are unreasonable, the project is rejected.
- After a project is funded, the EDA Construction Review Division gives the contractor, the architects, and the engineers a specific procedure to follow that includes competitive bidding for construction and the ongoing detailing of expenses. The EDA delegates construction oversight responsibility to the private architects and engineers; however, at regular intervals, EDA engineers do partial and full inspections of work on-site. EDA staff are present at virtually all bidding.

"Trust but verify" is the EDA way.

An effective national infrastructure investment strategy requires comparable professional oversight and a willingness to punish violators. Such hard steps are the only way to break the culture of corruption in public construction.

The first step in that process is discovering the fraud. President Abraham Lincoln solved part of that problem during the Civil War (1863), when he persuaded Congress to enact the False Claims Act, which has now been on the books for almost 150 years. The law's purpose is to encourage people who are aware of fraud against the government to bring the information forward. While this is now known as whistle-blowing, the more elegant term is *qui tam,* Latin for "who pursues the action on our Lord the King's behalf as well as his own."

As the definition suggests, individuals are permitted to file lawsuits alleging fraud on behalf of the government. The cases are filed under seal while the Justice Department decides whether to participate. If the government chooses not to join the action, the individual can proceed and collect up to 30 percent of any monies recaptured on behalf of the government. In recent years, the federal government has received almost $13 billion in settlements and judgments from *qui tam* and related cases.

Congress should increase funding for the FBI and the Justice Department to pursue these cases, since they offer the means of recouping billions of dollars. As more *qui tam* cases are filed, potential miscreants will know they have an increased risk of being exposed by coworkers and others.

The administration of George W. Bush, however, was reluctant to join in *qui tam* cases, and by January 2008 the Justice Department had a backlog of more than nine hundred cases under seal, which means they were stopped. Almost a quarter of these dealt with procurement fraud, mostly at the Defense Department. Thirty cases involved fraud in Iraq.

The stimulus bill enacted in February 2009 contains $330.5 million for oversight of infrastructure expenditures. Of this, $25 million will be used to hire one hundred additional lawyers, accountants, and analysts at the General Accountability Office. Another $84 million will go to a new accountability board. The remaining $221 million will be allocated to the inspectors general at agencies that fund projects.

This approach is long overdue. In a year or so, we will know better if this works or if additional hands-on involvement is needed, as with the EDA programs at the Commerce Department. The point is that explicit attention to potential fraud is essential for any national public works program. Also, a side benefit of cleaning up fraud in federal projects will be similar oversight at the state and local levels.

Warranties on public infrastructure will also protect taxpayers and cover the replacement of defective work at little or no public cost. If a project is defective, the contractor must pay for a correction. Warranties are worthless unless enforced, and procedures must be in place to enforce them. Procedures are also required for explicit and public waiving of a warranty by public officials when it is not to be exercised.

A major benefit of demanding warranties of design, engineering, and construction will be reduced insurance costs. While warranties will add a small cost to projects, the inspections and reviews required by insurance companies will better protect the public against fraud.

In our 1981 book, Susan Walter and I made six basic recommendations on strengthening infrastructure accountability. They remain valid almost thirty years later.

First, the level of government mandating a requirement must be prepared to pay for it. Federal mandates on state and local governments for various types of infrastructure investment are a principal cause of fiscal stress on state governments, which often pass the responsibility on to city and county governments.

Second, functions that are in the national interest should not be imposed on state and local governments lacking the capacity to finance the work. Washington needs to finance such projects with federal revenues.

Third, federal funding should not, as a rule, supplant state or local responsibilities. Federal financing should only be used to support those responsibilities and capacities that are beyond the capacities of the jurisdictions involved.

Fourth, federal infrastructure financing must also promote maintenance rather than focus solely on new construction. For decades, public leaders have raised funds to build projects that almost instantly are forgotten in repair, maintenance, and operations budgets. A plan for financing the operation, maintenance, and repair of projects must be an integral part of any federal package.

Fifth, federal public works policy must be sufficiently flexible to accommodate the diversity of regional needs and problems and not impose rigid standardized approaches irrelevant to the realities of the individual regions. New York's highway needs are different from New Mexico's, as Florida's requirements for wastewater treatment differ from those of North Dakota.

Sixth and perhaps most important, state and local governments need to lessen their growing dependence on federal aid by assuming responsibility for the financing and delivery of those functions that are clearly assigned to them in terms of their capacity and jurisdiction. Too often, state and local governments have delayed projects while they pursued federal funding that never came.

A SPECIAL PROJECT

By spring 1933, more than half of young men age fifteen to twenty-five had only part-time work or none at all. To provide jobs for them, FDR devised the Civilian Conservation Corps (CCC), which quickly became one of the most popular New Deal programs. The CCC "boys," as they often called themselves, were mostly school dropouts. According to Robert D. Leighninger Jr. in his 2007 book, *Long-Range Public Investment: The Forgotten Legacy of the New Deal,* most had never had full-time jobs, few knew what they wanted to do with their lives, and many acknowledged they were headed for or already involved in criminal activity. Most knew little about their abilities. The CCC helped them develop purposeful lives.

The CCC existed from 1933 until 1942, the first year of World War II. Conservation was one of its twofold purposes, the other being relief. Leighninger lists the accomplishments of the CCC to include:

1. Bridges	46,854
2. Lodges and museums	204
3. Historic structures restored	3,980
4. Drinking fountains	1,865
5. Fire lookout towers	3,116
6. Wells and pump houses	8,065
7. Forest roads	2,500 miles

8. Roads and truck trails	7,442 miles
9. Cabins	1,477
10. Bathhouses	165
11. Large dams	197
12. Water supply lines	5,000 miles
13. Fences	27,191 miles
14. Fish-rearing ponds	4,622
15. Beaches improved	3,462
16. Trees planted	3 billion
17. Fires fought	6.5 million days (and a loss of 47 lives)

They did all this in nine years. The "boys" received room, board, clothing, and one dollar a day. Of the $30 they earned per month, they were required to send $25 home to their families. The CCC remittances helped many American families avoid starvation. As Leighninger notes, scores of books were written by the CCC boys in later years describing how the experience changed their lives for the better and enabled them to be productive, responsible men.

The same need for relief, a useful start in life, and conservation exists today. After years of neglect, many public parks and forests are in terrible shape. As of April 2009, America had 3.3 million young men and women between the ages of sixteen and twenty-four looking for jobs but unable to find them. It is a perfect match. Just as seventy-five years ago, a large portion of these young people have no plans, are dropouts, and need the structure a new CCC-type program could provide to help them develop their capabilities and create purpose-driven lives.

As documented in the beginning of this chapter, America has a huge backlog of conservation projects that would benefit from the work of a new CCC. Helping this young generation of Americans to make the nation's parks and forests sparkle again is a winning proposal.

. . .

Because decay in American public infrastructure is advanced and worsening, a major national program of infrastructure repair and construction that would create millions of well-paying jobs and prepare the nation for a better future is now appropriate. There is a place in such a program for young people as well. The starting point is for Congress and the president to create a national capital budget, fund it, and begin rebuilding America.

CHAPTER SIX

WORKERS

Edward, an accountant and friend of many years, is sixty-four years old. He had planned to retire in 2010 when he reached sixty-five, but recently decided that he would not be retiring next year or anytime soon. The Wall Street crash wiped out much of his retirement fund, and his broker calculates it will take seven to ten years to get back to the same financial position he had in 2007 before the American economy began to fall apart.

Edward did everything a prudent person was supposed to do. He invested steadily and for the long term. He used the research provided by his broker, did not speculate, and chose blue-ribbon investments. Then the gamblers in the money industry crashed the economy and wiped out a big part of his retirement savings. Edward says that he feels grateful to have what remains of his assets, his good health, and his practice.

His experience is neither unique nor extreme. The Labor Department reports that between 1977 and 2007, employment of workers sixty-five and older rose by 101 percent. For men, it was a 75 percent increase, while for women sixty-five years and older, it was 147 percent. The reason was obvious: Their income from Social Security, personal savings, and pensions did not provide them enough money to afford their retirement. And this was before the crash.

Thirty years ago, the retirement model was the three-legged stool—a retirement based on personal savings, a private pension, and Social Security. Now it is the four-legged stool—personal savings, a private pension, Social Security, and a part-time job.

The crash of 2008–9 has destroyed the retirement savings of tens of millions of Americans such as Edward, and their lives are unlikely to be the same. Others who have worked for the same companies for decades and are now preparing to retire, recently have had their corporate pension plans frozen, which will reduce their future benefits. Millions of union workers now face the prospect of pension cuts.

Simultaneously, more than 45 million Americans lack any health care insurance. The Medicaid system, which is supposed to help those who cannot afford health care, varies widely from state to state. Some governors and state legislators have acted punitively, denying services to the poor and children by raising eligibility standards and instituting long waiting periods. One out of six people in America lack any health care coverage and are very vulnerable to the economic effects of illness.

The problems of income and health care fall particularly hard on workers and families who are displaced from their jobs and then left to their own devices. The numbers are powerful. From January 1, 2005, to December 31, 2007, 3.6 million people who had worked for their employers three or more years lost their jobs, and an additional 4.6 million workers with less than three years of tenure also lost their jobs, a total of 8.2 million in that three-year period. A third of the long-term displaced workers were still out of a job when the Labor Department did its most recent survey in 2008. Between January 1, 2008, and March 2009, more than 5.4 million Americans joined the ranks of the out of work.

The February 2009 economic stimulus bill provided these millions of workers only $575 million of adjustment assistance, which is more a political placebo than an economic cure. By contrast, the money industry got more than $12 trillion of aid.

The question before President Obama now is the same one that FDR confronted in 1933: What must society do so its workers can ably respond to structural economic changes? Many actions are appropriate, but three are essential:

1. create a private, portable pension plan tied to the workers, not their employers, that will ensure substantial private savings for future retirees;
2. create a universal health care system for all Americans so that they can move between jobs and in and out of the workforce without worrying about medical care for themselves and their families; and
3. provide American workers the means to get the education, training, and workplace adjustments and transition income they need to stay productive and at work.

Franklin Roosevelt put part of that vision into place as part of the New Deal. Barack Obama's challenge is to bring the rest into being.

RETIREMENT

The American way of retirement—the three-legged stool—is a muddle of ill-defined and dysfunctional parts. Private pension plans, for instance, are often administered in a way that cheats the beneficiary of benefits. The Social Security system has been used since 1982 to generate revenue surpluses that have been diverted to the financing of massive federal deficits. Private savings have been destroyed by the failure of the federal government to regulate Wall Street. Consequently, most Americans over the age of forty can anticipate a less than happy and dignified retirement when they can no longer work.

The first U.S. private-sector pensions were created in the late nineteenth century by the railroad industry. The current form of the three-legged retirement stool began to take shape during World War II, when employers who were scrambling to find workers circumvented federally imposed wage freezes by instead offering pension and health care benefits, which were permitted. After the war, the demand for those benefits became part of negotiations between workers and employers.

The most common form of pension was a defined-benefit plan, which guaranteed workers a set amount of retirement based on their years of service to the employer. Many plans required the worker to stay for thirty or more years. Employers often abused the system by firing those who were nearing retirement, thus relieving themselves of any obligation to pay.

Even at those corporations that were more responsible, a break in service would devastate a worker's pension. In the 1980s, the National Bureau of Economic Research reported that workers who changed employers with equal pension plans just once by age thirty-one reduced the value of their pensions by 28 percent. Workers who shifted jobs twice at ages forty-one and fifty-one reduced their pensions by 57 percent. By the 1980s, workers could expect to change employers at least six times. This trend of faster job changes has only increased in the intervening quarter century, further reducing the value of pensions.

The seminal pension event of the past half century occurred in 1963 when Studebaker, then America's oldest major automaker, collapsed, leaving about eleven thousand workers without their pensions. In reaction, the federal government created the Pension Benefit Guaranty Corporation (PBGC), an agency that regulates private-sector health and defined-benefit pension plans. The PBGC sets standards and guarantees benefits for more than 44 million workers who are participating in more than twenty-nine thousand private-sector pension plans. It does not insure public-sector or church pension plans, nor does it insure defined-contribution plans—those whose benefits are limited to worker and employer contributions into it. The PBGC is a federal corporation financed by insurance premiums paid by those it serves. Most significant, the PBGC is not backed by the full faith and credit of the United States.

At the beginning of fiscal year 2009, the PBGC had assets of roughly $63 billion and liabilities of $74 billion, leaving it with a deficit of $11 billion. By May 2009, that deficit had grown to more than $33.5 billion. The failure of any major pension plan or many small plans during the current crisis will worsen that situation and ultimately leave lawmakers with the choice of cutting pensions or bailing out the agency.

As American corporations have withered under the heat of trade-related competition, they have shed their defined-benefit plans, particularly firms with one hundred workers or fewer. In 1985, more than 112,000 single-employer plans were in place. By the beginning of 2008, there were fewer than 29,000. Companies either paid out monies to workers or gave them annuities, changed to a defined-contribution approach, or dropped pensions altogether.

The disappearing defined-benefit pension is already adversely affecting millions of American workers. In January 2009, the Washington-based Urban Institute analyzed the consequences for four different groups of post–World War II workers. For the baby boomers born between 1946 and 1950, the shift is largely meaningless. They are near or at planned retirement age, and their benefits are frozen in either a defined-benefit or defined-contribution plan, thus they will lose relatively little. Even if their employer goes bankrupt, the PBGC guarantees payment of their pensions up to $54,000 annually if they retire at sixty-five.

The boomers born between 1951 and 1960, however, will lose up to a quarter of what they would have received. They are the in-between generation and do not have that many higher-income working years to make up their loss. The last wave of boomers, born between 1961 and 1965, have not been employed at corporations long enough to meet their elongated vesting periods. They have a chance to build defined-contribution accounts—that is, if the economy can recover and if they keep their jobs.

The big exception is union workers, who make up about 12

percent of America's wage and salary workforce. The AFL-CIO reports that 79 percent of union workers are covered by pension plans, versus 44 percent of nonunion workers, and 70 percent of union workers have defined-benefit retirement coverage, compared with 16 percent of nonunion workers. Thus, most union workers will get a definite level of retirement income, despite swings in the market such as those that devastated many defined-contribution plans last year.

The crash of 2008 created major losses in the funds held by defined-benefit pension plans. At the end of 2007, the one hundred largest private pension plans had 109 percent of the assets needed to meet their obligations. A year later, they had 79 cents on the dollar available. In other words, the one hundred largest corporations with defined-benefit plans had a funding surplus of $60 billion at the end of 2007, but a deficit of $265 billion a year later.

The Pension Protection Act of 2006 was enacted to make sure defined-benefit pension plans can pay the benefits they promise and to ensure the PBGC does not become insolvent. A key feature of the legislation is that corporations are obligated to contribute to their plans when the holdings fall below specific levels. After the 2008 election, however, a group of the largest U.S. corporations persuaded Congress to enact legislation—which it did on December 23, 2008—that delayed the mandatory-contribution feature of the law.

Defined-contribution plan investments have lost a third or more of their value in the crash of 2008, so that is what the beneficiaries will get. Of course, that is what such plans are about, the elimination of any additional employer contributions.

America's counties, cities, and states have vastly underfunded their public pension plans, which are now their principal financial liability. In 2008 and the first three months of 2009, public pension plans lost more than $1.3 trillion. *BusinessWeek* reported in April 2009 that 59 state pension plans alone had a shortfall of more than $237 billion. This did not include county and municipal pension funds, which cover more workers than the states.

Already, states are taking drastic action. The California Public Employees' Retirement System, America's largest, is considering raising employers' contributions. So too is Arizona. Kentucky set a minimum retirement age and is putting into place a two-tier program that provides smaller pensions for new workers.

In their desperation to make up lost assets, several state pension funds are considering buying the toxic assets the Treasury will be trying to sell through the Public-Private Investment Program (PPIP) to purchase legacy assets. Under this arrangement, the states would buy a portion of the positions of private investment firms that will buy these assets, hoping that they are eventually worth more than the price. This is risky, as the packagers of these deals are usually the same people who put the state funds into the failed investments that have cost them so much.

Also, there is a corruption factor. Many private investment funds pay huge fees to well-connected insiders to help raise monies from public pension funds. Sometimes these monies wind up as political contributions for the state officials or in special projects for "friends" of the pension managers. The attorney general of New York has a large ongoing investigation into such practices, which have been common there as well as in many other states. Investing state pension funds in sold-off toxic assets may be an acceptable venture for risk takers, but that hardly seems the appropriate way to make up the lost monies needed to pay pensions for teachers, firefighters, police, and other civil servants.

Social Security, the third leg of the retirement stool, is in very good fiscal condition, contrary to many alarmist cries. The 1983 amendments to the Social Security Act produced more revenues than were expended for more than two decades. The goal back then was to build a large trust fund that could help finance the system when the baby boom generation began to retire. Building that retirement surplus was one of the great achievements of that generation of Americans—they deferred consumption to save for their retirement.

Sometime between 2013 and 2019, the trust fund outlays will exceed its income from payroll taxes. A decade later, the outlays will exceed the income from tax contributions and interest. At that point, Social Security will be beginning to pull down funds from the trust. Under existing assumptions, the drawdowns will exhaust the trust fund around the year 2039, at which time retirees will still receive roughly 80 percent of their Social Security benefits.

The Social Security Trust Fund today has more than $2 trillion in special series, nonmarketable Treasury securities that are backed by the full faith and credit of the U.S. government. Wall Street tried during the George W. Bush administration to shift part of this to private accounts that the money industry would manage. Fortunately, Congress did not translate the idea into law, and millions of Americans lost nothing in future Social Security benefits when the financial markets collapsed in 2008.

Despite the vast reserves in the Social Security Trust Fund and its long-term projected fiscal health, the money industry is exerting great political pressure to solve the Social Security "entitlement crisis"—an effort that again will inevitably lead to recommendations to privatize all or parts of the program.

Fortunately, less radical means exist to keep the Social Security Trust Fund solvent and able to meet all its obligations for the balance of this century. Other nations are addressing their solvency problems by putting into place new automatic adjustment mechanisms including tax increases or changes in the early and normal retirement ages. These countries are deciding in advance how to deal with anticipated shifts. The United Kingdom, for instance, links eligibility age for future retirees to projected alterations in life expectancy and gives workers at least fifteen years' notice of adjustment in eligibility age. Sweden uses life expectancy indexing and the automatic adjustment of benefits. France is increasing the years of service and the years of contribution needed to receive full benefits. Again, the point is that very modest changes now can ensure that Social Security remains fully solvent and functioning for the lifetime of every person who is at work today in America.

Retirement savings are low or nonexistent for an overwhelming majority of American workers. Even though about 60 percent of workers, public and private, participate in some form of pension plan, for most the benefits will be small when they retire. Only Social Security is capable of providing its promised benefits over the next several decades.

What the overwhelming majority of American workers lack, but badly need, is a portable pension that is tied to the worker and not the job—one that will allow unhampered job transfers and permit leaving and entering the workforce while pensions continue to accrue.

Over the past half century, several major proposals to provide portable pensions have been advanced, none of which have been enacted. The Committee on Corporate Pension Funds and Other Private Retirement and Welfare Programs, which was originally formed by President Kennedy, presented the first in 1965. The main feature of this proposal was a central portable pension fund. When a worker left a job, the employer would be able to contribute to the fund an amount equal to the worker's vested pension rights. In so doing, the employer would be released from future pension-related administrative and financial obligations, while the worker could either transfer the money to the plan of a new employer or leave it in the portable fund until retirement.

Senator Jacob K. Javits (R-NY) made the second major proposal in 1974 during negotiations that eventually led to the Employee Retirement Income Security Act (ERISA). Workers who changed jobs could transfer the value of their pension rights into a central account managed by ERISA. The central fund would invest these monies in government obligations or interest-bearing accounts in savings and local banks or credit unions. Workers could transfer their funds to a qualified pension plan or a new employer on a tax-free basis. If the money remained in the fund until retirement (no earlier than age fifty-nine and a half and no later than age seventy), the employee would receive either a lump sum payment or an annuity contract. As with the other proposals, if a worker became disabled, payment would be made immediately, and in the case of death, payment would go to the worker's estate. The Javits proposal was passed by the Senate but was subsequently dropped during the passage of ERISA.

In the late 1970s, Jimmy Carter established the Presidential Commission on Pension Policy, which proposed creation of a portable Minimum Universal Pension System (MUPS). Unlike the previous proposals, MUPS would make participation mandatory. All workers over the age of twenty-five who had one year of service or one thousand hours of employment would be eligible, and vesting of benefits would be immediate. MUPS would supplement Social Security but could not be integrated with it. Employers would be encouraged to maintain the MUPS funds of workers in pension trusts or other secure arrangements. But if employers did not wish to administer these funds, they could forward the money to a portable trust fund in the Social Security Administration; a board of trustees appointed by the president would administer it.

The George H. W. Bush administration did improve portability by making it easier for employees to qualify for tax-free rollover of their pension monies when they changed jobs. The Clinton administration offered several pension portability proposals that Congress refused to enact. George W. Bush tried to make partial privatization of the Social Security System—a means for Americans to divert a portion of their Social Security tax into private investments—an option. The idea was a centerpiece of his domestic agenda, but it was a low priority for the GOP-controlled House of Representatives and it died.

During the 2008 campaign President Obama proposed the creation of a mandatory pension plan whereby employers that offer no pension plan enroll employees in a direct-deposit IRA account. When a worker changes employers, funds would automatically roll over into the new employer's system. Under the Obama plan, businesses would choose an investment portfolio with low fees that would not include company stock.

Each of these proposals contains practical features that remain relevant today. By combining key elements from each with some new features, a new approach—a portable pension plan (PPP)—is possible. The PPP would provide portable, private coverage for all workers, much like Social Security.

The PPP should be a restricted defined-contribution pension plan—that is, funds could not be withdrawn before retirement, but then the worker could take either a lump sum payment or an annuity contract based on the value of the contributions. As with an IRA, the contributions would be tax-deductible and the federal government would not tax the returns until the worker retired and began taking out money. The tax rate would be at capital gains level. Annual contributions would be small, perhaps 3 percent of a worker's wage or salary, which the employer would match. Through years of contributions and the magic of compound interest, a worker would build a substantial retirement.

The central feature of the PPP would be portability. The Pension Benefit Guaranty Corporation, the Treasury, or the Social Security Administration would administer it. The federal government would establish a PPP account for all workers when they enrolled for Social Security. Contributions would begin with a worker's first Social Security contribution, and full vesting in the PPP would be immediate.

Workers would build up guaranteed pensions throughout their careers, regardless of their employment situation. During a period when a worker was employed by a firm with an ERISA-approved pension plan but was unvested, the firm would pay into the worker's PPP that part of the wages used for financing the company's pension plan up to the PPP limit, and the worker would provide a matching contribution. This feature would end the widespread subsidization of corporate pension plans by non-vested employees. Once the worker became vested, however, both worker and employer contributions to the PPP would cease if the value of the private plan was greater than the PPP. If it was not, the worker and the employer would contribute the difference to the PPP.

Workers who become self-employed would be required to continue contributions to their PPP. Workers who leave the workforce would be permitted to continue making IRA-like tax-deductible contributions to their PPP up to some limit if they desire. This latter feature would be particularly useful for women who temporarily leave the workforce to have and care for children.

The PPP would also provide both workers and their employers a means of transferring pension monies between various plans. Upon separation from an employer, a worker could deposit to the PPP an amount equal to the value of the worker's pension. The administering agency would invest the PPP funds in low-risk, high-rated federal, state, or local government bonds or private funds of equal safety.

The PPP would be simple to administer and easy to understand. For workers whose employers do not provide a pension program, the PPP would offer an efficient, cost-effective, and financially prudent plan. It would ensure workers would not lose savings because of job changes.

The plan would also provide a major new means of increasing national savings. It would eliminate as well the problem that often arises with pension plans that are "integrated" with Social Security, whereby Social Security benefits are deducted from the pension, a practice that often leaves the recipient with little more than the Social Security. Equally important, the PPP would permit the Social Security system to revert to its original role as a source of supplemental retirement income. Finally, the PPP would facilitate greater worker mobility.

The PPP, coupled with Social Security, would provide the next generations of American workers a dignified retirement—something the three-legged stool failed to deliver.

HEALTH CARE

Health care is the cottage industry that has eaten much of the American economy after World War II. In 2009, however, more than 45 million Americans are without any health insurance and at least as many have only marginal coverage. More than 40 percent of American adults go without health care annually because they cannot afford the cost. The U.S. infant mortality rate is the highest of all industrial countries and is double that of Japan, Sweden, Norway, and France.

The issue is about more than money. The United States spends almost 17 percent of its annual GDP on health care, which is almost 25 percent more than Switzerland, number two in GDP use. The U.S. per capita expenditure on health care is double that of Germany, Canada, the United Kingdom, and Australia. Yet, as difficult as it may be to believe, the measured quality of U.S. health care lags behind that of all these nations.

The issue is not the cost of medicines, which constitutes only 10 percent of the $2.4 trillion America spends on health care each year.

One of the major issues in our hodgepodge approach to health care is administration. The Congressional Budget Office reports that Medicare, the single-payer insurance for Americans sixty-five and older, has an administrative cost of less than 2 percent, versus 11 percent for private plans administrated by Medicare Advantage. Some plans spend 25 percent or more on administrative expenses. A 2006 study sponsored by the Council for Affordable Health Insurance, an association of insurance carriers, challenged those numbers. Merrill Matthews, the author, concluded that Medicare's actual administrative costs were 5.2 percent and private insurance costs were 16.7 percent when commission, premium tax, and profit were included. The difference was still significant.

For the fourth time in seventy-five years, there is now a presidentially led effort to provide universal health coverage to the American people. The best, simplest, and least expensive approach would be for the United States to extend Medicare to all Americans through a government-operated single-payer insurance system. The principal obstacles to such rationality are politically powerful fiefdoms in the health care industry and free-market absolutists, both of which oppose such a simplified approach.

America's quest for universal health care insurance began in June 1934, when President Roosevelt appointed Secretary of Labor Frances Perkins to chair the Advisory Committee for Economic Security. The committee was a cabinet-level group of more than one hundred advisors drawn from a broad range of disciplines including actuaries, physicians, public health experts, hospital administrators, dentists, and public welfare specialists. After five months, FDR met with the committee and its advisors at the Mayflower Hotel in Washington, where they discussed the creation of a new public insurance system that would provide American workers unemployment insurance, retirement benefits, and health care.

The American Medical Association (AMA), then as now one of the most influential lobbying organizations in the United States, aggressively opposed medical insurance in any form, private or public. Its position was that any third-party involvement in medical care would detract from doctors' medical control of patient care and risk harming the quality of the services they provided.

By 1934, AMA members were in a fighting mood, afraid they would lose control of their profession. They were already worried because five years earlier Baylor University College of Medicine in Dallas had offered teachers in the area the first group health insurance in the United States. The price was 50 cents a month for twenty-one days of medical care at the Baylor hospital. This became the Blue Cross plan, one based on claims from the overall group rather than the health of any individual teacher.

The Baylor plan was immediately successful, and in 1931, the American Hospital Association began introducing nonprofit group insurance in other states. A member of Blue Cross in one place was eligible for service in all other places. AMA opposition to Blue Cross was so intense in the early 1930s that physicians who participated were shunned and risked loss of professional privileges. As this attitude suggests, the medical profession of that era was still a cottage industry, and its leaders were notorious free-market absolutists out to protect their perceived interests.

Meeting with his advisory committee, FDR said, "Whether we come to this form of insurance soon or later on, I am confident that we can devise a system which will enhance and not hinder the remarkable progress which has been made and is being made in the practice of the profession of medicine and surgery in the United States."

By 1935, AMA opposition was almost fanatical. Doctors bombarded Congress with cards, letters, ads, editorials, and visits. Their opposition was so significant that FDR concluded the AMA might kill his entire Social Security legislation; thus, he dropped the medical insurance provision from the bill he sent to Congress in 1935.

The final legislation was a compromise that excluded many groups, such as agricultural workers, and discriminated against women and minorities, but it was the best FDR could get through a Congress dominated by powerful members from the South, including many racial bigots and misogynists. One of FDR's post–World War II goals was to include national health insurance in Social Security, but he died in April 1945. President Harry Truman, his successor, picked up the health care baton, but failed in 1948 to enact legislation.

The need, however, remained. After President Johnson's overwhelming victory in the 1964 election, he persuaded Congress to modify Social Security and provide government-sponsored health care for those sixty-five and older (Medicare), plus health care for the poor (Medicaid). A quarter century later, President Clinton attempted to expand national insurance to all other Americans, but opponents in Congress killed his program.

As a result, America's health care system is a combination of public and private programs, enmeshed in ways that represent thousands of political compromises. At the high end, U.S. health services are unsurpassed, but for the overwhelming majority of Americans they are a complex hodgepodge that is difficult to understand or traverse, producing passable services. The complexity is reflected in the chart prepared by the Organization of Economic Cooperation and Development (OECD) that tries to explain how American health care is financed.

The ultimate question is, does the system work well for most of the American people? The answer is not as well as the systems in most other countries. The Commonwealth Fund has conducted three major national studies that compared U.S. health care with the systems of Germany, Canada, Australia, New Zealand, and the United Kingdom.

As to efficiency of medical care, the United States ranks last among the six countries, with high administrative costs, sometimes of 25 percent or greater. The United States is also last in the critical arena of managing data records, even though Americans invented the computer and business productivity has surged

UNITED STATES: Financing of Health Care, 2003

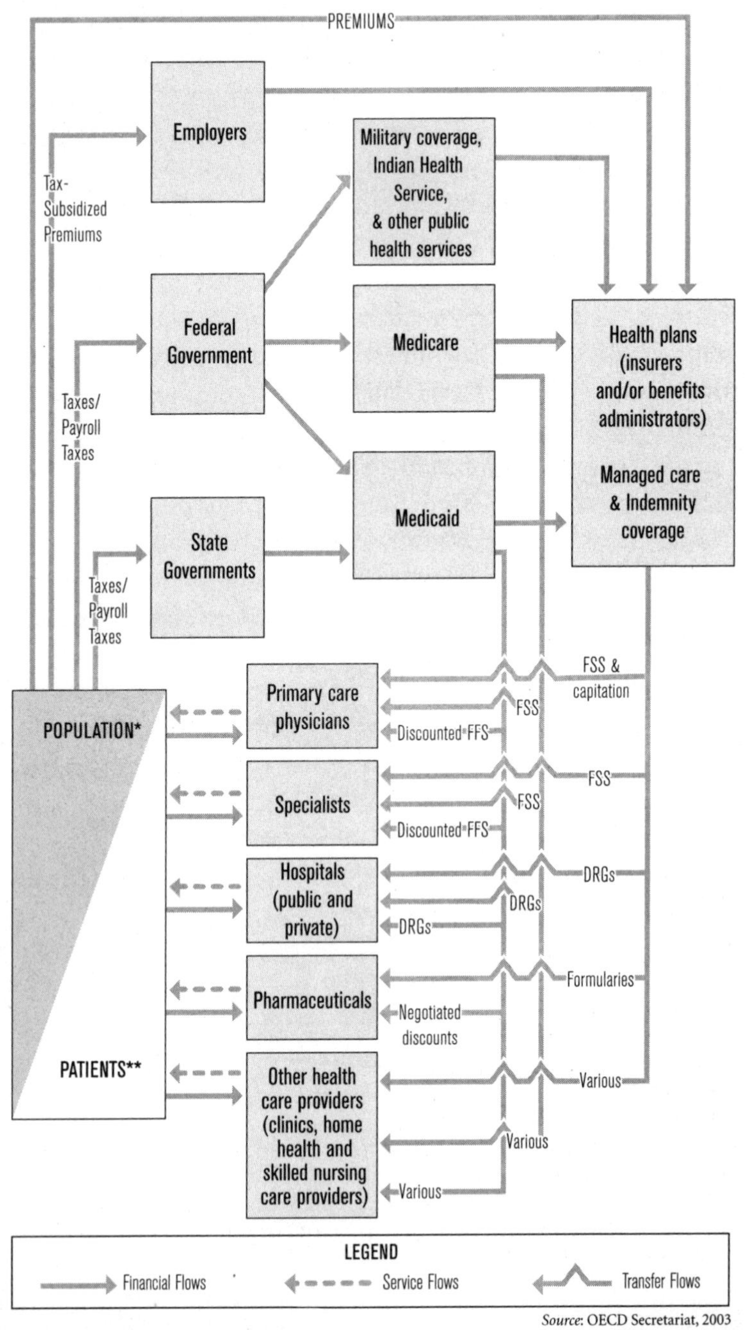

PREMIUMS
Employers
Tax-Subsidized Premiums
Military coverage, Indian Health Service, & other public health services
Federal Government
Medicare
Health plans (insurers and/or benefits administrators)
Managed care & Indemnity coverage
Taxes/ Payroll Taxes
Medicaid
State Governments
Taxes/ Payroll Taxes
FSS & capitation
POPULATION*
Primary care physicians
FSS
Discounted FFS
Specialists
FSS
FSS
Discounted FFS
Hospitals (public and private)
DRGs
DRGs
DRGs
Pharmaceuticals
Formularies
Negotiated discounts
PATIENTS**
Other health care providers (clinics, home health and skilled nursing care providers)
Various
Various
Various
LEGEND
Financial Flows
Service Flows
Transfer Flows

Source: OECD Secretariat, 2003

because of the enthusiastic application of new technologies. In health care records management, America is barely out of the age of the quill pen.

The United States has missed many opportunities to upgrade. The year Bill Gates dropped out of Harvard (1975), a Florida inventor named Charles Harder devised an electronic Medical Alert Network to manage a wide range of medical information on computers, create an electronic Personal Medical Profile for individuals, and store that information on a central computer that could be accessed and updated by patients and physicians. The chief of public affairs at the Department of Health, Education, and Welfare wrote Harder in December 1976, "To the best of my knowledge, the service offered by Medical Alert Network is unique." Ultimately, Harder was unable to raise enough interest and capital for the venture, even as other nations such as Canada and Japan digitized their medical records.

As the Defense Department prepared for the invasion of Iraq in late 2002 and early 2003, Ross Perot offered the armed forces a special gift, a dog tag–size digitized, encrypted copy of the entire medical record, including X-rays, of every military person involved in that war. The data would be on lightweight, bulletproof, fireproof, flexible material that portable scanners could read. Perot also offered to provide the scanners. He believed that instant access to medical records would help doctors in the field save the lives of American fighters. Yet the Defense Department was unable to accept the gift because it had not digitized the

Table Notes

FFS is fee-for-service payment. DRGs are case-based payments to hospitals based on a diagnosis-related group system.

*Health care for the 14% of the population lacking health insurance coverage is financed by publicly subsidized charity care and patients' out-of-pocket payments to health care providers.

**Patient cost-sharing arrangements vary widely by type of coverage. Indemnity coverage generally includes deductibles and coinsurance. Managed care plans often require copayments for certain services.

medical records of America's armed forces. It had spent trillions of dollars on advanced weapons but still kept medical records on paper filed and stored in boxes.

The National Center for Health Statistics reported in December 2008 that only 38 percent of U.S. physicians use electronic medical records. More significant, only 4 percent of the two thousand physicians surveyed reported fully functional systems. Digitized medical records in other nations drastically reduce administration costs, resulting in improved quality of care, fewer medical errors, and improved analysis of medical information.

President Obama's February 2009 economic stimulus program provided federal monies to begin digitizing America's medical records, but this will take years to implement.

Another problem in the existing system is fraud, waste, and abuse, which are at staggering levels. As of 2009, more than 1,500 insurance companies were involved in some way with health care. Their employer, hospital, billing, payment, and purchasing forms, plus dozens of administrative activities, provide numerous opportunities for fraud, which is estimated to take one of every ten dollars spent on health care.

While President Obama once supported the concept of a single-payer plan, his health care proposal is now evolving. As of June 2009, he intended to build on the existing system, provide tax credits to business, make partial federal payments for catastrophic health costs, work with insurance companies to make malpractice insurance less expensive, improve administrative efficiencies through improved data management, and create a public insurance program. He proposed to pay for much of this by rolling back the Bush administration's tax cuts for Americans earning more than $250,000 per year and retaining the estate tax at its 2009 level.

This plan is so complex, involves so many variables, and is so dependent on opponents being willing to sacrifice their interests that it is unlikely to be the final version. If it is, it is unlikely to become law. If Obama fails to enact a national health care plan, as presidents Roosevelt, Truman, and Clinton also failed, Americans can expect health care costs to rise above 20 percent of the GDP in less than a decade, and millions more Americans will be without any care. The stakes are enormous.

The advantages of a single-payer plan are so numerous that it is the obvious choice. At its core, it is an extension of Medicare to the whole of America. Medicare is far from perfect. Yet in a single-payer plan, administrative costs will be a fraction of current costs, closer to Medicare's barely 2 percent or 5.2 percent if all costs are included as per the Matthews study. There will be less fraud, and it will be easier to catch. The plan will cover everyone. Individuals will be able to choose their physicians and purchase more or different services with their own money. Patients will get the medicines they need. Physicians will be relieved of the heavy administrative and red-tape burdens they now carry. Finally, the overall cost to everyone will drop.

Politicians can explain a single-payer plan to the American people, who will be able to understand it. As Medicare was one of the most successful public programs of the twentieth century, universal health care insurance can be its counterpart in the next century.

Good health care for America involves more than creating universal coverage and a sound method for paying for it. Expanded funding for the Public Health Service would allow it to expand coverage for immunizations and other programs. Increased funding for basic and applied research would allow our universities, private research institutes, and the National Institutes of Health to study diseases and seek solutions that can transform health care just as the eradication of polio, measles, and smallpox did in the past.

New incentives to the pharmaceutical industry will stimulate the development of new medicines. One promising approach, as described in chapter four, Innovation, would be to lengthen the life of patents so that they would have a better cost-benefit basis for investment. For many "niche" and other rare diseases, pharmaceutical companies cannot afford to invest adequate R&D, because the prospective market is too small and the time of exclusive use of a new drug is too limited. Expanding the effective term of a patent to twenty-five or thirty years, from today's seventeen to twenty, can radically alter the economics of research and development in favor of seeking new solutions. The cost to the government would be zero.

The cost of liability insurance for the medical profession is a major problem in the United States. A new digital record system will better assess the competence of those involved and facilitate setting up primary or supplemental liability insurance programs doctors can afford. The goals are fewer incompetent medical personnel, the payment of compensation to patients when mistakes are made, and no exploitation of the medical profession with unwarranted lawsuits.

The principal opposition to a single-payer system will appear to be ideological. As so often happens, though, that ideology will be a screen for the insurance industry, which profits from the present approach. The main objection will be that a single-payer program is socialism, which it is not.

Great Britain has a socialized medical system: The government owns the hospitals and equipment; hires the doctors, nurses, and technicians; and operates it all. The Veterans Administration hospital system is socialized medicine. Its 153 medical centers, 755 community-based outpatient clinics, and 232 counseling centers serve 7.9 million veterans with doctors and caregivers who work for the federal government in government-owned facilities. Even though the VA system wins awards and provides better care than most private facilities, no one is proposing such a system for the rest of the United States.

A single-payer system also is not one in which the government tells patients which doctors they may and may not see, as do most private corporations that operate health maintenance organizations.

Like Medicare, single-payer is a medical financing system that uses private contractors to administer its program. Doctors, nurses, specialists, and laboratories will be the same profit and nonprofit providers that now exist, and medicines and equipment will be purchased from private companies, as they are now.

Health care for members and workers in Congress is paid for by a government-financed program, as is federal employee health care. Neither is socialized medicine. The public provides the money and the beneficiaries choose who gives them care. Ideally, these two programs will be made part of the larger single-payer plan, ensuring that public servants get the same level of health care as other American taxpayers.

To deliberately be redundant, doctors in private practice who accept Medicare are not federal government employees, nor are those who work in privately owned pharmacies or hospitals. The insurance payments they receive from Medicare are just like those they receive from private insurance companies such as Prudential, Blue Cross, or Aetna.

A single-payer system is a government-run insurance program that collects fees from employers and individuals and pays them out for health care costs. Most employers would pay less under a single-payer system than they do now by self-insuring or buying private insurance. Under this new system, employers would not make payments for insurance; instead, they would pay a modest payroll tax and employees would provide some matching funds. Most of those insured would pay less than they do now.

The transition from today's system to single-payer would be easy; the health care industry would simply bill the single-payer agency as they do Medicare now. Medicare would be the ideal agency to administer this new program because it is experienced and has a large core staff that the government can expand.

The idea of paying 10 to 12 percent of our GDP on health care, and getting 100 percent coverage of excellent medical care for the people of America seems almost too good to be true. Yet other nations do it.

We have much to learn from the experiences of other countries, many of which spend far less of their GDP on health care and get far more for their money than does America. The United States should seek knowledge from the experiences of other nations concerning functions such as cost reduction, software utilization, planning, forecasting, budgeting, and human resources management.

The U.S. government would particularly benefit from comparing any proposed new single-payer plan to the health care systems of Germany, Japan, Sweden, the Netherlands, the United Kingdom, and Canada. If the United States can improve health care and cut its cost to 10 to 12 percent of GDP (as opposed to today's 17 percent) by, for example, lowering administrative and medical costs, it could save $1 trillion or more per year. There are many other uses for that money.

BYE-BYE, BOOMERS, SO LONG

When World War II ended, most of the 16 million Americans in uniform counted their blessings to be alive, returned to civilian life, and tried to resume normal lives. Americans married in record numbers, and between 1946 and 1964, the country had the largest baby boom in its history. In 2005, as the first boomers approached their sixtieth birthdays, more than 78 million were alive.

The boomers changed America at every phase of their lives, creating unprecedented demand for diapers, elementary schools, and then colleges. Their hearty lifestyles propelled six decades of consumption of everything from hula hoops to personal flights into space. In 2005, America had twelve thousand specialty stores selling them cosmetic and antiaging skin care products and almost twenty-eight thousand fitness and recreation centers helping them stay young and fit.

The boomers energized America. They went to work in record numbers between the late 1960s and early 1980s, expanding the labor force by an annual rate of 2.6 percent in the 1970s and 1.6 percent in the 1980s. Their education levels were high, and by virtually every measure, America in the age of the boomers has been the hardest-working industrial country in the world, with workers putting in more hours per year than their competitors in Japan and Europe. For more than two decades, these tens of millions of energetic workers, on the job during their most productive years, have given America a demographic advantage in global competition.

Yet time takes its toll. The boomers will live and work longer than their parents, but nonetheless they are aging and beginning to retire. By 2030, however, more than 57 million of them will still be here. As always, the next phase of their lives, the long good-bye, will be another unique experience for America.

As the boomers depart and are replaced, the American workforce will grow far more slowly; between 2015 and 2020, the projected rate is only .2 percent annually. The combination of fewer new workers and the long phaseout of the boomers will create another era of about fifteen to twenty years during which most of the American workforce will be composed of aged boomers and the post-1965 population cohort just behind them. The workforce will have a median age of about forty-five by 2025. Thus, about 90 percent of workers then will be people who are at work now.

The boomers' departure creates some unique challenges. First, they will leave with critical know-how, skills, and institutional knowledge. America has no experience of having so many highly educated and skilled people leaving the workforce in such a brief period. These people make America work. The challenge will be to transfer their institutional knowledge between generations in a timely manner.

The second challenge will be preparing enough people to replace them. In these opening years of the twenty-first century, the fastest-growing portions of our workforce will also be our least educated. America is about to reap a bitter harvest from its long-term racial discrimination, failed education systems, and political indifference.

African American and Latino population cohorts will increase from 28 percent of the working-age (twenty-five to sixty-four) population in 2000 to more than 37 percent by 2020, while the white portion of that cohort will decline from 72 to 63 percent. The disparity in the educational rates between whites and minorities, therefore, is large and of enormous consequence.

A gauge of these differences is how well ninth graders do over time in the education pipeline from the start of high school to completion of college. Of every one hundred ninth graders from each population cohort, 75 percent of whites, 53 percent of Latinos, and 49 percent of African Americans finish high school within four years. This difference has major implications.

As for those who go on to college immediately after finishing high school, the percentages are 48 percent for whites and 27 percent for African Americans and Latinos. Of those who finish and graduate from college with an associate's or bachelor's degree, whites graduate 23 percent of the time versus 9 percent for African Americans and 10 percent for Latinos.

If America is to meet the economic challenges of the coming century, the nation must focus on raising these completion rates for African Americans and Latinos. Today the single largest barrier to college entry for 50 percent of African Americans and Latinos is lack of a high school education. While elementary and secondary education reform is not the topic of this book, the issue is so important to America's future that the point merits special attention here.

Interestingly, American workers possess more knowledge and greater skills than what will be required for the new jobs that are projected to be available in 2025. With the outsourcing of goods production and high-end service work abroad, America is quickly becoming a place where future job and income opportunities are going to be limited—unless, of course, we act now. The math tells the story.

The most extensive and best occupation projections are those prepared by the Bureau of Labor Statistics (BLS) every two years. In the past, the BLS has been accurate in spotting the direction of occupational change, identifying fast- and slow-growing occupations, and forecasting aggregate numbers of jobs and workers.

The BLS projects that from 2006 to 2016, the United States will create 15.6 million new jobs. Most of this growth (8.1 million) is projected to be in professional and business services, health care, and social assistance. The thirty largest growth occupations include registered nurse, home health aide, postsecondary teacher, home health assistant, janitor, child care worker, and computer specialist. Of the thirty occupations, two require vocational education or an associate's degree, three require a bachelor's degree, and only one requires a doctoral degree. The other twenty-five (83 percent) require only short-term on-the-job training.

The BLS also estimates the education and training levels the economy will need by 2016 to fill these job openings. It projects that 19.1 percent of the jobs will require a bachelor's degree or higher, about 9.6 percent will require an associate's degree or postsecondary vocational training, 16.9 percent will require work experience in a related profession or long-term on-the-job training, and, finally, 52 percent of the jobs will demand only moderate to short-term on-the-job training.

The education level of America's nonagricultural civilian workforce in 2009 is already higher than what the majority of these new jobs will require. Of 132 million Americans, the BLS reports that almost 45 million hold a bachelor's degree or higher

(35 percent), 37 million have some college or an associate's degree (27 percent), and 50 million (38 percent) have a high school education or less. Already, America has college-educated graduates competing for jobs with those with associate's degrees and those with associate's degrees and vocational training competing with those who need long-term or moderate training.

The BLS projects that the service sectors will be the source of most U.S. employment growth. America has chosen to outsource goods production. Within the goods-producing sector—manufacturing, mining, farming—the BLS projects that only construction employment will grow, and that is because construction is not subject to import competition. Materials are, but the actual fabrication is done on-site.

As all this suggests, America is on the leading edge of a mass downscaling of educational and job skills. Any profession or occupation that is subject to international competition, including service jobs in the legal, accounting, and medical fields, is likely to have job losses under present U.S. policies on globalization.

This demography means that America will have a growing percentage of its workforce with less than a high school education, plus a decline in the portion with higher levels of education. Put into perspective, the country is now on the path to reversing almost seven decades of educational progress. The Census Bureau reports that more than four out of five American adults age twenty-five and over have at least a high school diploma or its equivalent, while more than one out of four have a bachelor's degree or greater. "This is a threefold increase in high school attainment and more than a fivefold increase in college attainment since the Census Bureau first collected educational attainment data in 1940."

Ultimately, what matters in global competition is how the United States compares with other nations. In 2005, The National Center for Public Policy and Higher Education compared the percentage of young Canadians (age twenty-five to thirty-four) with associate's degrees or higher versus their American counterparts. Using Canada's attainment as the index score of 100, the U.S. score was 77.

The center predicted that "if current population trends continue and states do not improve the education of all racial/ethnic groups, the skills of the workforce and the incomes of U.S. residents are projected to decline over the next two decades."

It could have added that if current U.S. globalization policies continue, a decline in the education and skills of American workers will not matter greatly, because large numbers of the kinds of jobs that require knowledge and skills and that pay well will not be available in the United States.

Even with such depressing prospects, workers still will need to keep pace with the changing demands of their jobs. Thus, they will need periodic booster shots of education and training throughout their working careers. Of the many obstacles to such a course of action, several are paramount:

- Public education and training programs generally ignore upgrade education or training.
- Employers have few incentives to invest in worker training, because they fear their expenditures are likely to benefit other employers after the education and training are completed.
- America still lacks a comprehensive worker adjustment program. As discussed earlier, programs to really help the millions of workers who are losing their jobs because of outsourcing or the economic crisis do not exist.

America needs an inclusive adjustment and training program to boost the skills and flexibility of the 155 million people now in the workforce to prepare them for and help them cope with change. This would include remedial education and reentry-level training for disadvantaged and impaired workers, entry-level training for the hundreds of thousands of new workers coming into the labor force each year, continuing training and education for workers on the job, and special assistance for displaced workers.

According to the National Center for Public Policy and Higher Education, the United States has lost its leadership role as the most highly educated nation in the world. Moreover, the center reports we are losing ground to several nations, particularly with respect to our younger population, which represents our future workforce. We cannot remain a great nation with an undereducated population and an unskilled workforce.

Ultimately, America faces a hard choice: Accept economic decline or prepare our people and get the economy moving again. If we choose the latter, America will need a national training and education strategy. Most of all, however, America needs more and better jobs for our people, which is the topic of the next chapter.

CHAPTER SEVEN

JOBS

"Does the United States need an auto industry?" The *New York Times*' editors asked a panel of experts and its readers this question on April 30, 2009, on its Room for Debate blog as two of the Big Three U.S. automobile manufacturers faced possible bankruptcy, reorganization, sale, or even nationalization at the hands of the federal government. Opinions differed wildly.

Certainly, Americans do not need Ford, Chrysler, or General Motors merely to provide them with vehicles. In 2008, Japanese car companies built three million cars and trucks in the United States and brought in another two million from Japan. Korean automakers imported 615,000 and produced another 237,000 in their U.S. plants. Germany exported to America more than 208,000 vehicles in 2008 and produced another 328,000 in their U.S. affiliates. By 2011, foreign makers from Asia and Europe will have more North American production than Ford, Chrysler, and GM combined. And soon China's automakers will be flooding the U.S. market with their low-priced, high-quality vehicles, which will include knockoffs of all the best features from all their rivals. American consumers have no lack of choice when selecting an automobile.

All these foreign companies are from state-capitalist economies. Their governments support the automobile industry and other large industries, in turn generating business for dozens of their domestic supplier industries including steel, glass, plastics, tires, semiconductors, software, and fabrics. Auto production supports the entire manufacturing sector in many nations, creating demand for dies, machine tools, robotics, and all manner of new technology.

If China, Japan, Korea, and Germany eventually take over the entire U.S. automobile market, they will cartelize the industry and work out among themselves the details of sharing the spoils. Working together—and not against one another—they will control sales, prices, distribution, model changes, and even options. They will provide all the vehicles Americans want and can afford. The United States will not need a home-owned auto industry.

The same *New York Times* question can be asked about other industries as well, including those thought to be basic to the U.S. economy. Does the United States need an agricultural industry? Surprisingly, the answer is no. If *need* means there is no alternative supply, then America does not need its farms and ranches. The United States can import all the food and fiber it consumes and is well on the way to doing so. Between 2000 and 2008, the value of U.S. agricultural imports more than doubled, rising from $39 billion to more than $80 billion.

Because the worldwide food industry is so highly concentrated, a handful of commodity dealers such as Archer Daniels Midland and Cargill could easily supply the United States with a wide variety of foods from around the world. Beef producers in Australia, Canada, New Zealand, Mexico, and Uruguay already provide American supermarkets almost half a billion pounds of beef carcasses per month. China, India, and Brazil can sell the United States all the cotton it needs and are eager to do so. Garlic, apple juice, and peanuts, among other agricultural products, are imported in vast quantities from China. The European Union sends America wine, oils, cut flowers, and dairy products.

America's big agricultural exports are wheat, corn, soybeans, rice, and cotton. Most of this is production subsidized by the Department of Agriculture, which distributes up to $30 billion in cash subsidies to farmers and landowners annually, more than 90 percent of it going to the producers of these five crops.

Does the United States need a defense industrial base? Again, other nations already supply a large portion of the materials and weapons the United States relies on for its defense. In the mid-1990s, the Clinton administration directed the Defense Department to seek out reliable foreign companies in order to get the most competitive prices.

Distance is not a consideration in such bidding, according to Defense Department directives. China, Japan, Korea, and Taiwan can produce all the boots, clothing, and armor needed by the U.S. military. Israel, Great Britain, France, Germany, and Italy make first-class weapons and ammunition. Japanese, Taiwanese, and Korean shipyards can easily best their U.S. counterparts on price and delivery times of naval ships. Europe's Airbus won the competition to furnish the next generation of U.S. Air Force tanker planes, although that decision has been contested. Much of the electronics used in our most modern weapons comes from Japan, Taiwan, and China.

Only a few unique weapons systems, such as nuclear submarines, missiles, advanced fighter aircraft, and satellites, absolutely need to be made in the United States, but if given the opportunity, other countries would be delighted to take U.S. designs and manufacture them. Dozens of other nations already rely on foreign arms makers to provide them with their defense needs.

The *New York Times* question about need is not new. Over the past thirty years, policy makers have repeatedly asked themselves whether or not America really needs this or that particular industry. If *need* means there is no alternative supply, the answer repeatedly has been no. The manufacture of shoes, textiles, apparel, chemicals, medicines, radios, televisions, machine tools, aircraft, ships, imaging devices, computers, and appliances are among the dozens of industries U.S. policy makers have decided we do not need to provide ourselves because foreign producers can provide those goods, often at lower cost.

Policy makers can pose the same question for all remaining industries. If alternative supplies at low prices eliminate need, then America's existing industries are, in fact, not needed. Other countries are ready, willing, and able to provide the country with anything it needs.

One of the great hopes of globalization was that other nations would take the industries and jobs that Americans did not need or want, freeing up the American workforce for high-knowledge and high-paying service industry jobs. Certainly that was a promise made by lawmakers when they enacted laws and policies that supported the outsourcing of so many industries.

Taking tens of millions of U.S. workers with high school educations or less and converting them into high-technology workers was, of course, a pipe dream. Indeed, it was a cruel hoax even the most intellectually uncurious members of Congress easily should have figured out was nothing but propaganda from banks and corporations wanting to outsource jobs to nations with low wages. It was a thin political rationalization, for sure, but for many in Congress and a succession of presidents it was thick enough.

Official U.S. trade data expose what a great deception it was. The goods-producing industries had the jobs the United States did not need or want; the services industries, such as telecommunications, banking, insurance, and logistics, supposedly were going to create high-paying replacement jobs. In 2008, the United States exported $139 billion more in services than it imported and imported $820 billion more in goods than it exported. By a ratio of six to one, the value of goods the United States imported exceeded the value of the services it exported. This deception on the public is comparable to Wall Street's repackaging subprime mortgages and selling them as triple-A bonds.

The question of not needing some particular industry or not wanting some types of jobs, such as apparel making, ignores the central problem of how 155 million working Americans, increasingly lacking education and skills, will make a living and pay their bills. One answer is to provide them with more education and training. But training for what? The promised high-knowledge-based service industry jobs simply are not there in sufficient quantities, and they never will be in our lifetimes.

Yet America needs millions of new jobs. For June 2009, the Labor Department reported that 14.7 million of the 155 million workers in the labor force were unemployed, placing the official unemployment rate at 9.5 percent. But the federal data did not include

- those who had been unemployed fifteen weeks or longer and still wanted a job;
- workers employed in temporary work but still seeking a full-time job;
- displaced workers who were still unemployed; or
- discouraged workers who had given up looking but still wanted a job.

If the above categories also are included, an additional 13 million workers go into the ranks of the unemployed. Thus, the real number of unemployed in June 2009 was about 28 million workers and the real unemployment rate was 17.9 percent, up from the Labor Department's official figure of 9.5 percent in June 2009. This means about one of six American workers is unemployed and cannot find a job.

For those who see no need for American manufacturing, the ultimate questions are, what replacement jobs will there be for America's 12 million manufacturing workers, and who will create them? Everyone requires clothing, housing, furniture, appliances, transportation, electronics, computers, and other consumer goods. How will unemployed Americans pay for what they and their families must have?

For those who see no need for the agricultural industry, the questions are many. Will foreign imports be safe? If there are shortages in producing countries caused by drought or pestilence, will the leaders of those nations sacrifice the interests of their people for those of the United States? How will three million displaced U.S. agricultural workers find jobs? And, perhaps most important, is surrendering U.S. food self-sufficiency a wise policy, even if imported foods are cheaper?

As for the question of the need for a defense industrial base, the intriguing paradox is that our top military officers annually report that China is a rising military threat to the United States, while civilian defense executives claim that China is a reliable supplier of many of the components used to make American weapons. Who is right?

These and dozens of other questions have long been ignored by our leaders because they assumed U.S. industry was so strong and American workers were so productive they could never be overwhelmed in open competition. Accordingly, our government has worked to impose global trade rules that provide equal access for all nations. They have acted as if economic competition were a sport in which everybody plays fairly by the rules.

Other nations, notably those with state-capitalist models, see economics as war in which all is fair. They generally are willing to promise anything, pay any price, enter any treaty, and meet any burden that will lead to success and power in global trade. Our politically appointed treasury secretaries, secretaries of state, and trade representatives are no match for the career negotiators from nations such as China and Japan.

There is an American job crisis. Near-term employment, particularly in manufacturing and service trades subject to foreign competition, is falling to Depression-era levels. Displaced workers need income, health care, and employment services now. The longer the unemployed remain out of work, the more difficult it will be for them to return to work.

Over the longer term, the economic crisis is going to worsen. Countries with state-capitalist economies are aggressively working to gain advantage. While most European and Asian automakers, for instance, have suffered similar declines in sales as Ford, Chrysler, and General Motors, they have the complete support of their governments and are racing to exploit the current downturn in the business cycle and grab market share from the Big Three. They are reorganizing and expanding production in the United States as a means of moving quickly to compete against their real future competitors, one another. It is economics as war, and the United States is the battlefield.

Meanwhile, U.S. automakers are sidelined at precisely the moment they should be investing in R&D, developing more efficient production methods, and creating effective marketing programs. Banks are unwilling to lend them money, and political appointees from Washington are setting their longer-term strategies for them. What the U.S. automobile industry really needs is a respite from imports and time for the Big Three, Washington, and Wall Street to adjust to new economic realities.

SHORT-TERM IMPORT RELIEF

Fortunately, U.S. law already allows for a respite from imports for a brief period so that industry and government responses can be planned and begun. The law is Section 201 of the Trade Act of 1974—the "safeguard" provision.

Terence Stewart, an experienced Washington trade lawyer and one of the principal legal advisors during Chrysler's restructuring in the early 1980s, notes:

> *In an environment where a fundamental disequilibrium, caused by factors not effectively addressed multilaterally—VAT, currency, etc.—exists, the government may be the only*

protector of the manufacturing sector. The distortions lead companies to shift technology and jobs offshore, not because of intrinsic comparative advantage but because the distortions have not self-corrected through exchange rate movements, as economists typically predict they will. Failure to shift offshore leads to the loss of market to foreign producers or those who have moved. Section 201 is a tool that can be used during the gap period between recognition of the problem and resolution. The president or USTR can invoke its application as can a resolution by the House Ways and Means Committee or the Senate Finance Committee or by the ITC itself. There would likely be a number of important industries where such actions could be taken.

Under this law, which is congruent with U.S. obligations at the World Trade Organization, a domestic industry seriously injured or threatened with serious injury by increased imports may petition the International Trade Commission (ITC), a quasi-judicial U.S. agency, for import relief for a limited period so the industry can adjust itself.

If the commission makes an affirmative determination, it recommends to the president remedies to the injury and actions needed by the industry to adjust to the import competition. The final decisions on whether or not and how to act reside with the president. The use of such relief is a long-standing and standard practice accepted and used by all U.S. trading partners.

The ITC determination does not require a finding of unfair trade practices, but the law requires that the ITC find the injury or threatened injury to be "serious" and increased imports to be an important cause of the existing or prospective damage.

The process is fast, usually with determinations made within 120 days of the petition being filed or no later than 180 days of filing. The period of relief is limited to only four years, with the remote possibility of an extension for another four.

As Stewart notes, the petition can originate from one of several sources, including

- a trade association,
- a firm,
- a certified or recognized union,
- a group of workers representative of a domestic industry,
- the president of the United States,
- the United States trade representative,
- a resolution by the House Committee on Ways and Means,
- the Senate Committee on Finance, and
- the ITC upon its own motion.

Relief may be in the form of one or a combination of measures, including temporary tariff increases on imports, quantitative restrictions, or an orderly marketing agreement with other governments.

The experience of Harley-Davidson, the motorcycle maker, illustrates how useful and powerful this law can be. In the early 1970s, Harley-Davidson dominated the large-engine motorcycle market in the United States. Then Japanese manufacturers aggressively entered the market with deeply discounted prices and large inventories. The Japanese companies, working with their government, made a concentrated attack, selling substantial numbers of their products at low prices, backed by their ability to charge a premium in Japan's closed home market.

In 1981, Japanese makers sold 739,000 machines in the United States, compared with 41,000 Harleys. The surge of imports overwhelmed the U.S. maker, and in 1982 Harley filed a Section 201 relief petition at the ITC. The subsequent investigation found the rise of Japanese imports, coupled with an additional year's worth of inventory of Japanese machines in the United States, virtually guaranteed that Harley would not recover without safeguard relief.

The ITC recommended to President Reagan that tariffs on the imports of large-engine motorcycles be raised for five years, enough time for Harley to recover. The first year the recommended tariff was 45 percent; it was 35 percent the second year, 20 percent the third, 15 percent the fourth, and 10 percent the fifth. The president accepted the ITC recommendations and Harley got its relief.

Harley used the time well, improving its product and marketing, diversifying its product line, and putting its financing on a sound basis. Four years later, in 1987, Harley had 47 percent of the big-engine market and it was doing so well it requested that the fifth-year tariff be lifted. In succeeding years, Harley prospered. In 2008, it employed 8,600 people; provided its workers with strong benefits and pensions; sold 303,000 machines, a third of which were exported; and had revenues of $5.59 billion and a net income of $654 million. Like most other U.S. corporations, of course, Harley is now dealing with a weakened market for its products caused by the current economic downturn, but in 2009 it is a strong enterprise.

Thousands of American companies in dozens of industries now face bleak futures just as Harley did in 1982. Many can recover if given breathing space and if the government changes its policies to be more responsive to economic challenges created by state capitalism. First among these is the auto industry, in which imports counted for more than 40 percent of U.S. consumption in 2007–2008, up from about 30 percent in 2004.

The auto industry is not alone. Even before the crash of 2008, imports were overwhelming numerous major sectors across the U.S. economy. The electronic products sector had a $176 billion trade deficit in 2008. In the textile and apparel industries, imports exceeded exports by more than $86 billion. The chemical industry and related industries had a $33 billion deficit, and for machinery manufacturers it was $35 billion. Imports may soon completely destroy these industries and take away millions of well-paying jobs.

Losses of these sizes, across the range of U.S. industries engaged in global trade, are not the consequence of a few incompetent corporate executives or unproductive workers. This reflects a structural incompatibility between our market capitalism and the state capitalism that increasingly dominates the global economy.

If America is not to lose the balance of its manufacturing and high-value service industries and the millions of jobs they provide, the Obama administration needs to quickly initiate both emergency and long-term remedial measures.

In the near term, to prevent imports from permanently damaging our economy even further, invoking the safeguard provisions of Section 201 is required. This will not necessitate a finding by the ITC of unfair trade practices by other nations, but simply a recognition that the flow of imports over the past several years imperils certain domestic industries and the jobs they create. Not all industries will be affected, though many will. Trade and other economic data available from the Commerce and Labor departments can quickly and clearly identify the companies that, like Harley-Davidson, can adjust for import competition if given time and attention.

LONGER-TERM INDUSTRIAL POLICIES

As previously discussed, the United States has dozens of policies for a multitude of industries and situations, but unlike the policies of other nations, they are neither explicit nor coherent. Rather, they are an accumulation of random decisions that affect specific parts of the economy, often in powerful ways.

Many other nations consider certain industries so important that those countries have long devised special policies to ensure their success. Airbus is a glaring example of a government-subsidized corporation. Spain, France, and Germany subsidize the design, production, and sale of passenger aircraft not only to compete in international aviation but also as a means of retaining an active presence in dozens of related areas, including materials and advanced computers.

All Japanese industries of virtually any economic significance are the result of industrial planning, subsidies, and provision of a sanctuary home market by their government. The Munitions Ministry, the World War II agency with a brilliant staff of bureaucrats that ran Japan's wartime industrial policy, was renamed the Ministry of Commerce and Industry on August 26, 1945, just a week after Japan's surrender and four days before General Douglas MacArthur's arrival in Tokyo as supreme commander of occupational forces. Later renaming it the Ministry of Economy, Trade, and Industry (METI), the same bureaucrats immediately shifted from wartime production to rebuilding Japan's economy and then to pursuit of global domination in key industries.

China's list of targeted industries is explicit in its five-year plans. Beijing has identified 161 central industries on its priority list, with 30 to 50 targeted to become national champions, behemoth corporations with the size and reach of companies such as Microsoft and GE. Many of these industries are termed "lifeline" sectors: oil, coal, petrochemicals, metallurgy, power, telecommunications, defense, ocean shipping, air transport, and scientific instruments. Dozens of other high-priority subordinate industries are listed under these sectors, including auto production, civilian satellites, large-equipment manufacturing, large-scale integrated circuits, and equipment for the Internet.

Germany is far more circumspect, but its government supports industries that are considered national priorities, such as automobile and machine tool manufacturing.

U.S. corporations that face such favored competitors in the global marketplace cannot survive for long without the backing of the U.S. government. The economic battlefield is littered with U.S. corporations, even entire industries, that tried to go it alone and failed against such policies.

Car manufacturing is sure to be on any list of industries that would benefit from a comprehensive government industrial policy. Automobiles are a major component of the GDP. The industry provides an essential product for which demand will always exist and is a key customer of dozens of other important industries. It provides mass employment, heavily concentrated in a few places in the United States, for individuals ranging from scientists and engineers with advanced specialties to day laborers with few skills and little education. The Chinese, German, Japanese, French, Italian, and Korean governments have selected their automobile industries for favored treatment. If the United States wants a successful domestic auto industry, we must fight for it and do the same.

Now that the federal government has taken control of the U.S. auto industry, the importance of a coherent approach in its future development will become increasingly obvious. President Obama and his subordinates no doubt will come to understand the realities and frustrations corporations in a market economy face when competing with corporations that are part of state-capitalist systems.

Many people, including the federal officials now in charge of the GM and Chrysler recoveries, may be surprised to learn that the Big Three automakers are building some of the highest-quality cars in the world. In 2007, Ford won 102 quality awards, including *AutoPacific* magazine's Ideal Vehicle Award for three models and the Auto 1 of Europe Award (given by *AutoBild*, Germany's largest car magazine) for the S-MAX model. Of the fifteen global finalists for the 2008 *Motor Trend* Car of the Year, the Big Three manufactured nine, the Japanese four, and the Europeans two. The 2008 winner was GM's Cadillac CTS, which *Motor Trend* described as "proof America can take on Europe's best."

Many people probably will also be surprised to learn that the Big Three, particularly GM and Ford, are among the world's leading innovators. General Motors, Ford, and Chrysler invest almost $12 billion annually on R&D, making them a major source of technology development. In 2007, the USPTO granted the three corporations 1,030 patents. According to several recent studies, those patents are the most valuable assets the Big Three own.

James E. Malackowski, CEO of Ocean Tomo LLC, a merchant bank that specializes in valuations of intellectual property products and services, recently compared the green, clean, and energy-efficient patent portfolios held by the fifteen top global automakers. Malackowski examined four areas: (1) emission control, catalytic converters, and related chemistry; (2) fuel cells; (3) hybrid/electric vehicles, mostly motor and battery innovation; and (4) emerging related technologies, including solar, wind, and other green inventions.

According to Malackowski, GM has higher average quality and newer green technology and patents than the other fourteen auto manufacturers combined. Ford and GM hold approximately one-third of all green-technology patents and their related value. Moreover, GM owns 70 percent of patents in the emerging technology category; this share increases to 85 percent if Ford's patents are added. Finally, Ford owns 30 percent of all patents in emission control innovation. These Big Three technology holdings have great potential for stimulating overall U.S. economic and job growth and creating greener and more fuel-efficient cars. They could save the U.S. automobile industry.

The Big Three, however, carry legacy pension and health care costs not borne by European and Asian automobile producers. The current restructuring of the industry will shift much of the health care cost to the United Auto Workers union. Converting corporate debt, including U.S. debt, to equity will reduce the automakers' debt service and help their cash flow. An operational U.S. government industrial policy for the car industry can make these things happen.

As discussed in the chapter two, Taxes, a big disadvantage to

U.S. carmakers is the value-added tax (VAT) rebate Asian and European car manufacturers receive from their governments on every vehicle they export to the United States. U.S. companies do not receive a VAT rebate, nor do they receive credit for corporate taxes they pay in the United States on their exported vehicles. Instead, they must pay a local VAT on each vehicle they import as well as U.S. corporate taxes. This disadvantage, moreover, is not a function of production, but one of politics and policy at the highest levels between the United States and foreign governments.

Unlike the previous corporate management of the auto industry, the Obama administration will be able to examine the U.S. tax returns of Asian and European corporations that import vehicles into the American market. Through a complex set of accounting maneuvers, they generally shift their profits elsewhere, thereby paying few corporate taxes in the United States. This too has given them another advantage.

The administration will also discover that foreign producers have benefited from billions of dollars in tax breaks and other gifts from state governments. Alabama gave Mercedes-Benz $253 million and Honda $248 million to build facilities there. Tennessee provided Volkswagen with land, tax breaks, and other benefits worth $577 million and Nissan $197 million to locate their headquarters in that state. South Carolina presented BMW $150 million in benefits, Mississippi paid Nissan $363 million, and Kia got $415 million from Georgia to build new plant facilities. Unfortunately, among the ways these southern states pay for such incentives is by cutting back on expenditures for education, Medicaid, and other public services.

President Obama has repeatedly stated that a revived U.S. auto industry will produce vehicles that are safer, more fuel efficient, and minimally damaging to the environment. These are precisely the vehicles customers in Japan and Korea want. Already many American-made models are superior to those produced in Japan and Korea, yet the Japanese and Korean governments keep foreign cars out of their markets through a variety of strategies and barriers.

Although Japanese producers sold 6 million vehicles in the United States in 2007 and the Koreans sold almost 615,000, Japan accepted fewer than 17,000 made in the United States and Korea took fewer than 7,000. Their automobile markets are reserved almost exclusively for their own producers.

More than twenty years ago, TRW Inc., a major parts maker, tried to penetrate the Japanese replacement auto parts market. Unable to find distributors for its products, TRW located a small Japanese distributor that was willing to sell itself to TRW for an exorbitant price. The Japanese company never completed the sale because the Ministry of Finance ruled it would carry a 100 percent capital gains tax, one not applied to other similar transactions between the Japanese. This illustrates how closed the Japanese market was and still is.

U.S. carmakers have had many similar experiences in their attempts to operate and sell in Japan, and they generally have given up trying to penetrate its closed auto market. The Obama administration's attempts to get U.S.-made automobiles onto the Japanese market no doubt will be challenging, but they will be essential if GM and Chrysler are to become globally competitive.

The administration will also discover that Japanese automakers in the United States generally use Japanese-made parts or parts made by Japanese companies in the United States. They reject parts made in the United States regardless of quality, price, service, marketing, innovation, or reputation. A few token U.S. suppliers do exist, but they are exceptions. Since auto parts are the largest portion of the industry and the largest employer, breaking into that closed relationship will be crucial to the U.S.-owned and -operated suppliers who produce more of their goods in the United States and correspondingly employ more American workers.

The most important discovery the Obama administration is going to make is that federal money loaned to or invested in the U.S. auto industry really is a rescue, not a bailout. If Wall Street had not collapsed, the market and financing for new vehicles would not have dried up, GM and Chrysler would have reorganized themselves, and they would not have needed federal monies.

If President Obama fails to revive the U.S. auto industry, there will be Depression-level unemployment in the states of Wisconsin, Indiana, Michigan, and Ohio, and hundreds of thousands of people will have their homes foreclosed. Asian and European car manufacturers located in the South, moreover, will not be accepting many of the hundreds of thousands of displaced workers from the above states. Such workers are generally UAW members, and those companies are strictly nonunion employers.

Federal control of the auto industry is a high-stakes political and economic matter. Ironically, an ITC Section 201 safeguard order against imports most likely will encourage a shift of more foreign production into the United States as a means of avoiding import controls. Today most foreign cars that are "made in the USA" are actually car kits sent from Japan, Korea, or Europe that are then assembled by American workers. The real value contained in those kits is produced in Japan, Korea, and Europe.

Giveaways by states help foreigners at the expense of domestic enterprises. A simple way to stop such misuse of taxpayer funds is a 100 percent federal tax on the money. Many politicians will oppose this, but such opposition can be surmounted. Cutting services to poor residents of those states to enrich foreign corporations is unacceptable.

Concerning the larger issue of confronting the VAT disadvantage, representatives of the president should negotiate an exemption to the VAT concerning the auto trade with Germany, Japan, Korea, France, Italy, and China. The United States has been very generous to those countries, including financing much of the defense of the first five, and this demand should be more than acceptable to those now free and prosperous countries.

The Obama administration needs to confront the unequal trade and investment relationships between Japan and Korea and the United States through plurilateral negotiations. Reciprocity is a golden rule in trade, yet those nations are denying it to the United States.

A start in this effort would be for Japanese and Korean automakers to market GM, Ford, and Chrysler vehicles in their countries. American dealers have long sold foreign-made vehicles alongside those made in the United States, a practice that helped Asian producers break into the U.S. market. The Big Three should have the same market share in Japan and Korea, perhaps in a decade, that Japanese and Korean producers enjoy here.

In Japan, an existing practice will facilitate this. The country imposes regulatory restrictions on cars, resulting in almost the entire domestic fleet being replaced roughly every four years. There are no old automobiles in Japan. As this turnover occurs, the marketing of superior American-made vehicles would be possible. Japanese companies, of course, would be compensated by equal access to the U.S. market, which they already enjoy. Reciprocity is not charity.

Moving away from the automobile industry, another major target that will create good jobs under a coordinated U.S. industrial policy is the production of materials and equipment necessary for a national infrastructure investment program—steel, concrete, controls, and aluminum, among dozens of other items. A major program, as suggested in chapter five, Infrastructure, would create sixteen thousand new jobs of a year's duration for every $1 billion of investment. In turn, buying components made in America would invigorate many related supply industries. Such a step, moreover, is congruent with U.S. obligations under the World Trade Organization, because relying on domestic-based suppliers is neither protectionist nor illegal.

The most visible opponents of the "Buy American" provisions are the U.S. Chamber of Commerce, the National Association of Manufacturers, and the Business Roundtable—the three large associations that represent domestically and foreign-headquartered transnational corporations. These companies have much of their production outside the United States, and we no longer can think of them as American companies. As many of them repeatedly point out, they are global corporations. If they return production to the United States, of course, they could qualify under the Buy American provisions.

In their opposition to the Buy American provisions, these companies and the think tanks and lobbying organizations they support, plus the editorial pages of several leading newspapers, portray the enactment of laws that require purchases from U.S.-based producers as a violation of U.S. obligations under international trade agreements. Such laws are not.

Today only thirty-nine nations other than the United States are participants in Government Procurement Agreements. The United States carefully negotiated those provisions, and the authorization of the Buy American provisions will be administered in compliance with those obligations. The United States does not have similar obligations to 113 other nations that are also members of the WTO. An analysis of how the Buy American provisions are congruent with our international obligations is available on the Internet at http://www.americanmanufacturing.org.

The goals of a massive infrastructure development program, using Buy American provisions, would be the same as President Roosevelt's during the 1930s: create new jobs, provide needed domestic civil works, and build recreational facilities for the people.

The philosophy behind this is the same as that espoused in comments by the renowned nineteenth-century American orator Robert Green Ingersoll: "If we purchase a ton of steel rails from England for twenty dollars, then we have the rails and

England the money. But if we buy a ton of steel rails from an American for twenty-five dollars, then America has both the rails and the money."

During the past three decades of market absolutism, the Antitrust Division of the Justice Department and the Federal Trade Commission have sat on the sidelines as one industry after another was monopolized, often by foreign corporations. As economic theory suggests, some of the largest U.S.-headquartered global corporations are actively engaging in anticompetitive behavior against smaller, weaker competitors. The high-technology sector of the U.S. economy is the leading example.

Microsoft, Intel, Cisco, Apple, HP, and a handful of other corporations dominate high-tech industries worldwide, holding two-thirds or more of the global market share in many product lines. For instance, Microsoft holds a 90 percent market share in operating systems, Intel's semiconductors are used 85 percent of the time globally, Cisco dominates the Internet equipment sector, and Apple is strong in the music download industry.

In the absence of effective antitrust enforcement, several of these companies expanded rapidly during the past decade by purchasing their competitors. This allowed them to innovate through acquisition. HP's revenues surged from $49 billion in 2000 to more than $118 billion in 2008. During the same period Microsoft's revenues went from $23 billion to more than $60 billion and Oracle grew from $10 billion to $22 billion.

The aggressive business strategies these and other big tech corporations employ frequently cross the line into illegality. As discussed in chapter four, Innovation, the fifteen corporations described there were defendants in 730 patent infringement lawsuits, plus 641 antitrust lawsuits from 1996 to 2008.

The 1,371 antitrust and patent infringement lawsuits filed against these companies reveal a pattern of anticompetitive practices. Their joint lobbying effort to weaken U.S. patent protections highlights their intentions to strip smaller competitors of their economic rights. Fines and sanctions seem meaningless to these corporate CEOs. Perhaps criminal indictments of corporate leaders would gain their attention and change their anticompetitive actions.

At the same moment, other nations have targeted these same companies for the jobs and wealth they create. The challenge for Washington is to devise an industrial policy that allows companies such as these fifteen to grow, prosper, create, and employ, while simultaneously ensuring they do not illegally retard the rise of competitors and ensuring that these same corporations do not become victims of the industrial policies of other nations. It will be a delicate balance.

Without such policies, these big U.S. corporations eventually will be overtaken by state capitalists from abroad, as was the American consumer electronics industry, or they will become global monopolists of such size and power that they will be beyond control, such as Exxon and other major oil producers.

An enduring myth about American business is that its leaders are largely ideologically unprepared to engage in proactive efforts with government. As we have seen over the past thirty years, they do it daily with foreign leaders and tyrants of all kinds. Capitalists are flexible. They can also work with leaders of our government to create long-term, sustainable, noninflationary competition policies that can compete with state capitalism.

The greater danger is not that they cannot work with government, but that so many CEOs are rarely willing to acknowledge that any success they have achieved is due to anything other than their own efforts. Too often U.S. businesspeople view struggling industries as corporate or personal failures, rather than as victims of state capitalism. Also too often, many of America's once top corporations have been ruined because they learned too late that they cannot compete against a foreign government and all its resources. Corporate hubris is a dangerous sin.

A great danger faced by America, and the Obama administration, will arrive in mid-2010 and early 2011 when today's economic stimulus expenditures begin to expire. The political urge will be to declare that prosperity is just around the corner when it is not.

Our economic reality now is national decline. Extraordinary emergency actions over many years are required. If they are not taken, millions more jobs will be lost, the national debt will continue to grow, and America's capacity to recuperate will be further diminished. Action now is the only sensible response.

EPILOGUE

FIRST THINGS FIRST

In his March 1933 inaugural address, President Franklin D. Roosevelt said of his approach to confronting the Great Depression, "I favor as a practical policy the putting of first things first." Those first things were for the United States to (1) put its own national house in order (2) make income balance outgo, and (3) put people to work. He also announced that he would "spare no effort to restore world trade by international economic readjustment, but the emergency at home cannot wait on that accomplishment."

"First things first" is a sensible way for us to battle the current depression. Again, our house is badly out of order. The financial system is crippled, focused on the wrong priorities, and infused with corruption. Our national trade and tax policies encourage employers to seek offshore production and jobs, which is draining national wealth and risking national security. The nation's economic infrastructure is wearing out faster than we are repairing or replacing it. The social contract with America's working people is increasingly Darwinian and fails to provide tens of millions of citizens with health care, training, and pensions. America's largest, most technologically advanced corporations are leaving the United States, even as they are lobbying Congress to weaken the U.S. system of innovation upon which the creation of new jobs depends.

The federal income certainly does not balance its outgo. The massive federal debts imperil America's solvency and with that its economic and political sovereignty. Our highest federal officials' begging trips to China, Japan, and elsewhere in pursuit of enormous loans to finance federal deficits are a national indignity and highlight how dire the situation has become. The total public debt outstanding on July 4, 2009, exceeded $11.5 trillion—more than eleven times greater than in 1980. Soon the rest of the world will be unwilling to lend any more money to a nation whose people cannot control their government's spending.

As for putting Americans to work, more than 26 million workers who wanted a job could not find one in mid-2009. The consensus of many economists is that unemployment will be at double-digit levels until at least 2011.

The stimulus package proposed by President Obama and enacted by Congress in February 2009 is too little and too fundamentally misdirected to reignite the U.S. and global economies. While it is slowing the pace of decline, restoration of the economy will require stronger actions taken over a much longer term. For all its good intentions, the package comes from an outdated economic playbook and cannot bring order to our economic house by restoring U.S. fiscal soundness, putting massive numbers of people to work, or restoring self-sustaining, noninflationary growth.

American needs an audacious systemic change that will enable it to compete against state capitalism. This book recommends six game-changing actions that are within the political and fiscal capacity of this nation to undertake.

While the need for regulation of the financial sector is imperative, the bailout of the past year has done little more than recapitalized the gamblers and kept our financial oligarchs in power. As was said of the Bourbons of France, the bankers and their political allies seem to have neither forgotten nor learned anything. Wall Street today is fully capable of creating another worldwide economic meltdown.

When the next opportunity for financial reform comes, the priority should be reform first and bailouts second. U.S. regulators need to rid the financial industry of its gamblers, thieves, and incompetents; control the industry's excesses; and refocus back to the original purposes of safeguarding people's money and making prudent loans that will support a productive U.S. economy.

Because the American people are now the lenders of last resort for the financial industry, because they saved it from its own greed and incompetence, and because they are part owners, these are legitimate priorities the president and the Congress should enforce.

The national failure to match outgo with income is leading not only to an increasing foreign resistance to financing U.S. debt, but also to a growing unwillingness to accept payment in dollars. If the United States squanders the privilege of having its dollar as the world's reserve currency, another Great Depression is inevitable. President Obama and the U.S. Congress face no greater economic challenge than bringing the federal budget into balance quickly, regardless of the political and economic pain that will be felt in the United States.

The U.S. corporate and income tax systems are beyond repair and cannot produce the revenues needed to balance the federal budget and reduce the national debt. The demands for government services, moreover, are so deep that major, deficit-balancing cuts are unlikely. This book argues for scrapping the existing tax system and replacing it with a VAT, which will produce large revenues, eliminate most of the present tax evasion, and do it all at a lower cost and in a more equitable way than the current systems.

Another danger faced by the nation is the continued hollowing out of the U.S. industrial base, including portions that produce America's tools of war. The nation cannot balance its trade accounts and reignite the economy until it brings back its manufacturing base.

The idea that these manufacturing industries will never return or cannot return is simply self-serving nonsense put forth by the outsourcers and their propagandists. The producers should bring the work and jobs back to the United States, or domestic-based suppliers should be encouraged to take their places. Building a state-of-the-art U.S. manufacturing economy would be a quick way to reignite the economy.

Rebuilding the U.S. infrastructure, providing universal health care, guaranteeing every worker an adequate and portable pension plan, strengthening unemployment insurance, and providing education and job-training opportunities are elementary necessities for people in a functioning, flexible market economy. Any indignation about such investments should be because the United States failed to put them in place long ago.

Reciprocity is the golden rule of global trade, and a U.S. trade policy that adheres to strict reciprocity is another key to rebuilding the U.S. economy. The goal must be balanced U.S. trade accounts with exports counterbalancing imports.

Trade is business. The United States built its economy over two centuries by dealing with others as they were, not as it wished them to be. Market capitalism is America's way, just as other nations find that state capitalism or other approaches best fit their needs. U.S. leaders need to accept that as pragmatic wisdom and then move on to capturing the jobs and opportunities that global commerce offers.

America's future is ours to make. Thus, this book begins and ends with the same defining quote from President Barack Obama's inauguration:

> *We remain the most prosperous, powerful nation on earth. Our workers are no less productive than when this crisis began. Our minds are no less inventive, our goods and services no less needed than they were last week or last month or last year. Our capacity remains undiminished.*

But our time of standing pat, of protecting narrow interests and putting off unpleasant decisions—that time has surely passed. Starting today, we must pick ourselves up, dust ourselves off, and begin again the work of remaking America.

ACKNOWLEDGMENTS

This book evolved quickly from concept to manuscript because many people were generous with their time and contributions. Ashbel Green, my longtime editor and friend, offered numerous suggestions that are found throughout the book. Jeff Alexander, my editor at Vintage, has helped me shape the book in ways too numerous to mention, including meeting a tight schedule. The copy editors and support staff at Vintage are remarkably good, and I am a beneficiary of their skills and dedication to book publishing.

The support of John Davis, my friend and neighbor, who has gone through this book numerous times with editorial suggestions and recommendations, was invaluable, particularly as we were working on such a tight deadline. Allan Rexinger's insights after reading the various drafts were, as always, to the point and are greatly appreciated.

Dan Leckrone provided special insights on innovation, patents, and the battle between large and small-entity inventors. He is also a skilled editor, as chapter four, Innovation, illustrates.

Eamonn Fingleton, Jock Nash, and Kathi Dutilh read the manuscript in progress and offered helpful suggestions.

Because a few parts of this book are drawn from earlier works, the acknowledgments would be incomplete without thanking Gail Schwartz, Susan Walter, and Juyne Linger for all I have learned from them as coauthors on those previous books. Parts of the commentary on rescuing the U.S. auto industry came from an article that Kara Hopkins, executive editor of *The American Conservative*, invited me to write for the December 2008 edition. Her insights are reflected herein.

Bruce Stokes, Terence Stewart, and William Frymoyer contributed greatly to my education about trade and the value-added tax. Mark Blaxill and Ralph Eckardt generously shared materials about the prior actions of the Federal Trade Commission, and Kevin Rivette expanded my knowledge about the intricacies of the U.S. patent system.

Others helped me but prefer to remain anonymous. I will thank them individually.

Kay Casey Choate's counsel, support, and wonderful spirit are priceless. I dedicate this book to her.

APPENDIX

TABLE 1. THE (VAT) INDIRECT TAX DISTORTION TO U.S. TRADE, BY NATION
(Millions of Dollars)
(2007)

Country	2007 Indirect Tax Rate (%)	U.S. 2007 Exports	U.S. 2007 Imports	Assessment on U.S. Exports	Rebate to U.S. Imports	Total Distortion	% of Total
Afghanistan	3.5	473	75	16.6	2.6	19.2	0.005
Albania	20	33	10	6.6	1.9	8.5	0.002
Algeria	17	1,626	17,397	276.5	2,957.5	3,234.0	0.909
Angola	10	1,264	12,211	126.4	1,221.1	1,347.5	0.379
Argentina	21	5,115	4,258	1,074.1	894.2	1,968.3	0.554
Armenia	20	101	33	20.2	6.5	26.7	0.008
Australia	10	17,917	8,633	1,791.7	863.3	2,655.0	0.747
Austria	20	2,958	7,736	591.6	1,547.2	2,138.8	0.601
Azerbaijan	18	175	1,727	31.4	310.9	342.3	0.096
Bahamas*	7	2,423	394	169.6	0.0	169.6	0.048
Bangladesh	15	451	3,429	67.7	514.4	582.0	0.164
Barbados	15	418	38	62.7	5.7	68.4	0.019
Belarus	18	95	1,033	17.1	185.9	203.0	0.057
Belgium	21	22,977	15,270	4,825.2	3,206.7	8,031.9	2.259
Belize	10	228	87	22.8	8.7	31.5	0.009

Country	2007 Indirect Tax Rate (%)	U.S. 2007 Exports	U.S. 2007 Imports	Assessment on U.S. Exports	Rebate to U.S. Imports	Total Distortion	% of Total
Benin	18	280	5	50.5	0.9	51.4	0.014
Bhutan	17.5	2	1	0.4	0.1	0.6	0.000
Bolivia	13	263	334	34.1	43.4	77.5	0.022
Bosnia-Herzegovina	17	18	25	3.1	4.2	7.3	0.002
Botswana	10	52	187	5.2	18.7	24.0	0.007
Brazil	17.5	21,684	25,018	3,794.7	4,378.1	8,172.8	2.298
Bulgaria	20	296	425	59.3	85.1	144.3	0.041
Burkina Faso	18	32	1	5.8	0.3	6.1	0.002
Burma	12.5	8	0	1.1	0.0	1.1	0.000
Cambodia	10	138	2,464	13.8	246.4	260.1	0.073
Cameroon	19.25	131	307	25.3	59.0	84.4	0.024
Canada	7	213,119	312,505	14,918.3	21,875.3	36,793.6	10.347
Cape Verde	15	5	2	0.7	0.3	1.1	0.000
Cent. Afr. Rep.	18	20	3	3.5	0.5	4.1	0.001
Chad	18	71	2,238	12.8	402.9	415.7	0.117
Chile	19	7,610	8,969	1,445.9	1,704.2	3,150.1	0.886
China**	17	61,013	323,085	10,372.2	42,001.1	52,373.3	14.728
Colombia	16	7,884	9,251	1,261.5	1,480.2	2,741.7	0.771

Comoros	10	0	0	0.0	0.0	0.1	0.000
Congo (DROC)	18.7	110	206	20.6	38.6	59.2	0.017
Congo (ROC)	18	139	3,099	25.0	557.8	582.8	0.164
Costa Rica	13	4,224	3,916	549.2	509.0	1,058.2	0.298
Côte d'Ivoire	18	156	585	28.1	105.4	133.5	0.038
Croatia	22	239	332	52.5	73.1	125.6	0.035
Cyprus	15	156	17	23.3	2.5	25.8	0.007
Czech Republic	19	1,124	2,417	213.5	459.2	672.7	0.189
Denmark	25	2,653	6,109	663.2	1,527.2	2,190.3	0.616
Djibouti	28.2	58	4	16.4	1.3	17.6	0.005
Dominica Island	15	82	2	12.2	0.3	12.5	0.004
Dominican Republic	12	5,793	4,214	695.2	505.7	1,200.9	0.338
Ecuador	12	2,709	6,131	325.1	735.7	1,060.8	0.298
Egypt	10	5,311	2,380	531.1	238.0	769.1	0.216
El Salvador	13	2,210	2,044	287.2	265.7	553.0	0.156
Equatorial Guinea	15	234	1,683	35.2	252.4	287.6	0.081
Estonia	18	227	296	40.9	53.2	94.1	0.026
Ethiopia	15	166	88	24.9	13.2	38.1	0.011
Faeroe Islands	25	3	7	0.7	1.8	2.5	0.001
Fiji	12.5	28	153	3.5	19.1	22.6	0.006

Country	2007 Indirect Tax Rate (%)	U.S. 2007 Exports	U.S. 2007 Imports	Assessment on U.S. Exports	Rebate to U.S. Imports	Total Distortion	% of Total
Finland	22	2,731	5,290	600.8	1,163.7	1,764.5	0.496
France	19.6	25,784	41,237	5,053.7	8,082.4	13,136.1	3.694
Gabon	18	474	2,147	85.3	386.4	471.7	0.133
Gambia	15	19	0	2.9	0.0	2.9	0.001
Georgia	18	266	188	47.9	33.8	81.7	0.023
Germany	16	44,294	94,416	7,087.1	15,106.6	22,193.7	6.241
Ghana	12.5	404	199	50.5	24.8	75.3	0.021
Greece	19	2,058	1,197	390.9	227.5	618.4	0.174
Guatemala	12	3,872	3,031	464.7	363.8	828.5	0.233
Guinea	18	72	96	12.9	17.2	30.1	0.008
Guinea-Bissau	10	7	0	0.7	0.0	0.7	0.000
Haiti	10	696	488	69.6	48.8	118.4	0.033
Honduras	12	4,328	3,943	519.4	473.1	992.5	0.279
Hungary	20	1,112	2,799	222.5	559.7	782.2	0.220
Iceland	24.5	616	207	151.0	50.8	201.8	0.057
India	12.5	16,309	23,857	2,038.6	2,982.1	5,020.7	1.412
Indonesia	10	4,133	14,411	413.3	1,441.1	1,854.3	0.521
Ireland	21	8,427	30,292	1,769.6	6,361.3	8,130.9	2.287

Israel	15.5	9,940	20,817	1,540.7	3,226.6	4,767.4	1.341
Italy	20	12,538	35,020	2,507.5	7,004.1	9,511.6	2.675
Jamaica	15	2,237	685	335.5	102.8	438.3	0.123
Japan	5	58,096	144,928	2,904.8	7,246.4	10,151.2	2.855
Jordan	16	832	1,333	133.1	213.3	346.4	0.097
Kazakhstan	15	731	1,241	109.6	186.1	295.7	0.083
Kenya	16	576	326	92.2	52.2	144.4	0.041
Korea	10	33,012	45,368	3,301.2	4,536.8	7,838.0	2.204
Kyrgyzstan	20	47	2	9.4	0.3	9.8	0.003
Laos	10	13	20	1.3	2.0	3.3	0.001
Latvia	18	355	329	63.9	59.2	123.1	0.035
Lebanon	10	789	105	78.9	10.5	89.4	0.025
Lesotho	14	8	443	1.1	62.0	63.1	0.018
Liechtenstein	7.6	11	278	0.8	21.2	22.0	0.006
Lithuania	18	662	464	119.2	83.5	202.7	0.057
Luxembourg	15	972	527	145.8	79.1	224.9	0.063
Macedonia	18	30	73	5.5	13.1	18.6	0.005
Madagascar	20	32	338	6.4	67.6	73.9	0.021
Malawi	17.5	51	69	8.9	12.1	21.0	0.006
Malaysia	10	10,215	32,755	1,021.5	3,275.5	4,297.0	1.208

Country	2007 Indirect Tax Rate (%)	U.S. 2007 Exports	U.S. 2007 Imports	Assessment on U.S. Exports	Rebate to U.S. Imports	Total Distortion	% of Total
Mali	18	30	10	5.5	1.7	7.2	0.002
Malta	18	203	315	36.5	56.7	93.2	0.026
Mauretania	14	102	1	14.3	0.1	14.4	0.004
Mauritius	15	40	187	5.9	28.1	34.0	0.010
Mexico	15	119,381	210,159	17,907.2	31,523.8	49,431.0	13.901
Moldova	20	51	23	10.1	4.6	14.7	0.004
Mongolia	15	26	83	3.9	12.5	16.4	0.005
Montenegro	18	44	5	8.0	1.0	9.0	0.003
Morocco	20	1,334	626	266.8	125.2	391.9	0.110
Mozambique	17	114	5	19.3	0.9	20.2	0.006
Namibia	15	116	220	17.5	33.0	50.4	0.014
Nepal	13	27	90	3.5	11.7	15.2	0.004
Netherlands	19	30,536	19,260	5,801.8	3,659.3	9,461.1	2.661
New Zealand	12.5	2,681	3,093	335.2	386.7	721.8	0.203
Nicaragua	15	847	1,608	127.0	241.3	368.3	0.104
Niger	19	63	9	12.0	1.7	13.7	0.004
Nigeria*	5	2,689	32,525	134.4	0.0	134.4	0.038
Norway	25	2,920	7,244	729.9	1,810.9	2,540.8	0.715

Pakistan	15	2,013	3,578	301.9	536.6	838.5	0.236
Panama	5	3,492	361	174.6	18.1	192.7	0.054
Papua New Guinea	10	62	107	6.2	10.7	16.9	0.005
Paraguay	10	1,168	66	116.8	6.6	123.4	0.035
Peru	19	3,764	5,207	715.2	989.3	1,704.6	0.479
Philippines	12	7,336	9,397	880.3	1,127.7	2,008.0	0.565
Poland	22	3,011	2,211	662.5	486.5	1,149.0	0.323
Portugal	21	2,422	3,072	508.7	645.0	1,153.8	0.324
Romania	19	650	1,064	123.6	202.1	325.6	0.092
Russia	18	6,681	19,143	1,202.6	3,445.7	4,648.3	1.307
Rwanda	18	14	13	2.6	2.3	4.8	0.001
Samoa*	10	17	5	1.7	0.0	1.7	0.000
Senegal	18	151	19	27.1	3.4	30.5	0.009
Serbia	18	104	58	18.6	10.5	29.1	0.008
Singapore	5	23,577	19,080	1,178.8	954.0	2,132.9	0.600
Slovak Republic	19	657	1,561	124.9	296.5	421.5	0.119
Slovenia	20	278	488	55.6	97.6	153.2	0.043
South Africa	14	5,204	9,132	728.6	1,278.5	2,007.1	0.564
Spain	16	9,651	10,499	1,544.1	1,679.9	3,224.0	0.907
Sri Lanka	12.5	215	2,060	26.8	257.5	284.4	0.080

Country	2007 Indirect Tax Rate (%)	U.S. 2007 Exports	U.S. 2007 Imports	Assessment on U.S. Exports	Rebate to U.S. Imports	Total Distortion	% of Total
Sudan	10	67	7	6.7	0.7	7.4	0.002
Suriname*	10	296	129	29.6	0.0	29.6	0.008
Sweden	25	4,084	13,007	1,021.0	3,251.7	4,272.7	1.202
Switzerland	7.6	15,056	14,761	1,144.3	1,121.8	2,266.1	0.637
Taiwan	5	24,541	38,052	1,227.1	1,902.6	3,129.7	0.880
Tajikistan	20	52	0	10.4	0.1	10.5	0.003
Tanzania	20	172	46	34.4	9.2	43.6	0.012
Thailand	7	7,837	22,685	548.6	1,587.9	2,136.5	0.601
Togo	18	285	5	51.4	0.9	52.3	0.015
Tonga	15	13	5	2.0	0.8	2.8	0.001
Trinidad and Tobago	15	1,679	8,764	251.9	1,314.6	1,566.5	0.441
Tunisia	18	395	448	71.1	80.7	151.8	0.043
Turkey	18	6,443	4,616	1,159.7	830.8	1,990.5	0.560
Turkmenistan	15	183	219	27.5	32.9	60.4	0.017
Uganda	18	75	27	13.6	4.8	18.4	0.005
Ukraine	20	1,282	1,236	256.5	247.2	503.7	0.142
United Kingdom	17.5	45,436	56,873	7,951.2	9,952.7	17,904.0	5.035
Uruguay	23	542	492	124.6	113.2	237.8	0.067

Uzbekistan	20	87	165	17.5	33.0	50.4	0.014
Vanuatu	12.5	24	1	3.0	0.1	3.1	0.001
Venezuela	15	9,762	37,582	1,464.3	5,637.3	7,101.6	1.997
Vietnam	10	1,823	10,541	182.3	1,054.1	1,236.5	0.348
Zambia	17.5	67	49	11.8	8.5	20.3	0.006
Zimbabwe	15	104	71	15.5	10.7	26.3	0.007
Total		993,227	1,872,120	125,491	230,108	355,599	100.000
U.S. Trade with World		1,045,929	1,942,863				
% Trade Affected		94.96%	96.36%		Total Distortion:		
Avg Rate on U.S. Exports		12.63%			$356 Billion		
Avg Rate on U.S. Imports			12.29%				
Avg Unweighted Tax Rate		15.62%					

Source: Compiled and calculated by the Law Offices of Stewart and Stewart, Washington, D.C., August 2008.

Tax distortion figures are estimates for each country equal to the product of the country's standard indirect tax rate and the value of U.S. trade with that country. Lower or higher tax rates for individual products are not accounted for, nor is the fact that border assessments at the indirect tax rate are generally assessed on the U.S. export's landed duty-paid value rather than the FAS value. Where the tax rate for a particular year is not available for a country, the most recent available rate is used.

*Country does not zero-rate exports, and thus the rebate to U.S. imports is calculated at zero.

**China's export rebate is calculated at the 13% rebate rate that is more prevalent for exports rather than the standard 17% VAT rate assessed on most imports.

TABLE 2. SUMMARY DATA FOR COALITION PATENT FAIRNESS 14 PRINCIPAL CORPORATIONS, PLUS IBM

(Millions of Dollars)

CONSOLIDATED STATISTICS $MM

	13-Year Period (1996–2008)	Y1996
Net Sales or Revenues	$4,148,811.0	$176,849.2
Cost of Goods Sold	$2,243,175.3	$96,763.4
Gross Income	$1,886,530.7	$78,604.8
Gross Margin	45.5%	44.4%
Operating Income	$679,589.5	$26,841.3
Net Income	$491,973.1	$17,607.9

PATENT SUIT INFO

	13-Year Period (1996–2008)	Y1996
Patent Suit Settlement Amount (Millions of USD)	$3,955.3	$-
% of Revenue	0.10%	0.00%
% of Operating Income (Profits)	0.58%	0.00%
% of Net Income	0.80%	0.00%

RESEARCH & DEVELOPMENT

	13-Year Period (1996–2008)	Y1996
R&D Expenditure (Millions USD)	$335,176.4	$12,457.6
% of Revenue	8.1%	7.0%
% of Operating Income	49.3%	46.4%
% of Net Income	68.1%	70.8%

Y1997	Y1998	Y1999	Y2000	Y2001
$197,963.0	$219,693.1	$242,442.3	$275,439.2	$263,941.3
$105,049.8	$118,740.5	$129,668.2	$143,285.7	$142,818.0
$91,465.2	$99,458.6	$110,953.1	$130,188.6	$119,430.3
46.2%	45.3%	45.8%	47.3%	45.2%
$33,055.5	$33,918.4	$44,012.3	$51,284.9	$33,499.9
$22,265.5	$24,359.9	$32,724.5	$46,126.1	$19,553.8

Y1997	Y1998	Y1999	Y2000	Y2001
$-	$400.0	$(0.7)	$-	$14.0
0.00%	0.18%	0.00%	0.00%	0.01%
0.00%	1.18%	0.00%	0.00%	0.04%
0.00%	1.64%	0.00%	0.00%	0.07%

Y1997	Y1998	Y1999	Y2000	Y2001
$14,754.0	$16,844.4	$18,337.2	$22,895.0	$24,336.4
7.5%	7.7%	7.6%	8.3%	9.2%
44.6%	49.7%	41.7%	44.6%	72.6%
66.3%	69.1%	56.0%	49.6%	124.5%

(*continues*)

SUMMARY DATA FOR COALITION PATENT FAIRNESS 14 PRINCIPAL CORPORATIONS, PLUS IBM

(Millions of Dollars)

(*continued*)

CONSOLIDATED STATISTICS $MM

	Y2002	Y2003
Net Sales or Revenues	$276,757.2	$317,311.3
Cost of Goods Sold	$149,587.1	$173,203.7
Gross Income	$125,754.2	$142,858.6
Gross Margin	45.4%	45.0%
Operating Income	$30,685.2	$43,861.2
Net Income	$17,109.7	$30,739.6

PATENT SUIT INFO

	Y2002	Y2003
Patent Suit Settlement Amount (Millions of USD)	$475.0	$348.0
% of Revenue	0.17%	0.11%
% of Operating Income (Profits)	1.55%	0.79%
% of Net Income	2.78%	1.13%

RESEARCH & DEVELOPMENT

	Y2002	Y2003
R&D Expenditure (Millions USD)	$25,674.1	$27,497.4
% of Revenue	9.3%	8.7%
% of Operating Income	83.7%	62.7%
% of Net Income	150.1%	89.5%

Y2004	Y2005	Y2006	Y2007	Y2008
$359,060.4	$390,423.7	$418,428.1	$475,746.2	$534,755.9
$196,529.6	$210,626.3	$224,092.7	$263,646.3	$289,164.0
$161,484.8	$178,706.5	$193,153.5	$210,465.8	$244,006.9
45.0%	45.8%	46.2%	44.2%	45.6%
$56,623.1	$67,663.3	$71,527.4	$84,257.6	$102,359.1
$40,487.5	$49,253.2	$55,023.6	$64,477.1	$72,244.5

Y2004	Y2005	Y2006	Y2007	Y2008
$1,057.5	$660.0	$445.5	$65.0	$491.0
0.29%	0.17%	0.11%	0.01%	0.09%
1.87%	0.98%	0.62%	0.08%	0.48%
2.61%	1.34%	0.81%	0.10%	0.68%

Y2004	Y2005	Y2006	Y2007	Y2008
$30,276.8	$29,593.5	$34,179.5	$37,368.4	$40,962.1
8.4%	7.6%	8.2%	7.9%	7.7%
53.5%	43.7%	47.8%	44.4%	40.0%
74.8%	60.1%	62.1%	58.0%	56.7%

TABLE 3. CPF, PLUS IBM, ALL COURTS AS PLAINTIFFS IN PATENT INFRINGEMENT CASES (1996–2008)

All Courts as Plaintiffs	1996	1997	1998	1999	2000	2001	2002	2003	2004	2005	2006	2007	2008	Total
Apple	1	2	0	0	1	0	0	1	1	2	5	0	2	15
Cisco	0	0	1	0	0	2	0	2	2	3	1	10	0	21
Dell	0	0	0	0	0	0	0	0	1	2	1	0	0	4
HP	0	2	5	6	2	5	2	3	8	7	2	3	4	49
Intel	0	4	0	3	1	3	5	1	1	7	3	0	2	30
Micron	1	1	2	1	2	0	1	0	2	1	1	0	0	12
Oracle	0	0	0	0	0	0	0	1	2	0	3	0	1	7
Palm	0	0	0	0	0	0	0	0	0	0	0	0	0	0
RIM	0	0	0	0	0	1	3	2	0	2	0	5	4	17
Symantec	0	0	0	0	0	0	2	0	1	0	0	0	0	3
SAP	0	0	0	1	0	0	0	0	0	0	0	3	1	5
Google	0	0	0	0	0	0	0	0	4	1	0	0	2	7
Autodesk	0	0	0	0	1	0	0	0	0	0	0	0	0	1
Microsoft	0	1	1	1	1	0	2	1	0	4	2	4	2	19
IBM	0	0	0	0	1	1	0	0	2	2	3	0	0	9
Total	2	10	9	12	9	12	15	11	24	31	21	25	18	199

Rocket Docket as Plaintiffs	1996	1997	1998	1999	2000	2001	2002	2003	2004	2005	2006	2007	2008	Total
Apple	0	1	0	0	0	0	0	1	1	0	4	0	1	8
Cisco	0	0	0	0	0	1	0	2	0	2	1	8	0	14
Dell	0	0	0	0	0	0	0	0	1	0	1	0	0	2
HP	0	0	0	1	0	0	0	0	4	2	1	3	0	11
Intel	0	1	0	0	1	2	0	1	0	5	3	0	1	14
Micron	0	0	0	1	1	0	0	0	2	1	0	0	0	5
Oracle	0	0	0	0	0	0	0	0	1	0	1	0	0	2
Palm	0	0	0	0	0	0	0	0	0	0	0	0	0	0
RIM	0	0	0	0	0	1	2	0	0	0	0	4	0	7
Symantec	0	0	0	0	0	0	0	0	1	0	0	0	0	1
SAP	0	0	0	1	0	0	0	0	0	0	0	0	0	1
Google	0	0	0	0	0	0	0	0	0	0	0	0	0	0
Autodesk	0	0	0	0	0	0	0	0	0	0	0	0	0	0
Microsoft	0	0	0	0	0	0	0	0	0	0	1	2	0	3
IBM	0	0	0	0	1	1	0	0	2	1	2	0	0	7
Total	0	2	0	3	3	5	2	4	12	11	14	17	2	75

TABLE 4. CPF, PLUS IBM, ALL COURTS AS DEFENDANTS IN PATENT INFRINGEMENT CASES (1996–2008)

All Courts as Defendants	1996	1997	1998	1999	2000	2001	2002	2003	2004	2005	2006	2007	2008	Total
Apple	1	0	1	1	1	6	1	5	9	8	5	15	11	64
Cisco	2	0	2	3	3	3	5	3	5	4	1	13	6	50
Dell	0	1	1	0	2	3	5	8	11	11	10	15	8	75
HP	2	5	6	8	7	6	9	1	11	8	8	15	14	100
Intel	3	3	5	1	7	1	6	2	11	10	6	3	5	63
Micron	0	0	3	1	1	2	4	0	2	2	4	0	1	20
Oracle	0	0	0	0	2	0	1	2	5	3	6	3	7	29
Palm	0	0	0	0	1	0	0	2	0	3	5	5	10	26
RIM	0	0	0	1	0	0	1	2	0	7	3	6	12	32
Symantec	0	3	1	2	0	0	1	1	1	0	3	1	2	15
SAP	0	0	0	0	0	0	0	0	0	2	6	10	3	21
Google	0	0	0	0	0	0	2	0	4	1	4	15	9	35
Autodesk	1	0	0	0	0	0	0	0	1	0	3	0	0	5
Microsoft	1	2	4	10	7	4	14	14	16	9	17	26	7	131
IBM	3	3	2	5	3	2	6	5	5	8	3	14	5	64
Total	13	17	25	32	34	27	55	45	81	76	84	141	100	730

Rocket Docket as Defendants	1996	1997	1998	1999	2000	2001	2002	2003	2004	2005	2006	2007	2008	Total
Apple	0	0	1	0	0	4	0	2	3	1	2	11	6	30
Cisco	0	0	1	0	0	0	1	1	2	3	0	9	6	23
Dell	0	0	1	0	1	1	2	3	4	3	8	11	5	39
HP	2	1	0	0	1	1	3	1	6	3	5	11	10	44
Intel	0	0	1	0	2	0	1	1	4	3	3	3	3	21
Micron	0	0	2	1	0	0	0	0	1	2	1	0	0	7
Oracle	0	0	0	0	0	0	0	1	1	2	5	2	6	17
Palm	0	0	0	0	1	0	0	1	0	1	4	3	8	18
RIM	0	0	0	1	0	0	0	2	0	4	3	5	9	24
Symantec	0	0	1	0	0	0	0	0	1	0	1	1	0	4
SAP	0	0	0	0	0	0	0	0	0	2	6	9	2	19
Google	0	0	0	0	0	0	0	0	1	0	2	10	7	20
Autodesk	0	0	0	0	0	0	0	0	1	0	3	0	0	4
Microsoft	0	1	0	0	0	2	2	1	4	6	11	18	4	49
IBM	0	3	0	0	1	1	3	3	3	3	2	12	1	32
Total	2	5	7	2	6	9	12	16	31	33	56	105	67	351

TABLE 5. CPF, PLUS IBM, ALL COURTS AS DEFENDANTS OR PLAINTIFFS IN ANTITRUST ACTIONS (1996–2008)

All Courts as Defendants	1996	1997	1998	1999	2000	2001	2002	2003	2004	2005	2006	2007	2008	2009	Total
Apple	0	1	1	0	0	0	0	0	0	2	1	4	0	0	9
Cisco	0	0	0	0	0	2	0	1	0	0	0	0	1	0	4
Dell	0	0	0	1	2	0	0	1	1	0	0	0	0	0	5
HP	0	0	0	0	0	0	0	0	0	0	0	0	0	0	0
Intel	0	0	0	1	0	0	0	0	0	70	30	3	10	0	114
Micron	0	0	0	0	1	0	18	5	5	25	59	118	1	0	232
Oracle	0	0	0	0	0	0	0	1	1	0	0	0	0	0	2
Palm	0	0	0	0	0	0	0	0	0	0	0	0	0	0	0
RIM	0	0	0	0	0	0	0	0	0	0	0	0	1	0	1
Symantec	0	0	0	0	0	0	0	0	0	0	0	0	0	0	0
SAP	0	0	0	0	0	0	0	0	0	0	0	0	0	0	0
Google	0	0	0	0	0	0	0	0	0	0	2	0	0	1	3
Autodesk	0	0	0	0	0	0	0	0	0	0	0	0	0	0	0
Microsoft	1	3	4	34	103	4	36	42	7	11	3	0	0	1	249
IBM	0	1	0	2	3	0	2	0	0	1	11	4	0	0	24
Total	1	5	5	38	109	6	56	50	14	109	106	129	13	2	641

All Courts as Plaintiffs	1996	1997	1998	1999	2000	2001	2002	2003	2004	2005	2006	2007	2008	2009	Total
Apple	0	0	0	0	0	0	0	0	0	0	0	0	0	0	0
Cisco	0	0	0	0	0	0	0	0	0	0	0	0	0	0	0
Dell	0	0	0	0	0	0	0	0	0	0	0	0	0	0	0
HP	0	0	0	0	0	0	0	0	0	0	0	0	0	0	0
Intel	0	0	0	0	0	0	0	0	0	0	0	0	0	0	0
Micron	0	0	0	0	1	0	0	0	0	0	0	0	0	0	1
Oracle	0	0	0	0	0	0	0	0	0	0	0	0	0	0	0
Palm	0	0	0	0	0	0	0	0	0	0	0	0	0	0	0
RIM	0	0	0	0	0	0	0	0	0	0	0	0	0	0	0
Symantec	0	0	0	0	0	0	0	0	0	0	0	0	0	0	0
SAP	0	0	0	0	0	0	0	0	0	0	0	0	0	0	0
Google	0	0	0	0	0	0	0	0	0	0	0	0	0	0	0
Autodesk	0	0	0	0	0	0	0	0	0	0	0	0	0	0	0
Microsoft	0	0	0	0	0	0	0	0	0	0	0	0	0	0	0
IBM	0	0	0	0	0	0	0	0	0	0	0	0	0	0	0
Total	0	0	0	0	1	0	0	0	0	0	0	0	0	0	1

TABLE 6: FISCAL STIMULUS BANG PER BUCK

Stimulus	**Return per Dollar Spent**
TAX CUTS	
Nonrefundable Lump-Sum Tax Rebate	1.01
Refundable Lump-Sum Tax Rebate	1.22
Temporary Tax Cuts	
Payroll Tax Holiday	1.28
Across-the-Board Tax Cut	1.03
Accelerated Depreciation	0.25
Loss Carryback	0.19
Housing Tax Credit	0.90
Permanent Tax Cuts	
Extend Alternative Minimum Tax Patch	0.49
Make Bush Income Tax Cuts Permanent	0.31
Make Dividend and Capital Gains Tax Cuts Permanent	0.38
Cut in Corporate Tax Rate	0.30
SPENDING INCREASES	
Extending Unemployment Insurance Benefits	1.63
Temporary Increase in Food Stamps	1.73
General Aid to State Governments	1.38
Increased Infrastructure Spending	1.59

Note: The bang for the buck is estimated by the one-year $ change in GDP for a given $ reduction in federal tax revenue or increase in spending.

Source: Mark Zandi, "Expand the Housing Tax Credit," Moody's Economy.com, June 16, 2009.

NOTES

PROLOGUE

xi Economists Barry: Barry Eichengreen and Kevin H. O'Rourke, "A Tale of Two Depressions II," http://www.voxeu.org/index.php?q=node/3421 (accessed July 29, 2009).

xiv By April 2009: Rasmussen Reports, http://www.rasmussenreports.com/public_content/politics/general_politics/just_53_say_capitalism_better_than_socialism (accessed June 6, 2009).

CHAPTER ONE: MONEY

3 By April: Peter S. Goodman and Jack Healy, "Housing Market Being Pounded by New Wave of Foreclosures," *New York Times,* May 25, 2009; Jack Healy, "More Homeowners Facing Foreclosure," *New York Times,* May 29, 2009.

3 Despite federal commitments: "Adding Up the Government's Total Bailout Tab," *New York Times,* February 4, 2009; Ben S. Bernanke, "The Crisis and the Policy Response" (Stamp Lecture, London School of Economics, London, England, January 13, 2009).

5 Walter Wriston: Ann Crittenden, "In for a Dime, In for a Dollar," *New York Times,* July 8, 1984.

6 A Washington Post Book: Roger J. Vaughan and Edward Hill, *Banking on the Brink* (Washington Post Book Company, 1992).

6 Despite the rhetoric: Kevin Phillips, *American Theocracy* (New York, Viking: 2006), 287.

7 Misfeasance: Charles P. Kindleberger, *Manias, Panics, and Crashes: A History of Financial Crises,* Fourth Edition, (New York, John Wiley & Sons, Inc.: 2000), 7. Kindleberger observed that these were the historic characteristics of a time of swindles and defalcations. This era fits the description.

8 Between 1981: Bureau of Labor Statistics, "Employees on Nonfarm Payrolls by Major Industry Sector, 1959 to Date," U.S. Department of Labor, http://www.bls.gov/news.release/empsit.t14.htm (accessed June 23, 2009).

9 "And the banks": Glenn Greenwald, "Top Senate Democrat: Bankers 'own'

the U.S. Congress," *Salon*, April 30, 2009, http://www.salon.com/opinion/greenwald/2009/04/30/ownership/.

9 In March 2009: Robert Weissman and James Donahue, *Sold Out: How Wall Street and Washington Betrayed America*, http://www.wallstreetwatch.org/reports/sold_out.pdf, 6–13.

10 While advising: Richard A. McCormack, "Multi-millionaires Populate Obama's Economic Team: None Need Worry About Losing Their Jobs," *Manufacturing & Technology News*, May 18, 2009. The author replicates the Public Financial Disclosure Report, 2008, filed by this individual with the U.S. Office of Government Ethics.

10 His chief of staff: "Mark Patterson," Who Runs Gov, http://www.whorunsgov.com/Profiles/Mark_Patterson.

10 the resulting vacuum: Peter H. Stone, "Lobbyist Paese Moves to Goldman Sachs," *National Journal*, April 29, 2009, http://undertheinfluence.nationaljournal.com/2009/04/lobbyist-pease-moves-to-goldma.php.

10 After leaving office: Julie Scuderi, "Gore's $5 Billion Hedge Fund Restricts New Investors," http://www.hedgeco.net/03/2008gores-5-billion-hedge-fund-restricts-new-investors.html.

10 The giant: Reuters, "Alan Greenspan to Join Paulson & Co. Inc. Advisory Board," January 15, 2008.

11 This fund: "Alternatives Manager of the Year—Paulson & Co.," *Money Management Letter*, May 30, 2009, http://www.moneymanagementletter.com.

11 Henry Paulson: Leo W. Gerard, president of the United Steelworkers Union, letter to Henry M. Paulson Jr., secretary of the treasury, October 28, 2008.

11 The deal: Marco Trbovich, "Paulson Cuts Goldman Sachs a Sweetheart Deal," *Huffington Post*, October 29, 2008, http://www.huffingtonpost.com/marco-trbovich/paulson-cuts-goldman-sach_b_138862.html.

12 President George W. Bush's: "Joshua B. Bolten," *New York Times*, May 30, 2009, http://topics.nytimes.com/top/reference/timestopics/people/b/joshua_b_bolten/index.html.

12 He served: "Biography: Robert B. Zoellick," World Bank, http://web.worldbank.org/WBSITE/EXTERNAL/EXTABOUTUS/ORGANIZATION/EXTPRESIDENT2007/0,,contentMDK:21394208~menuPK:64822289~pagePK:64821878~piPK:64821912~theSitePK:3916065,00.html (accessed May 30, 2009).

12 He was: Lindsay Renick Mayer, "Obama's Pick for Chief of Staff Tops Recipients of Wall Street Money," Capital Eye Blog, November 5, 2008, http://www.opensecrets.org/news/2008/11/obamas-pick-for-chief-of-staff.html (accessed May 30, 2009).

13 As part of a: Dennis Bernstein, "Obama's Campaign Finance Chair Has Links to Subprime Debacle," *Asian Week*, http://amok.asianweek.com/

2008/02/28/obamas-campaign-finance-chair-has-links-to-subprime-debacle/ (accessed May 30, 2009).

14 In the crash: Conrad Black, *Roosevelt: Champion of Freedom* (Cambridge, MA: Public Affairs, 2003).

14 Between 1934: Federal Deposit Insurance Corporation, *A Brief History of Deposit Insurance in the United States,* September 1998, http://www.fdic.gov/bank/historical/brief/brhist.pdf (accessed May 30, 2009).

14 They finally got: U.S. Senate Committee on Banking, Housing, and Urban Affairs, "Information Regarding the Gramm-Leach-Bliley Act of 1999," http://banking.senate.gov/conf/ (accessed May 30, 2009).

15 The Heritage: Ronald D. Utt, "Subprime Mortgage Problems: A Quick Tour Through the Rubble," The Heritage Foundation, April 3, 2008, http://www.heritage.org/Research/Economy/wm1881.cfm, 1–2.

15 The *New York Times:* "Derivatives," *New York Times,* May 31, 2009.

16 Treasury Secretary Rubin: Manuel Roig-Franzia, "Credit Crisis Cassandra," *Washington Post,* May 26, 2009.

17 The Houston-based: "Enron Corp. Bankruptcy Information," U.S. Bankruptcy Court, Southern District of New York, http://www.nysb.uscourts.gov/enron.html (accessed May 30, 2009).

17 AIG's liability: Gretchen Morgenson, "AIG, Where Taxpayers' Dollars Go to Die," *New York Times,* March 8, 2009.

17 Then the risk: Carrick Mollenkamp, Serena Ng, Liam Pleven, and Randall Smith, "Behind AIG's Fall, Risk Models Failed to Pass Real-World Test," *New York Times,* October 31, 2008.

18 The SEC: Stephen Labaton, "Agency's '04 Rule Let Banks Pile Up New Debt," *New York Times,* October 3, 2008.

18 By December 2008: Federal Deposit Insurance Corporation, *FDIC—Statistics on Depository Institutions Report* (Washington, D.C., March 2005).

18 Eric Dinallo: "Following the A.I.G. Money," editorial, *New York Times,* March 14, 2009.

18 Collectively: Comptroller of the Currency, Administrator of National Banks, *OCC's Quarterly Report on Bank Trading and Derivatives Activities, Third Quarter 2008* (Washington, D.C., January 2009), tables 1–12.

19 In March 2008, "Credit Crisis—the Essentials," *New York Times,* March 18, 2009.

19 On September 14: Ibid.

19 Six days later: Associated Press, "FBI Investigating Potential Fraud by Fannie Mae, Freddie Mac, Lehman, AIG," September 23, 2008.

20 In a move: Associated Press, "Tax Ruling May Have Aided Wells' Bid for Wachovia," October 6, 2008.

21 The bailout alternative: William M. Isaac, "A Better Way to Aid Banks," *Washington Post,* September 27, 2009.

24 This allowed: FDIC, Notice, "Temporary Liquidity Guarantee Program," *Federal Register* 73, no. 217 (November 7, 2008).
25 Both Joseph: Joseph E. Stiglitz, "Obama's Ersatz Capitalism," *New York Times,* April 1, 2009.
25 Their criticism: Paul Krugman, "Despair over Financial Policy," *New York Times,* March 21, 2009.
26 Another is: Andrew Rosenfield, "How to Clean a Dirty Bank," *New York Times,* April 6, 2009.
28 Led by Ferdinand: Ferdinand Pecora, *Wall Street Under Oath: The Story of Our Modern Money Changers* (New York: Augustus M. Kelley, 1968), 3–20.
28 The *New York Times:* Gretchen Morgenson and Don Van Natta Jr., "Even in Crisis, Banks Dig In for Fight Against Rules," *New York Times,* June 1, 2009.
30 In October 2004: "Statement of Chris Swecker," assistant director, Criminal Investigative Division, Federal Bureau of Investigation, before the House Financial Services Subcommittee on Housing and Community Opportunity, October 7, 2004, http://www.house.gov/financialservices/media/pdf/100704cs.pdf.
31 If fraudulent: Ibid.
31 It received: Federal Bureau of Investigation, *2007 Mortgage Fraud Report* (Washington D.C., 2008), 2–18; Federal Bureau of Investigation, "Mortgage Fraud—Just the Facts," 2009, http://www.fbi.gov/hq/mortgage_fraud.htm (accessed May 31, 2009).
31 Even with a reduced: FBI, "Mortgage Fraud—Just the Facts."
32 According to: "Transcript of Interview with William K. Black," *Bill Moyers Journal,* aired April 3, 2009, http://www.pbs.org/moyers/journal/04032009/transcript1.html (accessed May 31, 2009).
33 One of a board's: Carter McNamara, "Overview of Roles and Responsibilities of Corporate Board of Directors," Free Management Library, http://managementhelp.org/boards/brdrspon.htm (accessed May 31, 2009).
38 But Isaac says: William M. Isaac, "Bank Nationalization Isn't the Answer," *Wall Street Journal,* February 14, 2009.
41 Specifically: "Institutional Investors: Holdings of Corporate Equities in the U.S. by Type of Institution," Facts & Figures, NYSE Euronext, http://www.nyxdata.com/nysedata/Default.aspx?tabid=115 (accessed May 31, 2009).
42 In 1960: "NYSE Overview Statistics," Ibid.
42 But as of February 2009: "NYSE Group Turnover," Ibid.

CHAPTER TWO: TAXES

45 Now it is: "Table 7.1—Federal Debt at the End of Year: 1940–2013," *Historical Tables, Budget of the United States Government, Fiscal Year 2009* (Washington, D.C.: GPO), 127–28.

46 While President: Ibid.

46 Now the Congressional: Andrew Taylor, "Obama Budget Could Bring $9.2 Trillion in Deficits," *New York Times,* March 20, 2009.

46 Altogether, those: Department of the Treasury/Federal Reserve Board, "Major Foreign Holders of Treasury Securities," June 27, 2009, http://treas.gov/tic/mfh.txt.

47 Grover Norquist: Robert Dreyfuss, "Grover Norquist: 'Field Marshal' of the Bush Plan," *Nation,* April 26, 2001.

48 Specifically, Norquist's: "What Is the Taxpayer Protection Pledge?" Americans for Tax Reform, http://www.atr.org/taxpayer-protection-pledge-a2882 (accessed March 31, 2009).

52 Then the tax: "Brief History of IRS," Internal Revenue Service, United States Department of the Treasury, http://www.irs.gov/irs/article/0,,id=149200,00.html (accessed May 31, 2009).

52 Now the U.S.: "U.S. Tax Code On-Line," Fourmilab, http://www.fourmilab.ch/uscode/26usc/ (accessed May 31, 2009).

52 The administrative costs: U.S. Government Accountability Office, *Summary of Estimates of the Costs of the Federal Tax System* (Washington, D.C., August 2005).

52 The Cato Institute: Chris Edwards, "10 Outrageous Facts About the Income Tax," Cato Institute, April 15, 2003, http://www.cato.org/pub_display.php?pub_id=3063.

52 The complexity: Treasury Inspector General for Tax Administration, *Taxpayer Experience at the Taxpayer Assistance Centers Could Be Improved,* U.S. Department of the Treasury (Washington, D.C., September 2004), 1.

52 The IRS estimates: GAO, *Value-Added Taxes: Lessons Learned from Other Countries on Compliance Risks, Administrative Costs, Compliance Burden, and Transition,* April 2008, GAO-08-566, 1.

52 In September 2008: "$100 Billion the Country Could Use," *New York Times,* March 13, 2009.

53 Almost a century: Woodrow Wilson, *The New Freedom* (New York: Doubleday, Page, 1913), 139–40.

53 In 2009: Center for Responsive Politics, http://www.opensecrets.org/lobby/issuesum.php?lname=Taxes&year=2008 (accessed June 27, 2009).

54 In testimony: GAO, *Business Tax Reform: Simplification and Increased Uniformity of Taxation Would Yield Benefits,* Statement of David M. Walker, comptroller general of the United States, before the Committee on Finance, U.S. Senate, September 20, 2006, GAO-06-113I.

56 A 2008 report: GAO, *Value-Added Taxes,* 6–8.
59 Today a VAT: See calculations in appendix, table 1.
60 The same thing: Pat Choate, *Dangerous Business* (New York: Alfred A. Knopf, 2008), 187–89.
60 In 1998: Ibid.
61 A panel formed: Terence P. Stewart, "The Costs of Differential Tax Treatment," Law Offices of Stewart and Stewart (Washington, D.C., January 2007).
62 The flat tax: "Tax Reform: Flat Tax," About.com: US Government Info, March 13, 1998, http://usgovinfo.about.com/library/weekly/aa031398.htm (accessed May 31, 2009).
62 The leading alternative: "Tax Reform: National Retail Sales Tax Act," About.com: US Government Info, March 20, 1998, http://usgovinfo.about.com/library/weekly/aa032098.htm (accessed May 31, 2009).
63 The General Accountability Office: GAO, *Value-Added Taxes,* 4.
63 An analysis: Scott A. Hodge, "Tax Reform: Flat Tax or Fair Tax?" Tax Foundation, August 20, 2007, http://www.taxfoundation.org.news/show/22562.html.

CHAPTER THREE: TRADE

66 "A chance": "Emerging Markets Offer Golden Opportunity," *Nikkei Electronics Asia,* April 2009, http://techon.nikkeibp.co.jp/article/HONSHI/20090326/167808/ (accessed June 1, 2009).
66 The *Financial Times:* Martin Wolf, "The Brave New World of State Capitalism," *Financial Times,* October 17, 2007.
69 China is now: Choate, *Dangerous Business,* 28.
70 The Chinese government: "China Tightens Control Over Key State-Owned Industries," *China Times,* December 22, 2006.
70 One of these nine: "The State Council," Chinese Government's Official Web Portal, http://english.gov.cn/2008-03/16/content_921792.htm.
70 All have: Ibid.
71 In 2002: "SASAC's Responsibilities & Targets," *People's Daily,* May 22, 2003.
71 The chairman is: Li Rongrong, curriculum vitae, SASAC, http://www.sasac.gov.cn/n2963340/n2963378/2969259.html (accessed June 4, 2007).
71 At the first: "SASAC's Responsibilities & Targets."
72 In 2006: Peter Navarro, *Report of the China Price Project,* Merage School of Business, University of California-Irvine, 2006.
72 On a 100-point scale: Ibid., 17.
72 Navarro calculates: Ibid.
72 This contributes: Ibid.
73 Navarro calculates: Ibid.
73 Foreign companies: Terence P. Stewart, Esq., "China's Industrial Subsi-

dies Study: High Technology," Trade Lawyers Advisory Group LLC, 2007, http://www.uscc.gov/researchpapers/2008/TLAG%20Study%20-%20China's%20Industrial%20Subsidies%20High%20Technology.pdf (accessed June 27, 2009).

73 Overall, Professor: *Report of the China Price Project,* 17.

73 Navarro estimates: Ibid.

73 Navarro concludes: Ibid.

74 Navarro, taking: Ibid., 16.

74 Even then: Ibid., 17.

74 In 2008: "Trade in Goods (Imports, Exports and Trade Balance) with China," Foreign Trade Statistics, U.S. Census Bureau, http://www.census.gov/foreign-trade/balance/c5700.html#questions (accessed June 17, 2009).

74 Paul Otellini: Xinhua, "Intel Announces a $2.5 Billion Chip Project in China," March 23, 2007.

75 Overall, the United States: "ATP by Country" and "Country by ATP," Country and Product Trade Data, Foreign Trade Statistics, U.S. Census Bureau, http://www.census.gov/foreign-trade/statistics/country/index.html (accessed June 17, 2009).

77 Also, Bank of America: Cathy Chan and Adrian Cox, "China Gambit Paying Off for Goldman Sachs," *International Herald Tribune,* October 24, 2006.

78 This deindustrialization: "U.S. Trade in Goods and Services: Balance of Payments (BOP) Basis," U.S. Census Bureau, June 10, 2009, http://www.census.gov/foreign-trade/statistics/historical/gands.pdf.

83 The two nations: Margaret Thatcher, "The Language of Liberty" (speech to the English Speaking Union, New York, December 7, 1999).

83 This really was: Moisés Naím, "Washington Consensus or Washington Confusion?" *Foreign Policy,* spring 2000, 91.

85 On a visit: Anthony Failoa and Mary Jordan, "Developing Nations Set to Get More Say," *Washington Post,* March 31, 2009.

87 It is possible: Pat Choate and Juyne Linger: "Tailored Trade: Dealing with the World as It Is," *Harvard Business Review,* January–February 1988.

88 Between 1976: "U.S. Trade in Goods and Services."

88 The overwhelming majority: "Real Exports, Imports, and Balance of Goods, Petroleum and Non-Petroleum End-Use Commodity Category Totals," Foreign Trade Statistics, U.S. Census Bureau, http://www.census.gov/foreign-trade/Press-Release/current_press_release/exh11.pdf (accessed June 1, 2009).

89 The 547-page: Office of the United States Trade Representative, *2009 National Trade Estimate Report on Foreign Trade Barriers,* http://www.ustr.gov/sites/default/files/uploads/reports/2009/NTE/asset_upload_file405_15451.pdf.

91 Of the world's: Calculated from data provided in *The World Factbook,* Central Intelligence Agency, https://www.cia.gov/library/publications/the-world-factbook/index.html.

92 Multilateral negotiations: Choate and Linger, "Tailored Trade."

94 In 2008: "U.S. Data for Given Trade Partners in Rank Order of U.S. Goods Exports," Office of the United States Trade Representative, http://www.ustr.gov/sites/default/files/uploads/reports/2007/NTE/asset_upload_file670_10924.pdf (accessed June 1, 2009).

96 Though Japan: *Motor Vehicle Statistics of Japan* (Tokyo: Japan Automobile Manufacturers Association, 2008).

97 Canada and: "Top Trading Partners—Total Trade, Exports & Imports," Foreign Trade Statistics, U.S. Census Bureau, http://www.census.gov/foreign-trade/statistics/highlights/top/index.html.

97 Mexican importers: USTR, *2009 National Trade Estimate Report,* 335–42.

99 According to: Choate, *Dangerous Business,* 159–64.

102 "The system is": Ibid., 162–63.

CHAPTER FOUR: INNOVATION

108 The nation is: *The World Factbook,* Germany.

109 This nation is: *The World Factbook,* Japan.

109 The United States: Pat Choate, "The Global Publication of U.S. Patent Applications," Trade Lawyers Advisory Group, 2007.

109 The Small Business: Anthony Breitzman, Ph.D., and Diana Hicks, Ph.D., *An Analysis of Small Business Patents by Industry and Firm Size,* Small Business Research Summary, SBA Office of Advocacy, November 2008, http://www.sba.gov/advo/research/rs335tot.pdf.

109 in the twentieth: Len S. Smith, "Promoting the Progress of Science and America's Small Entity Inventors: Inventing an Improved U.S. Patent Application Publication Provision Out of the Prior Art," *Washington University Law Review* 77: 604.

109 Equally significant: Ibid.

110 According to: William J. Baumol, "Small Firms: Why Market-Driven Innovation Can't Get Along Without Them," SBA Office of Advocacy, http://www.sba.gov/advo/research/sbe_05_ch08.pdf (accessed June 2, 2009).

110 "Innovation is": Pat Choate, *Hot Property* (New York: Alfred A. Knopf, 2005), 241.

112 The revolutionaries': Ibid., 24–26.

113 In their book: Mark Blaxill and Ralph Eckardt, *The Invisible Edge: Taking Your Strategy to the Next Level Using Intellectual Property* (New York: Portfolio, 2009), 227–37.

115 The key provision: F. M. Scherer, "Technological Innovation and

Monopolization" (working paper, John F. Kennedy School of Government, Harvard University, October 2007), 31.

116 The amazing: F. M. Scherer, *Innovation and Growth: Schumpeterian Perspectives,* MIT Press Classics (Cambridge, MA: MIT Press, 1989), 210–12.

116 The *Wall Street:* Editorial, *Wall Street Journal,* January 27, 1956, quoted by F. M. Scherer, "The Political Economy of Patent Policy Reform in the United States" (working paper, John F. Kennedy School of Government, Harvard University, October 2007), 5.

117 Members: Scherer, *Innovation and Growth,* 5.

118 They obtained: Choate, *Hot Property,* 143.

120 In 1989: Pat Choate, *Agents of Influence* (New York: Alfred A. Knopf, 1990), 122.

120 Brown's first: Pat Choate, unpublished manuscript, 1999.

122 To no one's: "Workload Tables," *Annual Report,* U.S. Patent and Trademark Office, 2008.

124 In the summer: "Japan's System of Registering Intellectual Property Now Obsolete," *Yomiuri Shimbun,* July 1, 2005.

125 Today the: "Workload Tables."

125 The three top: *Report—Task Force on Industrial Competitiveness and Intellectual Property Policy,* Ministry of Economy, Trade and Industry (Tokyo, June 5, 2002), 3.

126 In October 2003: U.S. Federal Trade Commission, *To Promote Innovation: The Proper Balance of Competition and Patent Law and Policy* (Washington, D.C., October 2003).

133 An example is: Maureen O'Gara, "Microsoft Suffers Setback in Avistar Patent Challenge," CRM, June 9, 2008, http://crm.sys-con.com/node/584797 (accessed June 2, 2009).

133 Here is how: Pat Choate, "A Great Wall of Patents," testimony before the U.S. China Economic and Security Review Commission, Washington, D.C., November 7, 2005.

136 A widely distributed: "Important Changes in the USPTO Reexamination Process Warrant a Second Look from Innovative Companies Today: A Guide to How SoCal IP's Patent Assassins Can Leverage Reexamination to Minimize Patent Infringement Risk," SoCal IP Law Group LLP.

CHAPTER FIVE: INFRASTRUCTURE

142 While the United States: Calculated by author based on U.S. Bureau of Economic Analysis data on Gross Domestic Product, May 29, 2009.

142 In the same period: "Population of the United States," U.S. Census Bureau, http://www.census.gov/popest/national/national.html (accessed June 2, 2009).

143 The American Society of Civil Engineers: American Society of Civil

Engineers, *2009 Report Card for America's Infrastructure,* http://www.infrastructurereportcard.org/sites/default/files/RC2009_full_report.pdf.

143 America has approximately: Ibid., 41–47.

144 America has 85,000: Ibid., 15–23.

144 The United States: Ibid., 24–31, 57–62.

145 The average person: Ibid., 48–54.

145 America has: Ibid., 74–81, 98–104.

146 A goal of: Ibid., 64–73.

146 A single barge: Ibid., 82–88.

147 America's Class I: Ibid., 90–97.

147 No federal: Ibid., 124–31.

147 Hazardous waste: Ibid., 32–39.

148 America's federal: Ibid., 116–23.

149 In a press conference: "Nobelist and Economist Wassily Leontief Dies," *Harvard University Gazette,* February 11, 1999.

149 In March 2009, David Swenson, "Misunderstanding Economic Stimulus Multipliers," Web paper, University of Iowa, http://www.econ.iastate.edu/research/webpapers/paper_13050.pdf (accessed June 4, 2009).

151 Of course: Pat Choate and Susan Walter, *America in Ruins* (Durham, NC: Duke University Press, 1982), 3–20.

152 The federal government: Ibid., 68.

156 Another important: Ibid., 24–28.

158 The expense for: Dennis J. Enright, testimony before the Senate Finance Committee, Subcommittee on Energy, Natural Resources and Infrastructure, July 24, 2008.

159 A global association: "Corruption in the Construction Sector: The Nature and Scale of the Problem," Transparency International, Berlin, Germany, March 16, 2005.

159 Kessler: "Craft or Graft? The Insidious World of Construction Fraud," *Kessler Report* 10, no. 1: 1.

160 A special commission: Choate and Walter, *America in Ruins,* 2–6.

161 Many of the largest: Patrick Cockburn, "A fraud bigger than Madoff," *Independent,* February 16, 2009.

161 While U.S. officials: Stuart Bowen Jr., "Hard Lessons: The Iraq Reconstruction Experience," Foreign Press Center, U.S. Department of State, April 14, 2009.

163 The administration: Carrie Johnson, "A Backlog of Cases Alleging Fraud," *Washington Post,* July 2, 2008.

CHAPTER SIX: WORKERS

168 The Labor Department: "Older Workers," Spotlight on Statistics, Bureau of Labor Statistics, U.S. Department of Labor, July 2008, http://www.bls.gov/spotlight/2008/older_workers/.

169 Simultaneously: Paul Fronstin, *Sources of Health Insurance and Characteristics of the Uninsured: Analysis of the March 2008 Current Population Survey,* Employee Benefit Research Institute, Issue Brief no. 321, September 2008, 3.

169 From January 1: "Displaced Workers Summary," press release, Bureau of Labor Statistics, U.S. Department of Labor, August 20, 2008.

171 the National Bureau of: David A. Wise, "Labor Aspects of Pension Plans," *NBER Reporter,* winter 1984–85, 24.

171 The PBGC: "News and Highlights," Pension Benefit Guaranty Corporation, http://www.pbgc.gov/ (accessed June 4, 2009).

172 By May 2009: Ibid.

172 In January 2009: Barbara Butrica, Howard Iams, Karen E. Smith, and Eric Toder, *The Disappearing Defined Benefit Pension and Its Potential Impact on the Retirement Incomes of Boomers,* The Urban Institute (Washington, D.C., January 2009), 1–4.

173 a year later: Ibid.

173 *BusinessWeek:* Nanette Byres, "Should Public Pension Plans Go Toxic?" *BusinessWeek,* April 9, 2009.

174 The attorney general: Lauren Silva Laughlin, "Cuomo's Inquiry and Buyout Firms," *New York Times,* April 24, 2009.

175 Sometime between: "Projections of Future Financial Status," *2008 OASDI Trustees Report,* Social Security Administration (Washington, D.C., 2008).

175 Fortunately, less radical: Alison Shelton, *Reform Options for Social Security,* AARP Public Policy Institute (Washington, D.C., April 2008), 1.

176 The Committee: Pat Choate and Juyne Linger, *The High-Flex Society* (New York: Alfred A. Knopf, 1986), 247–50.

177 In the late 1970s: Ibid., 248.

180 In 2009: Fronstin, *Sources of Health Insurance.*

180 Yet, as difficult: Karen Davis, Ph.D., et al., *Mirror, Mirror on the Wall: An International Update on the Comparative Performance of American Health Care,* The Commonwealth Fund, May 15, 2007, http://www.commonwealthfund.org/Publications.aspx.

181 A 2006 study: Merrill Matthews, Ph.D., "Medicare's Hidden Administrative Costs: A Comparison of Medicare and the Private Sector, Physicians for a National Health Program (Chicago, Illinois, January 10, 2006), 1.

181 America's quest: Kirstin Downey, *The Woman Behind the New Deal: The Life of Frances Perkins, FDR's Secretary of Labor and His Moral Conscience* (New York: Doubleday, 2009), 230–45.

182 The price was: Norbert Goldfield, "The AMA Faces Down FDR and Wins," *Physician Executive,* January–February 1993, http://findarticles.com/p/search/?qa=Norbert%20Goldfield (accessed June 6, 2009).

182 Meeting with: Franklin D. Roosevelt, "Address to Advisory Council of

the Committee on Economic Security on the Problems of Economic and Social Security," November 14, 1934, Social Security Online, http://www.ssa.gov/history/fdrstmts.html#advisec.

183 The Commonwealth: Davis et al., *Mirror, Mirror on the Wall.*

185 The chief: Adrian W. Sybor, chief of Public Affairs Branch, Department of Health, Education and Welfare, letter to Charles Harder, December 10, 1976.

188 Its 153: "VA Fact Sheets," U.S. Department of Veteran Affairs, http://www1.va.gov/opa/fact/index.asp (accessed June 6, 2009).

190 In 2005: "Oldest Baby Boomers Turn 60!" press release, U.S. Census Bureau, January 3, 2006.

191 In 2005: Ibid.

191 By 2030: Ibid.

191 As the boomers: Mitra Toossi, "A Century of Change: The U.S. Labor Force, 1950–2050," *Monthly Labor Review* 125, no. 5 (May 2002): 18.

192 African American: "Income of U.S. Workforce Projected to Decline If Education Doesn't Improve," Policy Alert, The National Center for Public Policy and Higher Education (San Jose, CA, November 2005).

192 Of every one hundred: Ibid.

193 The BLS projects: Bureau of Labor Statistics, "Employment Projections: 2006–2016," U.S. Department of Labor (Washington, D.C., December 4, 2007).

194 The Census Bureau reports: U.S. Census Bureau, "Educational Attainment in the United States: 2007" (Washington, D.C., January 2009), 1.

195 Using Canada's: "Income of U.S. Workforce Projected to Decline."

196 According to: Patrick J. Kelly, *As America Becomes More Diverse: The Impact of State Higher Education Inequality,* National Center for Higher Education Management Systems (Boulder, CO, November 2005).

CHAPTER SEVEN: JOBS

197 In 2008: Office of Transportation and Machinery, "U.S. Motor Vehicle Industry Domestic and International Trade: Quick-Facts," U.S. Department of Commerce, 2009, http://www.trade.gov/wcm/groups/internet/@trade/@mas/@man/@aai/documents/web_content/auto_stats_mv_qfacts_pdf.pdf.

197 Korean: Ibid.

197 Germany: Ibid.

197 By 2011: Alan Ohnsman, "Honda May Pass Chrysler in North American Auto Output," update 1, Bloomberg.com, May 12, 2009, http://www.bloomberg.com/apps/news?pid=20601101&sid=ajAsCoCTXHOs.

198 Between: Economic Research Service, "Table 1: Value of U.S. Foreign Trade and Trade Balance (Agricultural and Non-Agricultural): U.S. Department of Agriculture, January–December, 1994–2008," http://www.ers.usda.gov/Data/FATUS/ (accessed June 27, 2009).

198 Most of this: Chris Edwards and Sally James, "Agricultural Policy," in *Cato Handbook for Policymakers,* 7th ed., ed. David Boaz (Washington, D.C.: Cato Institute, 2009), 193–99.

199 In the mid-1990s: Office of the Under Secretary of Defense for Acquisition and Technology, *Assessing Defense Industrial Capabilities: A DOD Handbook,* U.S. Department of Defense, April 25, 1996, DoD 5000.60-H, 34.

200 In 2008: "U.S. Trade in Goods and Services—Balance of Payments (BOP) Basis, 1960–2008," Foreign Trade Statistics, U.S. Census Bureau, June 10, 2009, http://www.census.gov/foreign-trade/statistics/historical/gands.pdf.

201 For May: Bureau of Labor Statistics, "The Employment Situation: June 2009," press release, U.S. Department of Labor, July 2, 2009.

203 Terence Stewart: Terence Stewart, e-mail message to author, April 12, 2009.

204 Under this law: U.S. International Trade Commission, "Trade Remedy Investigations: Section 201, Trade Act of 1974 (Global Safeguard Investigations), Import Relief for Domestic Industries," (Washington, D.C., June 2009), http://www.usitc.gov/trade_remedy/trao/us201.htm.

205 The experience: "Harley-Davidson, Inc.," FundingUniverse, http://www.fundinguniverse.com/company-histories/HarleyDavidson-Inc-Company-History.html (accessed June 6, 2009).

206 Even before the crash: United States International Trade Commission, "Sectors Quarterly Update: U.S. exports of domestic merchandise, imports for consumption, and merchandise trade balance, by major industry/commodity sectors, annual and year to date, January–March 2009," http://dataweb.usitc.gov/scripts/trade_shift/trade_by_sector_mv.asp.

209 Many people: Pat Choate, "Mom, Apple Pie, and Hyundai?" *American Conservative,* December 15, 2009.

210 James E. Malackowski: Ibid.

211 The administration: Mike Lillis, "Foreign Auto Makers Won Billions in Government Subsidies," *Washington Independent,* December 16, 2008.

ALSO AVAILABLE FROM
VINTAGE AND ANCHOR BOOKS

THE ORIGIN OF THE FINANCIAL CRISES
Central Banks, Credit Bubbles and the Efficient Market Fallacy
by George Cooper

In a series of disarmingly simple arguments, financial market analyst George Cooper challenges the core principles of today's economic orthodoxy and explains how we have pushed our economy into crisis. He examines the very foundations of today's economic philosophy and adds a compelling analysis of the forces behind economic crises. His goal is nothing less than preventing the seemingly endless procession of damaging boom-bust cycles, unsustainable economic bubbles, crippling credit crunches, and debilitating inflation. His direct, conscientious, and honest approach will captivate any reader and is an invaluable aid to understanding today's economy.

Business/Finance/978-0-307-47345-5

THE 21ST CENTURY ECONOMY: A BEGINNER'S GUIDE
by Randy Charles Epping

With recent economic turmoil monopolizing the headlines, it has become more important than ever to understand fundamental economic terms and concepts. *The 21st Century Economy: A Beginner's Guide* will give you all the knowledge you need to make sense of the latest headlines and the economic trends behind today's crises and tomorrow's opportunities. In his latest book, Randy Charles Epping uses compelling narratives and insightful analogies to clearly and concisely explain the rapidly changing way business is done in the twenty-first century.

Business/978-0-307-38790-5

THE SQUANDERING OF AMERICA
How the Failure of Our Politics Undermines Our Prosperity
by Robert Kuttner

The American economy is in peril. It has fallen hostage to a casino of financial speculation, creating instability as well as inequality. Here, Kuttner debunks alarmist claims about supposed economic hazards and exposes the genuine dangers: hedge funds and private equity run amok, sub-prime lenders, Wall Street middlemen, and America's dependence on foreign central banks. He then outlines a persuasive, bold alternative, a model of managed capitalism that can deliver security and opportunity, and rekindle democracy as we know it.

Current Affairs/978-1-4000-3363-8

THE MIND AND THE MARKET

Capitalism in Western Thought

by Jerry Z. Muller

Capitalism has never been a subject for economists alone. Philosophers, politicians, poets, and social scientists have debated the cultural, moral, and political effects of capitalism for centuries, and their claims have been many and diverse. *The Mind and the Market* is a remarkable history of how the idea of capitalism has developed in Western thought. Ranging across an ideological spectrum that includes Hobbes, Voltaire, Adam Smith, Edmund Burke, Hegel, Marx, and Matthew Arnold, as well as twentieth-century communist, fascist, and neoliberal intellectuals, historian Jerry Muller examines a fascinating thread of ideas about the ramifications of capitalism and its future implications.

History/Economics/978-0-385-72166-0

SUPERCAPITALISM

The Transformation of Business, Democracy, and Everyday Life

by Robert B. Reich

From one of America's foremost economic and political thinkers comes a vital analysis of our new hypercompetitive and turbocharged global economy and the effect it is having on American democracy. With his customary wit and insight, Reich shows how widening inequality of income and wealth, heightened job insecurity, and corporate corruption are merely the logical results of a system in which politicians are more beholden to the influence of business lobbyists than to the voters who elected them. Powerful and thought-provoking, *Supercapitalism* argues that a clear separation of politics and capitalism will foster an environment in which both business and government thrive, by putting capitalism in the service of democracy, and not the other way around.

Business/978-0-307-27799-2